O9-ABE-703

The Way of

INTEGRITY

Also by Martha Beck

Diana, Herself:
An Allegory of Awakening

Finding Your Own North Star:
Claiming the Life You Were Meant to Live

Finding Your Way in a Wild New World:
Reclaim Your True Nature to Live the Life You Want

Steering by Starlight:
Find Your Right Life No Matter What!

Expecting Adam: A True Story of Birth, Rebirth,
and Everyday Magic

Leaving the Saints:
How I Lost the Mormons and Found My Faith

The Four-Day Win:
End Your Diet War and Achieve Thinner Peace

The Joy Diet:
10 Daily Practices for a Happier Life

The Martha Beck Collection, Volume 1:
Essays for Creating Your Right Life

The Way of
INTEGRITY

FINDING THE PATH
TO YOUR TRUE SELF

MARTHA BECK

THE OPEN FIELD · PENGUIN LIFE

VIKING
An imprint of Penguin Random House LLC
penguinrandomhouse.com

Copyright © 2021 by Martha Beck
Penguin supports copyright. Copyright fuels creativity, encourages diverse
voices, promotes free speech, and creates a vibrant culture. Thank you for buying
an authorized edition of this book and for complying with copyright laws by
not reproducing, scanning, or distributing any part of it in any form
without permission. You are supporting writers and allowing
Penguin to continue to publish books for every reader.

The Open Field/A Penguin Life Book

Grateful acknowledgment is made for permission to reprint the following:

"Trust In Me" (The Python's Song) from *The Jungle Book*. Words and Music by
Richard M. Sherman and Robert B. Sherman. Copyright © 1966 Wonderland
Music Company, Inc. Copyright Renewed. All Rights Reserved. Used by
permission. Reprinted by permission of Hal Leonard LLC.

"Judge Your Neighbor" worksheet by Byron Katie. Copyright © 2019 by Byron
Katie International, Inc. Used with permission.

"The Turning" by Rowan Mangan. Used with permission of the author.

LIBRARY OF CONGRESS CATALOGING-IN-PUBLICATION DATA

Names: Beck, Martha Nibley, 1962–author.
Title: The way of integrity: finding the path to your true self / Martha Beck.
Description: New York: Penguin Life, 2021.
Identifiers: LCCN 2020038463 (print) | LCCN 2020038464 (ebook) |
ISBN 9781984881489 (hardcover) | ISBN 9781984881496 (ebook) |
ISBN 9780593298787 (international edition)
Subjects: LCSH: Self-confidence. | Meaning (Psychology) | Happiness.
Classification: LCC BF575.S39 B43 2021 (print) |
LCC BF575.S39 (ebook) |
DDC 158.1—dc23
LC record available at https://lccn.loc.gov/2020038463
LC ebook record available at https://lccn.loc.gov/2020038464

Printed in the United States of America
1st Printing

Designed by Amanda Dewey

All client names have been changed to protect
the privacy of the individuals involved.

Dear Reader,

The Open Field will commission and publish voices from all walks of life and areas of human endeavor that seek to inform, ignite, inspire, and move humanity forward—one person at a time.

The Open Field books are unique in look and feel, in mission and purpose. Each one is meant to carry your mind beyond judgments and troubles, into new reaches of peace and compassion.

You can expect inspiration and authenticity from The Open Field. You can trust that a book from this imprint will make a difference in your life and in your heart.

With gratitude,
Maria

To my family.
You light my way.

CONTENTS

INTRODUCTION

Even if you're not a frequent flier, this has probably happened to you. The plane is fully boarded. Everyone's laptops are stowed. The flight attendants have done their mandatory dance about the seat belts and the floor lights and the oxygen masks that will not inflate. Then, just as you expect to roll away from the gate, everything stops. The captain's sheepish voice crackles through the cabin. "Sorry, folks, we have a slight malfunction—probably just a glitch, but we need to call some mechanics to check. We're looking at a bit of a wait."

A ripple of woe runs through the passengers. Your heart sinks. How long will you be trapped in this uncomfortable seat, between a man who reeks of cheap cologne and a fretfully teething baby, before the plane finally flies? But after this initial burst of dismay, everyone heaves a sigh and settles in. You all approve of the crew's caution. You're about to travel five miles above Earth's surface in this mighty machine. No one, not even the baby, wants the plane taking off if it's not in perfect structural integrity.

This book, as you may have gleaned from the title, is all about integrity. But I don't mean this in a moralizing sense. The word *integrity* has taken on a slightly prim, judgmental nuance in modern English, but the word comes from the Latin *integer*, which simply means "intact." To be in integrity is to be one thing, whole and undivided. When a plane is in integrity, all its millions of parts work together smoothly and cooperatively. If it loses integrity, it may stall, falter, or crash. There's no judgment here. Just physics.

As above in aerodynamics, so below in our everyday lives. When you experience unity of intention, fascination, and purpose, you live like a bloodhound on a scent, joyfully doing what feels truest in each moment. Your daily work, whether it's writing computer code, gardening, or building houses, is so absorbing that at the end of the day you don't really want to stop. But when you do, you enjoy hanging out with loved ones so much, and sleep is so delicious you can't imagine anything sweeter. And when you wake up the next morning, the day ahead seems so enticing you practically bound out of bed.

If you're like many people I've coached, you may be rolling your eyes right now. It may sound like I'm wearing rose-colored glasses and munching antidepressants like jelly beans. You may never have felt the kind of sustained joie de vivre I'm describing. You might not believe that such a fulfilling life is possible.

It is.

Tragically, many people go their whole lives without ever

learning this, never experiencing the joyful ease that comes with full integrity. Some of these folks are massively misaligned, their lives an endless string of failures and crushed dreams. You may know a few: the friend from high school who keeps landing himself in prison, the cousin who marries one unfaithful scumbag after another, the colleague who seems to sabotage every project she undertakes. These folks are like airplanes whose major components, like wings and engines, are out of whack.

Your own life is probably somewhere between utterly blissful and completely wrecked. You have a vague sense of purpose, which you hope to follow someday. Though your job isn't perfect, it's good enough. And your relationships are fine. Mostly. Yes, there are times when someone—your spouse, your kids, your parents, your boss—makes you want to fake your own death and move to a hotel in the Cayman Islands. But honestly, it's *fine*. You don't feel bad, just vaguely anxious, uncomfortable, and disappointed. And it's perfectly normal that your mind tends to linger on regrets about plans that didn't work out and doubts that your dreams will ever come true.

When I meet clients who fit this description and suggest that their lives could be better, they often protest that they're doing fine, just *fine*. *Look,* they say: *Life is a bitch and then we die. Failure is much more common than success. We can't just flap our arms and fly.* They think they're simply accepting the bitter truth. But what I hear is the clank of stray bolts and loose parts, the sound of a human who has never experienced complete alignment of body, mind, heart, and soul.

Again, this isn't a moral judgment. If you don't always feel wonderful, it doesn't mean you're faulty or bad—in fact, I'd bet that you've spent your entire life trying to be good. And there's nothing defective about you. You're a highly functional, sophisticated creature. At the deepest level, you know what makes you happy and how to create your best possible life. That knowledge is coded into your very nature.

But your nature is forever colliding with a force that can tear it apart: culture.

By "culture" I don't mean opera or surrealist painting. I'm talking about any set of social standards that shapes the way people think and act. Every group of humans, from couples to families to cell blocks to sewing circles to armies, has cultural rules and expectations that help them cooperate. Some of these are explicit, like traffic laws or workplace dress codes. Others are implicit, like the assumption that when you go to a nice restaurant for dinner, you'll use silverware instead of plunging your face directly into your food like a truffle pig.

Humans create elaborate cultures because we are intensely social beings, dependent on the goodwill of others from the moment we're born. We also have an enormous capacity to absorb and replicate the behavior of people around us. From childhood, often without even noticing it, we learn exactly how to win approval and belonging in our particular cultural context. We act bubbly, quiet, or brave to please our families. We immediately begin to like whatever our friends say they like. We throw ourselves into schoolwork, babysitting, family feuds—whatever we believe will assure our place in the human world.

In this rush to conform, we often end up ignoring or overruling our genuine feelings—even intense ones, like longing or anguish—to please our cultures. At that point, we're divided against ourselves. We aren't in integrity (one thing) but in duplicity (two things). Or we may try to fit in with a number of different groups, living in multiplicity (many things). We abandon our true nature and become pawns of our culture: smiling politely, sitting attentively, wearing the "perfect" uncomfortable clothes. This is why a soldier will march into gunfire without complaint. It's why whole communities once thought it made sense to burn a few witches here and there. The extent to which people will defy nature to serve culture can be truly horrifying. But the whole thing works very well from the perspective of creating and sustaining human groups.

There's just one catch: nature does not give up without a fight.

If you've ever found yourself snapping at someone you dearly love, or sitting down to complete a work project only to spend five hours shopping for home tattoo kits online, it's probably because you're internally divided. You're trying to act in ways that don't feel right to you at the deepest level. Whenever we do this, our lives begin to go pear-shaped. Emotionally, we feel grumpy, sad, or numb. Physically, our immune systems and muscles weaken; we might get sick, and even if we don't, our energy flattens. Mentally, we lose focus and clarity. That's how it feels to be out of integrity.

All these inner reactions affect our outer lives. Since we can't concentrate, our work suffers. Irritability and gloominess make us bad company, weakening our relationships. Everything in and around us is negatively affected when we lose integrity. And because our true nature is serious about restoring us to wholeness, it hauls out the one tool that reliably gets our attention: suffering.

Personally, I do not enjoy suffering. It hurts me. If you're into it, I don't judge you—but I do want to make a crucial point: suffering is different from pain, at least in my lexicon. I once saw a sign in a medical clinic that read "Pain is inevitable. Suffering is optional." Physical pain comes from events. Psychological suffering comes from the way we deal with those events. It can grow exponentially in situations where pain is entirely absent. Even when you're curled up in a comfortable chair, suffering can make you wish you'd never been born. I know, because I spent years and years right up in it. This is what led me to an obsessive, decades-long quest to find my way to happiness.

I certainly didn't set out to be some kind of culture-busting maverick. Quite the opposite. I was born with the approval-seeking personality of an orphaned lapdog. Whenever my nature and my culture disagreed, I'd sell out my nature, and hard. It worked! I got all kinds of approval! On the other hand, I could barely tolerate things like, you know, being alive. In hindsight I'm grateful for this. It gave me an early start in struggling against suffering with every resource at my disposal.

Informal seeking led to years of formal study. I spent about a decade, from age seventeen to twenty-eight, getting three social-science degrees from Harvard. For a while after that, I taught subjects like career development and sociology. But my hidden agenda was always trying to figure out how I, and other people, could create lives we actually enjoyed.

Academia was a fine profession for me—honestly, *fine*—except for the parts I hated (navigating faculty politics or writing journal articles so boring the process felt like taking a cheese grater to my brain). Lecturing students was much less interesting to me than talking to them about their actual lives. Eventually some of them started paying me to do this. Hey, presto! I became a life coach before I'd ever heard the term.

This ramped up my quest to find "life design" strategies that really worked. I kept reading and also started writing: memoir, self-help, dozens and dozens of articles. I became a monthly columnist for *O, The Oprah Magazine.* I often appeared on TV, offering viewers tips for happier living. To test my methods, I coached wildly different people: rural South African villagers, erudite New Yorkers, heroin addicts just out of prison, billionaires, celebrities, random strangers I met in line at the DMV. And all these experiences, from my most intimate private encounters to my most diligent formal research, gradually coalesced to reveal one simple truth:

Integrity is the cure for unhappiness. Period.

Of all the strategies and skills I've ever learned, the ones that actually work are those that help people see where they've abandoned their own deep sense of truth and followed some other set of directives. This split from integrity is almost always unconscious. The people I know who experience it aren't wicked; in fact, most of them are perfectly lovely. They strive to cooperate with every rule for living they've learned from their respective cultures. Which is a terrific way to run your life if you like to look good and feel bad.

But there's another way, one that will lead you out of suffering and into levels of joy and purpose you may not yet realize are possible. I call it the way of integrity.

This book is meant to guide and accompany you along that way. Wherever you may be and however you may feel right now, the way of integrity will take you from this very spot to a life filled with meaning, enchantment, and fascination. I've helped hundreds of people experience this. I've also lived the whole process myself—and believe me, I was not an easy case. But after all that misery, the way of integrity took even me to a life that feels ridiculously blessed. This is not because I'm anything special. It's just because I know the way.

The word *way* can mean either a process or a path. In this book, it means both. If you don't know what to do next, the way of integrity will provide instructions, like a recipe. If you don't know where to go next, the way of integrity will show you the next step, like a map. If you follow the directions, you'll end up happy. Not because this path is virtuous, but because it aligns you with reality, with truth. Your life will work for the same reason a well-built plane will fly. Not a reward for good behavior. Just physics.

So if you're ready to abandon suffering, embrace your true nature, and experience the joy you know you're meant to feel, let's begin. What, you may ask, does the way of integrity actually look like? I will tell you. It looks like an epic medieval Italian fantasy adventure quest!

Stay with me. I'll explain.

Throughout my career as a writer and coach, I have repeatedly, zestfully, and unapologetically filched ideas from *The Divine Comedy*, written by Dante Alighieri in the early 1300s. This is not because I'm any sort of Dante scholar. I never took a course in Dante, can't speak Italian, don't know much about medieval history. As a young adult, I read *The Divine Comedy* for the only reason I read anything back then: I was looking for wisdom about how to feel better. And I found it.

Dante's masterpiece is quite simply the most powerful set of instructions I know for healing our psychological wounds, restoring us to integrity, and maximizing our capacity to feel good. *The Divine Comedy* takes us through the whole process, step by step. Yes, it's all framed as a story about one man having a mystical adventure. Yes, that man uses the imagery of a fourteenth-century European. But the psychological metaphors in Dante's epic still ring true today. They still show us the way. Plus, they're entertaining. Don't think that Dante is some pontificating drone. He's not. He's just a writer, standing in front of a reader, asking you to follow him out of misery and into happiness.

So for the rest of this book, I'll walk you along a way of integrity built around the framework Dante laid out in *The Divine Comedy*. You can take it slowly and gently, or go at it like an Olympic sprinter—whatever pace works for you. But however you decide to travel, you'll be passing through four stages. Just to give you the lay of the land, here's a summary of what you can expect.

Your quest for integrity will begin in "the dark wood of error," a place where we feel lost, exhausted, troubled, and unsure. This is Dante's metaphor for the misalignment in which most of us live. In some ways—possibly all ways—we feel that our lives aren't what they're meant to be. We don't know how we ended up so off course, or how to find our way out of confusion. Don't worry. We will.

Our next stage is Dante's famous "inferno." Passing through it, we'll find the parts of you that are suffering—the parts trapped in your inner hell—and set them free. The chisel you will use to break your own chains is your sense of truth. You'll see that psychological suffering always comes from internal splits between what your encultured mind believes and what feels deeply true to you. The way of integrity will help you heal these divisions. You'll start to experience more wholeness than ever before. The relief, most likely, will be tangible and immediate.

Once your inner life begins to heal, it's on to a form of Dante's "purgatory." This word simply means "cleansing." (I like to go on "integrity cleanses," by which I don't mean cleansing away integrity, but cleansing away everything else.) In this stage of your quest, you'll shift your external behavior to match your newfound inner truth. The further you go, the easier this becomes.

Finally, as your inner and outer lives approach complete integrity, you'll find yourself in metaphorical "paradise." There's no more work to do here, unless you count enjoying a life where everything—your psyche, your career, your love life—works smoothly. Fair warning: at this point you may begin experiencing things so exquisite our culture tells you they can't happen. Obviously, no one will have taught you how to navigate such wonders. No worries. You'll learn fast. You were born for it.

So that's our journey in broad strokes. As we go along, I'll not only touch on Dante's metaphors, but offer insights from recent science (psychology, sociology, neurology) that will help make the journey more accessible and potent. I'll tell you true stories about clients or friends of mine, people whose experiences can illustrate and clarify your own process. To show you how it all feels from the inside, I'll also recount some examples from my own lifelong integrity quest. And every now and then, I'll invite you to do some thought exercises to make your journey as quick and easy as possible.

In *The Divine Comedy*, Dante goes down into a huge pit (the inferno), then up a mountain (purgatory). He grows stronger and walks with less and less effort as he reaches the mountain's summit. Then, to his amazement, he finds himself rising upward. Flying. That's what happens when the misaligned parts of a human life come into integrity. Dante uses flight as a metaphor for a life that feels unlimited, literally heavenly.

Whenever I travel by air, no matter what problems and delays may occur, I'm astonished at the moment the plane takes off. It blows my mind that this huge machine can throw itself into the air and keep going, safe and sound, for thousands of miles. I feel the same way when I watch people come into integrity and take flight in their own unique ways, finding purpose, love, and success. Every day, I'm stunned to realize that it worked for me, too. It all feels like a dazzling, impossible miracle.

But it's not. It's just physics.

So if you're ready—even if you're just a bit curious—please make sure your seatbelt is fastened and your emotional baggage securely stowed under the seat in front of you. The way of integrity will take you to heights of happiness you've never dreamed possible. You are cleared for takeoff.

Stage One

THE DARK WOOD
OF ERROR

1.

Lost in the Woods

Like many compelling adventure stories, *The Divine Comedy* begins in the middle. "Midway through the journey of our life," says Dante, "I found myself in a dark forest, for the right way was lost." He doesn't mention how he got to the woods, what he was doing when he wandered off track, or how far he's gone. All this information is—literally—foggy. The only thing Dante really knows is that he's alone, adrift, and confused.

The experience of noticing we're on the wrong path, in what feels like the wrong life, comes to almost all of us at some point. A few years into a job, a relationship, or a living situation, we may suddenly realize that everything seems . . . off. Like Dante, we're a bit dim about exactly what's wrong, or how we got here. But in an empty moment when we've finally gotten the kids off to school, or we look up from our desks at the office and notice everyone else has gone home, or we've just had another ghastly fight with the person we thought we'd love forever, we stare into space and think, "What am I doing? What is this place? How did I get here? It wasn't supposed to be this way!"

This is often how people are feeling when they consult me. I've sat through countless first sessions with clients who are so baffled by their own dissatisfaction they can barely find words to describe it. They stammer, "I wish I knew my purpose," or "People say 'Follow your passion,' but I have no idea what mine is," or "I thought working hard and providing for my family was the right thing, but I feel so empty." A few of these people are clinically depressed or physically sick. But mostly, they're just lost.

The most common reason we end up feeling this way is by doing what we're "supposed to." We learn from our culture how a good person is supposed to behave, and we behave that way. Then we expect the promised rewards: happiness, health, prosperity, true love, solid self-esteem. But the equation fails to balance. Even after doing everything we can to *be* good, we don't *feel* good. Confused, we figure we're somehow not doing enough, or not doing it the right way. But the harder we work at finding the path to well-being, the less well we feel.

I've worked with many people who were so far gone in the dark wood they didn't remember anything else. By the time they came to me, their disorientation had become extreme. There was Jim, the physician who grew more and more repulsed by the thought of touching people until he finally had to close his practice. Or Evelyn, the magazine editor who, though a ravenous bookworm at home, gradually lost the energy to track simple paragraphs at work. Fran, a devoted mother of four, began forgetting so many of her children's playdates and school events that the whole family lived like a herd of spooked horses, nervous and jittery. None of these people was mentally ill, just far gone in a hazy wilderness.

I recognize this murky terrain. Know it well, in fact. I've been to the dark wood of error so many times I should have set up a hot dog stand somewhere in there. From childhood, my one overarching life directive was *Do whatever it takes to win approval.* Raised in a devout Mormon family, I obeyed every rule of my religion and worked hard at school. Then I went off to Harvard, which was about as far from my childhood culture as I could get without moving to Pluto. I managed by letting everyone I encountered assume that I agreed with them, passing for a devout Mormon at home and a rational atheist at school.

This strategy worked perfectly (approval everywhere!) except that after a while I couldn't move. Physically, I mean. At the ripe old age of eighteen, I developed mysterious, excruciating soft-tissue pain all over my body. I couldn't focus mentally. I started binge eating. I felt out of control and broken and borderline suicidal. I had to take a year off school, the better to focus on my complete physical and emotional deterioration. Oh, I was quite the little ray of sunshine.

Looking back at that experience and the stories of so many clients, I feel enormous gratitude for all our confusion, and despair. Those feelings meant that our internal guidance systems were working perfectly, signaling "WRONG WAY!" as clearly as they could. With nothing but the best of intentions, we'd lost the way of integrity. Suffering arose from our bodies and hearts as a result—and riveted our attention on fixing the problem.

DARK WOOD OF ERROR SYNDROME

There have probably been times when you, too, have departed from your own true path. At first, the resulting suffering may have been so mild you didn't even notice it. But no one can sleepwalk away from integrity indefinitely, because things get worse the further we travel in the wrong direction. Eventually, if we don't correct course, we begin displaying clusters of characteristic symptoms. You may have had them in the past. You may have them now.

I call any cluster of these symptoms "dark wood of error syndrome." Again, it's not a bad thing. It's the way our instincts motivate us to regain our integrity. It's the truth come to set us free. Which doesn't mean it's fun. In the remainder of this chapter, I'll describe the symptoms of this syndrome. As you read, ask yourself if you're experiencing any of them.

Dark wood of error symptom #1:
Feeling purposeless

The most common reason people give for hiring me as a coach is that they're desperate to find a sense of purpose. Very few actually want to die, but many tell me they see little point in living. They echo the Biblical lament in Ecclesiastes, "I have seen all the things that are done under the sun, and behold; all of them are meaningless, a chasing after the wind." In other words, "Life is *hard*. We're all going to *die*. *WTF*?" Without an authentic sense of purpose, it's hard to feel that the daily grind of a human existence is worth the trouble.

In modern Western culture, most of us believe that we can find a sense of purpose by achieving something. What something, exactly? That depends on how the people around us define "value."

My job is like watching a parade of the various things different cultures tell people to value. One day I coached a woman who believed that a purpose-driven life involved suing lots of people and wearing several pounds of diamond jewelry everywhere, including the dump. My next client was equally convinced that a purposeful life meant living in a cabin off the grid and using leaves as toilet paper. Some people think purpose means having a corner office. Others try to become movie stars, save the rain forests, or make viral videos of their pet hamsters.

Any of these ambitions might actually match your true purpose. If so, you'll feel a powerful inward compulsion to follow that particular path. You'll find the steps along the way fascinating and fulfilling, and as a result you'll be good at them. But if you pursue any course of action solely because *other* people think it's "purposeful," prepare to hit dense fog. You'll encounter baffling failures. You won't get along with people. You won't be able to drum up the energy to climb the success ladder—or for that matter, to wash your hair.

Maybe you're thinking, "Well, of course I feel awful—I never get the things I want!"

If so, I wish you could meet the people I know who've reached the pinnacle of our society's idealized achievements, only to realize that, as one woman told me, "There's no *there* there. I thought there was a position in the world that would make me feel good, but I got to that position and didn't find anything that made me happy. It all seemed pointless."

"So I won an Olympic gold," one client told me. "And as I climbed down from the podium, the only thought I could think was, 'What the hell do I do now?' It was awful, absolutely terrifying. It was like death—the worst feeling I'd ever had." A hard-working author said, "After a lifetime of trying, I finally had a book hit number one on the *New York Times* bestseller list. It made me really happy . . . for about ten minutes."

Our sense of purposelessness doesn't disappear in the face of culturally defined achievements. It remains a persistent, goading force, a biting fly that won't stop buzzing around our heads until we begin pursuing goals that truly fulfill us—in other words, following the way of integrity. And if the whine and sting of purposelessness isn't enough to shake us out of our sleepwalking, our subconscious minds will up the ante. They'll summon the megafauna, the mental wild beasts we call mood states.

Dark wood of error symptom #2:
Emotional misery

As if being lost weren't bad enough, carnivorous beasts attack Dante in the dark wood of error. The first is a ravenous leopard whose appetite can never be satisfied. Next comes a lion so terrifying Dante says "it seemed the air was afraid of him." Then he sees a wolf, the sight of which makes him so sad he "weeps in all his thought and is despondent." Neediness, panic, depression. Welcome to a few of the emotional states that may jump you as you wander through the dark wood of error.

When I stray from my integrity, the mood-monsters rear up almost immediately. One step away from my truth, I feel grasping, nervous, and morose. If I don't correct course, those feelings quickly escalate to clinginess, terror, and despair. Thank heavens! Without such ferocious attacks, I might still be following the self-contradictory ideals that made me such a royal mess at age eighteen.

Whenever you lose your integrity, you'll feel your own unique brew of bad moods, depending on your personality. You may tend, as I do, toward anxiety and depression. Or you may feel free-floating hostility, itching to punch everyone in your office, family, zip code. You may have full-on panic attacks, especially during special occasions (blind dates, parole hearings) when you most wish to appear relaxed and confident.

Whatever your repeated or persistent negative emotions, try

thinking of them as Dante's wild beasts, whose job it is to make your life unbearable when you stray from your true path. If the feelings don't go away even though you're taking your medication and meeting regularly with your therapist, you can be quite sure you're somehow out of integrity. The sooner you acknowledge this the better, because remaining in the dark wood of error may eventually cause you actual, physical harm.

Dark wood of error symptom #3: Physical deterioration

I believe that I was crippled by illness from age eighteen all the way into my thirties because my body was trying to help me find my way out of the dark wood of error. When I finally did that, my symptoms receded. Nothing else worked.

Obviously, bad health can affect people who live in total integrity. Bodies break down for many reasons. But from what I've seen, it's rare for someone who's internally split *not* to develop some kind of health problem. By the time people consult me, they're often suffering all kinds of physical distress, from headaches to terminal illness. They almost never see a connection between their physical condition and a lack of integrity. To most of them, that would seem—to use the scientific term—totally wackadoodle.

But speaking of science, solid research shows all sorts of links between living in harmony with our truth and maintaining good health. There's a whole field of medicine, psychoneuroimmunology, that focuses on the way psychological stress, including the stress of lying or keeping secrets, contributes to illness. Studies have linked deception and secret-keeping to elevated heart rate and blood pressure, increased stress hormones, higher bad-cholesterol and glucose levels, and reduced immune responses. The more significant our deceptive behavior, the worse the effect on health.

For example, in one study of gay men with HIV, researchers discovered that the more closeted the men were about their sexuality, the faster their disease progressed. There was a dose-response relationship between the level of concealment and immune status—in other words, the greater the concealment, the higher the rates of disease and death. "Don't ask, don't tell" sounds benign, but living in even tacit separation from our real identity can literally hasten our death.

Again, there are all kinds of physical ailments that affect people who *are* living in complete integrity. Everyone dies, and there's plenty of physical pain that has nothing to do with keeping secrets, telling lies, or wandering off true paths. Still, every time we make choices or assume appearances that don't align with our integrity, we really do become more vulnerable to physical problems, from back spasms to pneumonia. If you're inexplicably sick, weak, or accident-prone, your body may be trying to tell you you're lost in the dark wood.

My own illness defied all medical interventions. But when I began seeking my truth and reclaiming my integrity, all my supposedly "incurable" symptoms began to disappear. I've seen similar things happen to many clients. When you come into integrity, there's a solid chance it will happen to you.

Dark wood of error symptom #4:
Consistent relationship failures

It's simple logic: if you don't walk your true path, you don't find your true people. You end up in places you don't like, learning skills that don't fulfill you, adopting values and customs that feel wrong. The folks you meet along the way either genuinely love these things, or they're faking it as hard as you are. Either way, your connection with them will be artificial. You'll send out a pretend personality to meet other (potentially pretend) personalities, creating nothing but pretend relationships. I'll never forget one wealthy, beautiful celebrity who confided to me, after attending yet another glamorous party, "I'm exhausted by my own hypocrisy."

If you feel persistently disconnected and lonely, you're almost certainly (innocently) out of integrity. This goes double if you feel trapped with people you absolutely can't stand. When humans meet in the dark wood of error, all of them sleepwalking, the relationships they create tend to be shallow or toxic or both. These "friendships," "love affairs," and even familial bonds are rife with misunderstanding, hurt feelings, and mutual exploitation. Over the long run they tend to crumble into their sketchy foundations, leaving only hurt feelings behind.

If you feel constantly drained or betrayed in family, friendship, and romance, the relationships you're forming are probably based in the dark wood of error. We simply can't chart a course to happiness by linking up with others who are as lost as we are. The path to true love—true anything—is the way of integrity. No other person can ever find yours for you, much less give it to you. But you can always, no matter what your circumstances, find and follow it yourself.

Dark wood of error symptom #5: Consistent career failures

Your true self is intensely interested in your real life's work—but it could give a rat's ass about anything else. When you pursue a career that pulls you away from your true self, your talent and enthusiasm will quit on you like a bored intern. Every task will feel as distasteful as poisoned food, and leave you just as weak. You'll probably have a sequence of mistakes and unlucky breaks at work (actually these are *lucky* breaks, your true self stopping you from wandering further into the dark wood of error, but you won't see it that way at the time).

I've coached dozens of people who've gone into engineering because they loved inventing things, or academia because they loved learning, or journalism because they loved writing, and then got promoted into management or administration—which they hated. At that point, having left their integrity by doing things they didn't want to do, they flamed out spectacularly.

For example, one brilliant writer I'll call Edgar climbed the ranks of the publishing industry to become editor-in-chief of a prominent magazine. At that point he began drinking, heavily and openly. One fine morning, when I visited Edgar in his office, I was startled to find him guzzling his way through a case of wine he'd strategically installed right in front of him on his desk. He was out of that job within a year.

Another client, Chloe, loved her job as a forest ranger. She got into politics thinking it would help her protect the environment. After being elected to her local city council, Chloe developed a bizarre tendency to drowse off in committee meetings. Like, *all* committee meetings. Though she was getting a lot of rest, her new job became a tar pit of shame and embarrassment. People talked. Chloe never ran for reelection.

Our culture defines "success" as rising through bureaucracies, so these people didn't understand why they'd suddenly gone from high performance to crashing and burning. But from my perspective, these "inexplicable" failures made obvious sense: Edgar loved literature, not running a magazine. Chloe loved being out in the woods alone, not sitting around indoors with other people. Both had split themselves by aspiring to do things that, at another level, they knew they hated.

There are infinite ways to make a living. At some level—a deep, instinctive level—you know which of them will truly work for you. You can feel it immediately when a job requires you to push aside your true desires. Your awareness of your true career path may be buried deep under layers of acculturated false beliefs. But it's still there, like a flower trying to grow through toxic sludge. If you continue to resist your genuine impulses, you'll become slowly aware that what you're doing to make a living is turning you into the walking dead.

Dark wood of error symptom #6:
Bad habits you can't break

As you can see, the dark wood of error—*comment se dit*—sucks. So it's no surprise that when we're in there, we often grope for something to ease the pain. I'm a huge fan of better living through chemistry, and I will cheer lavishly when you use helpful medications under the supervision of your doctor. But many of us dark-wood denizens often go a step—or a mile—further along the psychopharmaceutical path. We hanker constantly for just a little more mood-altering . . . something. Anything. A little more beer, a little more nicotine, a little more cocaine, a little more all of the above.

The resulting chemical haze may let us wander very, very, *very* far from our true paths. I've coached people who numbed themselves senseless as they wandered through the dark wood of error, including one man who was gulping down over two hundred Oxycontin pills every day. He told me it was "almost enough."

When we're feeling fundamentally lost, afflicted by purposelessness, foul moods, and bad jobs, anything that stimulates the brain's pleasure centers can become an addiction. Some of the most common, aside from the dynamic duo of drugs and alcohol, are gambling, sex, intense relationship drama, shopping, binge eating, and staring at the internet day and night without pausing to sleep, eat, or pee. I myself have been known to spend hours solving urgent problems that existed only as pixels of colorful light on my smartphone. (Though, in my defense, all that candy wasn't going to crush itself.)

If you feel unable to stop an activity, if you're spending the rent money on it, if you hide it from others and feel a creeping obsession slowly consuming you, your first step toward integrity— a big one—might be acknowledging that you're addicted. From there you can begin regaining your integrity, if not only with the methods in this book, then with some form of rehab. Whatever happens, if you don't leave the dark wood of error, you'll find your bad habits almost impossible to break. Eventually, they may well break you.

The problems above aren't the only symptoms of having lost integrity, but as far as I've observed, they're the most common. They reveal places where we're in denial, out of alignment with our real perceptions, desires, and instinctive wisdom. Here's a little test to see whether you're a little (or a lot) lost in the dark wood of error.

EXERCISE:
Checking for dark wood of error syndrome

Answer the questions below as honestly as you can. If you find yourself fibbing in order to look more impressive and in control of your life, notice that. It means you're: (1) out of integrity and (2) unwilling to acknowledge it, even in a quiz no one else has to see. Take a deep breath and tell the truth.

As you do this assessment, please notice that the words "TRUE" and "FALSE" don't always appear in the same column. Make sure you circle the right response for each statement.

Circle the word "TRUE" or "FALSE" to accurately reflect your response to each statement.	Column 1	Column 2
1. In general, I see people as good and loveable.	(TRUE)	FALSE
2. I sometimes feel my daily activities are meaningless.	FALSE	(TRUE)
3. I adore the company of my friends and loved ones.	TRUE	(FALSE)
4. My job (includes the job of homemaker) feels like a heavy burden.	(FALSE)	TRUE
5. I feel "on purpose" and fulfilled even on the most ordinary day.	TRUE	(FALSE)
6. I have trouble sustaining loving relationships.	FALSE	(TRUE)
7. I have frequent infections (colds, flu, etc.) even when the people around me aren't sick.	(FALSE)	TRUE
8. There's an undercurrent of content-ment that supports me at all times.	(TRUE)	FALSE
9. I get to make a living doing something I love.	(TRUE)	FALSE
10. I don't feel really seen and understood by anybody.	(FALSE)	TRUE
11. I believe my presence is changing the world for the better, in small ways or large.	(TRUE)	FALSE
12. My relationships are often troubled by anger and mistrust.	(FALSE)	TRUE

13. I don't need any mood-altering substance or exciting activity to feel great.	(TRUE)	FALSE
14. Other people seem to be accomplishing great things, but I just don't measure up.	(FALSE)	TRUE
15. I have "friends" whose company I don't really enjoy.	FALSE	(TRUE)
16. I sleep deeply and restfully almost every night.	(TRUE)	FALSE
17. I can almost always count on my loved ones to understand me.	TRUE	(FALSE)
18. Though frightening things sometimes happen, I always feel basically safe.	(TRUE)	FALSE
19. I have aches, pains, and fatigue that limit my activities.	FALSE	(TRUE)
20. I frequently feel annoyed at whoever happens to be around me.	FALSE	(TRUE)
21. I love my job and can't wait to get to it.	(TRUE)	(FALSE)
22. I often feel so worried I don't sleep well.	(FALSE)	TRUE
23. My life is full of love and companionship.	TRUE	(FALSE)
24. I don't feel as if my work contributes anything important to the world.	(FALSE)	TRUE
25. Even when people around me get sick, I almost always stay healthy.	(TRUE)	FALSE
26. I often feel an underlying sense of sadness or despair.	(FALSE)	TRUE

27. I believe everyone's essence is basically good.	(TRUE)	FALSE
28. I feel angry, even when I'm alone.	(FALSE)	TRUE

Scoring

Count the words you circled in column 1 (the left-hand column).

Write the amount here: _17_

If this number is:

22–28

You live in an unusually high state of integrity. You may have spent time in the dark wood of error earlier in your life, but you know the way out. This book may be a nice refresher.

15–21

Your life is much happier than most, but there may be one or two areas where you're still divided from your true self. The way of integrity will fix that.

8–14

You are definitely spending some time in the dark wood of error. Please remember that this isn't your fault. Still, only reclaiming integrity will keep your areas of concern from getting worse.

0–7

Feeling lost and confused might seem "normal" to you, because you spend a lot of time hanging out in the dark wood of error. This book can help you access more peace and joy than you've felt for a long time—maybe ever. If you don't take steps toward integrity soon, things will just get worse.

WHAT TO DO WHEN YOU REALIZE YOU HAVE DARK WOOD OF ERROR SYMPTOMS

If your score on this quiz is lower than you'd like, don't panic. You aren't bad, and you haven't done anything wrong. You're just lost. By definition, that means you don't know where to go or what to do next. Fortunately, I can direct you to a surefire next step, the single step that will put you squarely on the way of integrity. It has never failed me or any of my clients. And it's so simple: just tell the truth about how lost you are.

I stumbled onto this step when I was eighteen, as I lay aching and depressed, unknowingly caught between two incompatible cultures. As months went by and I slowly followed my unhappiness to its root, I arrived at a fundamental realization that seemed to have nothing to do with physical illness, or even depression: I had no idea what was true. That realization, small and quiet though it was, felt strangely healing. In later years, as a coach, I would watch hundreds of other people who felt purposeless, anxious, angry, despairing, sick, lonely, or addicted sink into the truth "I am completely lost" as if it were the embrace of a loving parent.

This makes no sense to the ego, which always wants to feel righteous and in charge. But the true self relaxes when we stop sleepwalking and honestly assess our situation—even if, like Dante, we've woken up in a terrifying place. Our whole selves resonate with the simplest truths we can tell: "I don't like this place." "I don't know how I got here." "I'm frightened."

EXERCISE:
Finding integrity in the dark wood

Here is a simple exercise that will put your feet squarely on the way of integrity, no matter how lost you may feel. Below you'll find a list of simple statements. Your job is to say them out loud. Whisper them privately, proclaim them to a friend, shout them at the next telemarketer who interrupts your day. And just for a moment, as you say each sentence, tentatively accept that it might be true.

Now here's the important part: as you speak each sentence, feel what happens inside you. Your pride may sting, your inner critic may put its back up like a startled cat. But does your body relax a little, despite the apparent negativity of a given statement? Does your breath deepen? Do you feel a battle easing in your gut, your heart, your head? Just notice this. Don't worry about what comes next. Okay, go.

My life isn't perfect.
I don't like the way things are going.
I don't feel good.
I'm sad.
I'm angry.
I'm scared.
I'm not at peace.
I can't find my people.
I'm not sure where to go.
I don't know what to do.
I need help.

If you felt something settle in your body and emotions when you read one or more of the statements above, don't ignore it. That slight relaxation is your instinctive response to hearing—and, more importantly, speaking—the truth. If you can feel it, be proud of yourself. Things aren't perfect, but you're awake to the fact that they're not perfect, and that is *everything*. You're reconnecting parts of yourself that have been torn apart. Bravely done. You've taken the first step on the way of integrity.

2.

Desperate for Success

My friend Sonja once came up with some useful advice for men who would like to improve their performance in the bedroom. "Here's a hint," she said. "If whatever you're doing isn't working, *don't do it harder.*"

This applies in every area of life, but most of us don't seem to realize it. Our cultural assumption is that doing things harder is the way out of confusion and into happiness. With a bit more elbow grease and a solid grip on our own bootstraps, we should be able to yank ourselves straight out of suffering and into a fabulous life. Most of my clients, once they've admitted that their lives aren't really working, try to fix the problem by doing everything they've always done, but harder. They try to work better, look better, love better, eat better, just generally *be better, dammit!*

This is like waking up behind the wheel of the car, realizing you've drifted off the highway, and flooring the gas pedal in response. It can turn a precarious situation into a truly dangerous one. When we realize we're off course, the best thing we can do is slow down or even stop in our tracks. Then we can take stock of the situation and eventually find our way back to safety—a process you began by taking the quiz and trying the exercise in the previous chapter. If you found any murky areas in your life, you may have jumped to the conclusion that you need to try harder, be better. That almost certainly won't help.

Listen: the problem isn't how hard you're working, it's that you're working on things that aren't right for you. Your goals and motivations aren't harmonizing with your deepest truth. They didn't come from your own natural inclinations. They came from the two forces that drive us all off our true paths: trauma and socialization.

By "trauma" I don't just mean horrific tragedies like war or child abuse. I mean any painful experience that makes us feel blindsided and out of our depth. Being shamed by our parents or schoolmates can be traumatic. So can a financial downturn, an intense argument, the loss of a pet. Often our response to such events is to change our behavior to avoid repeating the experience. For example, if we're jilted in love or disappointed in our career, we may vow never to love again or never to trust our own aspirations.

The way we handle trauma is shaped by socialization. Not knowing what to do, we do what we know. We keep a stiff upper lip, or throw emotional tantrums to get attention from our loved ones, or go off by ourselves to brood. We repeat the pattern over and over, even when it doesn't make us feel one bit better. When we notice that it isn't working, we do it harder.

THE PROBLEM WITH "SUCCESS"

Dante wrote a vivid metaphor about this in *The Divine Comedy*. Shortly after realizing he's lost in the dark wood of error, the poet sees a mountain rising out of the murk, bathed in morning sunlight. It's so pretty and glowy that Dante calls it *dilettoso monte*, which translates to English as "Mount Delectable." It looks like the perfect way out of the dark wood, so although Dante is bone-tired, he sets out climbing . . . to no avail. Here come all those frightening beasts—remember them? They frighten, depress, and chase our hero back into the lowlands.

I see Mount Delectable as a symbol of all the ways to be "better" that we learn from our cultural context. For most people, this involves money: piles and piles of money. This basic golden substrate may be topped with layers of dazzling physical beauty, intellectual brilliance, artistic perfection, fairy-tale romance, or all of the above. "That! That! That!" we think. "Getting a Nobel Prize! Winning *all* the Oscars! Selling enough moonshine to keep Pawpaw in false teeth forever! *That* will make everything better!"

The problem with all our Mount Delectables is that they're still part of the dark wood of error that's making us miserable. Trying to climb the mountain of "better" almost always involves huge amounts of exhausting labor, when we're already dead tired.

Then, of course, there are those dreadful emotional states, the anxiety and depression and anger that accost us just when we seem to be making progress. They scuttle our best efforts, weaken our resolve, and land us back in the deepest parts of the dark wood.

I've clambered up the foothills of my own Mount Delectable several times. Even when I reached some of my target basecamps, it never made me feel better for more than a few days. As I've mentioned, I've coached people who seemed to live right up near the summit of Mount Delectable, but none of them expressed lasting contentment either. Because we're so indoctrinated to believe that "success" equals happiness, it's worth restating the point.

I remember getting a midnight call from a famous entrepreneur I'll call Keith, whose company had just gone public. Keith had made over two hundred million dollars the previous day. He phoned me from a celebration party, three sheets to the wind on fifty-year-old Scotch and a grab bag of fun pharmaceuticals. A famous band rocked and rolled in the background so hard I could barely hear Keith.

"YOU KNOW WHAT?" he screamed into the phone, "IT ISN'T ENOUGH! I THOUGHT IT WOULD BE ENOUGH, BUT IT'S NOT! WHEN IS IT EVER F*CKING GOING TO BE ENOUGH?"

It was a rhetorical question. Even if I'd tried to answer, Keith wouldn't have heard anything over the rock band in the room and the cultural messages in his head. Over and over, we'd talked about the fact that he was happiest doing simple things, like hiking. But Keith truly believed that if he did less of that and focused on getting even richer, he'd finally feel good enough. I hope it worked for him eventually. I have my doubts.

WHAT WE'RE TAUGHT TO WANT

At the heart of climbing Mount Delectable is what psychologists call "social comparison theory." It means that we tend to measure our own well-being not by how we feel, but by how our lives compare to other people's. An almost universal dark-wood error is believing that happiness will arrive when we're *above* others in some socially defined way. And because that way is shaped by culture, not nature, people can climb Mount Delectable by doing the weirdest things.

For example, for women in traditional China, climbing the social ladder required having teeny-tiny feet. Generations of girls and women had their feet bound and crushed, crippling them to make them *better*. In Victorian England, women wore fabrics dyed with arsenic that caused skin ulcers and had a tendency to burst into flames—a small price to pay for looking *better* than their fashion rivals! In our society, people will virtually kill themselves trying to be *better* by decorating the fanciest cake, or breeding the most standard of all standard poodles, or clubbing a tiny little ball into a tiny little hole.

You won't catch wild animals pouring their energy into such random activities. Some creatures compete for food, territory, and mates. Many love to play, and seem to enjoy their mock victories. But they don't pull out their own hair and feathers if they fail to accrue a billion times as much birdseed or dead rabbits as the next sparrow or coyote. Mount Delectable is built on the uniquely human characteristic of assigning "achievement" value to random things. It's all about culture, not nature.

Your true self, by contrast, is pure nature. It doesn't give a tinker's damn who wore it best, or if anyone wore it at all. Olympic medals and Pulitzer Prizes interest it only because they're shiny. Your true nature loves things for their capacity to bring genuine delight, right here, right now. It loves romps, friends, skin contact, sunlight, water, laughter, the smell of trees, the delicious stillness of deep sleep. Here's a little thought exercise that may help you feel the difference between an impulse that comes from culture and one that comes from nature.

EXERCISE:
Culture or nature?

First, recall the last time you saw some sort of advertising that really appealed to you. It might have been a television commercial, an ad on social media, or a display in a storefront. As it grabbed your attention, you might have felt strong desire for whatever was being advertised. Suddenly, you wanted—really wanted—the latest model of that smartphone, or that slick new car, or a trendier jacket than any you now own. Write down the thing you wanted. Foot bag

Something advertising made me want:

Football

For a moment, think about having this thing. Notice how your body feels as you hold the thought. Maybe you almost thirst to own this item. Maybe you feel a little racy with hope, or bitter with the conviction that you'll never have such an awesome object. As best you can, write down a description of the sensation you get when you let yourself want this item. What do you feel, physically and emotionally, when you think about getting it?

When I imagine getting the thing advertising made me want, I experience the following sensations:

Physical sensations:

Feet Relief

Emotional sensations:

hope

Now, shake it out. Literally. (Shaking your head, hands, or whole body, the way an animal might as it climbs out of water, can help clear your mind and emotions.) Let go of the advertising image. Notice if this is hard for you, if you're almost compelled to go place an order for the New Thing, or at least stare at images of it. Whenever you can let go of this wanting enough to feel centered in the present moment, answer the following question:

When you're alone in the quiet—say, lying awake at night—what do you yearn for? Not just want, *yearn* for. Write down the first thing that comes to mind.

Something I yearn for when I'm quiet:

Peace inside out

Allow the sensation of yearning for this thing to grow. Vividly imagine having it. How does this image affect your body and your emotions? List them below.

When I imagine getting the thing I yearn for when I'm quiet, I experience the following sensations:

Physical sensations:

Relaxed

Emotional sensations:

Dreamy

Can you pick up any differences? The exact experience will be particular to you, but people typically feel completely disparate sensations when they're triggered by advertising, as opposed to letting their desires emerge spontaneously from within.

This next point is important: to the extent that you're divided from your true self, you'll find that your wanting and your yearning are directed at different things.

When we aren't distracted by culture, we move directly toward fulfilling our innate longing. When we're craving things we've been taught to want, we lose track of our inner motivations entirely and may spend a lifetime pursuing rewards that never make us feel truly fulfilled.

I've used this exercise with many, many clients. Their wants are as widely divergent as their social conditioning. They want different kinds of clothes, houses, experiences, relationships. But they all *yearn* for just a few things, and those things are remarkably consistent, even among people from very different cultures. They include peace, freedom, love, comfort, and belonging.

Here's what I've noticed: if you spend your life pursuing culturally defined goals (climbing Mount Delectable), you may manage to get what you want, but you probably won't get what you yearn for. If you choose to leave Mount Delectable behind, you might not get what you want in that socially driven, craving kind of way. But you won't care, because your entire world will fill up—pressed down, shaken together, and running over, as the Good Book says—with all the things for which you yearn. And here is how to leave Mount Delectable behind: stop with the hustle.

THE CULTURAL HUSTLE

Mount Delectables arise out of the gloomy woods only when a group of people share common values. For example, in present-day America, crushing your daughter's feet down to four-inch "lily buds" (as they were known in China) would not propel you to the top of the social register; it would propel you to the top of the Child Welfare Service's most wanted list. Nor would your Facebook "Likes" go wild if you wore flammable, arsenic-dyed clothing. Your cultural group has to agree that your Mount Delectable accomplishments are desirable, since in nature's reality—including the reality of your own true nature—they mean nothing.

Humans are so tuned in to cultural values that once we start craving our way up Mount Delectable, we may go completely blind to our own real desires. We can't *lose* our true nature, since it's in our DNA, but we can divide ourselves from it to get better at various cultural games. My friend Rayya, who spent years on the street as a drug addict, called this "running a hustle." She did it for decades to procure drugs, or money to buy drugs. Long after getting clean and sober, she told me, "I can still walk into any room and read everyone's hustle. Because pretty much everyone is always hustling someone to get something."

According to my online dictionaries, *hustle* has a bevy of interesting meanings in modern English. Here are a few. These aren't in my own words; they're real quotes from dictionaries.

Definitions of "Hustle"
1. Have the courage, confidence, self-belief, and self-determination to go out there and work it out until you find the opportunities you want in life.
2. Force (someone) to move hurriedly in a specified direction.
3. Coerce or pressure someone into doing or choosing something.

4. Engage in prostitution.

5. Obtain by illicit action; swindle; cheat.

You can see a portrait of modern Western culture in this single word. Our social definition of "success" is all about hustle. We must rise above others, and that entails: (1) embodying confidence and self-determination, (2) going very fast, (3) pressuring other people into doing what we want, (4) selling ourselves, and (5) swindling and cheating. That, my friend, is how to climb Mount Delectable.

This way of going through life is incredibly effective for accruing *stuff*: land, gold, food, housing. It works so well that people who believed in it managed to colonize the whole damn planet. In the process, they (we) communicated the value of hustling to pretty much everyone we didn't manage to flat-out kill. So it's almost certain you've received some or all of your social training from this cultural tradition. You probably assume at a deep, unarticulated level, that to climb up to a happier place in life, you have no alternative but to join the hustle.

Anything you do solely to influence others, rather than to express your true nature, is a hustle. Being polite to get approval is a hustle. Flirting with people to make them feel special is a hustle. Sitting solemnly in church, consciously exuding piety, is a hustle. Acting a little bit stupid to avoid threatening others is a hustle. Using big words to impress is a hustle. Wearing certain clothes because you want to look professional, or sexy, or hip, or rich, or tall, or nonconformist, or demure—hustle, hustle, hustle.

Mind you, hustling doesn't mean you're bad. It means you're

well socialized, cooperating beautifully with culture. But it also means you're split from your true nature. In millions of small ways and some huge ones, you ignore what you naturally yearn for and hustle along to get the things you've been taught to want. Here's a little thought exercise to help you get a sense for this.

EXERCISE:
Feeling the difference

Think about three or four things you've done during the past week. They could be really small things, like brushing your teeth, or enormous things, like robbing a bank, or in-between things, like cooking breakfast or grooming a parrot. Choose one that, in hindsight, seems relatively pleasant.

Now let yourself vividly and carefully remember how you felt as you undertook this activity. Were you buoyed up, delighted, as you anticipated doing it? Once you got started, did you genuinely enjoy it? When you finished, were you pleased by the whole process? Make a note:

_____Swimming_____

Speedo ____X_____

Next, recall something you did during the past week that didn't thrill you. How did you feel, physically and emotionally, as you approached the task? How did you feel while doing it—depressed, tired, confused, annoyed, distracted? Write it down:

_____Hangout to God - Chapter_____
_____Bury)_____

Try toggling back and forth between these two sensations. Even if the difference is slight, notice it carefully. This is the difference between doing something from integrity and doing something to conform with a cultural hustle.

WHAT WE'RE TAUGHT TO IGNORE

Considering the two activities you've just used above, notice that there's only one reason you did the unpleasant thing: at some level *you thought you had to.* Maybe you did it out of fear, dreading what would happen if you didn't. Maybe you were trying to please someone. Maybe you have a whole set of acculturated rules sunk so deep in your brain that it never occurred to you it might have been possible to avoid this activity you dislike.

I'm not saying that all social conventions are bad. I don't think living in integrity means we should abandon cultural norms and run around naked, stealing food and humping attractive strangers. I just want you to be crystal clear about the difference between the behavior of your true self and your false self, between your joy and your hustle.

This is the second step on your way of integrity, a prelude to aligning your thoughts and actions with your truth. *It requires nothing of you except to recognize when you're doing something because it's prescribed by culture, and when an action arises from your true nature.* At this point there's no other action step.

NOTHING IS ABSOLUTELY TRUE

This is what I did after my massive crash at age eighteen. Since I'd found that not knowing what was true seemed to lie at the heart of my confusion, I set out to answer the question *What is true?* like a starving tiger sets out hunting. Still flat in bed, I read my way through several great works of Western philosophy, starting with the pre-Socratics and plowing on, in chronological order, through scores of incredibly dull books. Many just made me more depressed, because the philosophers in question often took a moment to affirm that all women are brainless, drooling, sinful, knuckle-dragging brood sows (I'm paraphrasing here).

After several months I finally reached Immanuel Kant's unspeakably dull masterwork, *The Critique of Pure Reason.* It bored the living crap out of me—and changed my life forever. Kant believed that our minds create all our experience, including space and time. There may be a reality out there, but we can perceive it only through the filter of our subjective perceptions, which means that *no one can ever know what's absolutely true.* Kant's reasoning felt right to me, and also mind-blowingly paradoxical: it's absolutely true that nothing is absolutely true, including this statement.

To me this felt like escaping from a cold, dark cave. It meant I could accommodate all cultural beliefs. The Mormons might be right about the nature of the universe, or they might be wrong. The good folks at Harvard might be right—or wrong—

in their utterly different version of reality. Who could ever be certain? Not yours truly. Whew! What a relief! Since everyone was making everything up as they went, I could go along with everyone while absolutely believing no one.

This proved to be a handy-dandy strategy for climbing Mount Delectable. I married another Mormon who was also educated at Harvard. Together we went about securing as many graduate degrees as we could, while still showing up as exemplary Latter-Day Saints. I had my first child and headed into my PhD program, like a pioneer woman whelping a young'un in the midst of plowing the fields. I was hustling *everybody*, including myself.

But I still had symptoms of dark-wood error. I felt hollow and anxious, addicted to continuous work. My exhausted body was still dragged down by insomnia, pain, and illness. I'd found a bit of my true nature, which really did enjoy learning and really did love my family. But the vast majority of my actions were responses to cultural pressures. I was halfway up Mount Delectable and climbing fast, toward nothing that made me genuinely happy.

EXERCISE:
Detecting your hustle

If you found out that some of the things you do every day come from culture, not your true nature, you're hustling up your own version of Mount Delectable. Are you ready to get radically honest about that? Then ask yourself the following questions, and pause after each until you can feel the real answer. (Again, you don't have to do anything except allow for internal recognition of the real situation. Just notice the difference between things you genuinely love to do and things you do for other reasons.)

- Do you ever hang out with people you don't truly enjoy? Who are they?

  _____ *yes - some in the pod*

  _____

  _____

- Do you consistently make yourself do anything (or many things) you don't really want to do? Make a list.

  _____ *cleaning for not*

  _____ *out to lunch - maybe*

  _____

- Are there things you do solely out of fear that *not* doing them will upset someone, or lower your value in someone else's eyes? What are they?

  _____ *sometimes -*

  _____

  _____

- Are there any times in your daily life where you're consistently pretending to be happier or more interested than you really are? In what areas (relationships, job activities, places) do you tend to do this?

  _____ *On the phone*

  _____

  _____

- Do you ever say things you know aren't true, or things you don't really, truly mean? What are they?

Not really

Read over everything you wrote down in the exercise, and you'll see a clutch of situations in which you're leaving your integrity to run a cultural hustle. You haven't done anything wrong, and there's no need to take any action at this point. Just notice how much of your life is spent hustling.

Often my clients feel a bit unmoored or even offended by this exercise. The unpleasant things they're forcing themselves to do, the areas where they lie about their feelings, the times they obey shame or threats of punishment are the very aspects of their behavior they believe to be most virtuous. If you're a stay-at-home mother who's never really enjoyed being around children, a firefighter who longs for quiet, intellectual work, or a soldier who doesn't thrive on routine, you may be proud that you've forced yourself to go against your nature and do what appears righteous to your culture. Now I'm telling you that this admirable effort is out of integrity.

What the hell?

Just breathe. I'm not saying that your efforts to fulfill cultural standards are bad. Quite the opposite. You're doing a Herculean job of living up to standards you truly believe are right and good. I admire that very much. It takes incredible self-discipline to go against your nature. If I scolded you about this effort, I'd just be administering another dose of punitive socialization. I'm not condemning you in the slightest. But I do want you to notice one thing:

Whenever you go against your true nature to serve your culture, you freaking hate it.

Remember, there's no change implication here, not yet. I encourage you to go right on living your life exactly as you've been doing so far. Keep running your hustle. Run as many hustles as you want. The only change to make at this point on your way of integrity is to admit—just to yourself—that some of your actions are designed to impress or fit in with other people. These actions aren't spontaneous, and they aren't in harmony with your truth. But at this point you don't need a revolution. What you do need is a teacher. Which, as destiny would have it, is the very next thing you'll encounter on the way of integrity.

3.

Meeting the Teacher

As Dante flees the slopes of Mount Delectable, he sees a human figure walking in the dark wood. He calls out, desperate for help but unnerved by the suspicion that this person may not be . . . what's the word? Oh, yes: alive. Sure enough, it turns out to be a ghost. But the best possible ghost: Publius Vergilius Maro, better known as Virgil. Yes, the guy's been dead for centuries, but on the plus side, he's Dante's favorite poet.

After introducing himself, Virgil asks why Dante isn't clambering up Mount Delectable with all the other kids. When Dante points out the bloodthirsty leopard that's been chasing him, Virgil seems to grasp the entire situation. He says that Dante will have to take an altogether different road to get out of the dark wood of error. Then he appoints himself as a travel companion and guide, saying he's been sent to help Dante through the journey.

HOW THE TEACHER ARRIVES

That's fantasy for you, am I right? In his worst hour, out in the middle of nowhere, Dante *just happens* to come across his favorite undead writer, who *just happens* to know exactly where Dante needs to go, and *just happens* to have the free time and the inclination to serve as a personal escort. If only the real world worked that way, right?

Well, here's the thing: it does.

I've watched this kind of small miracle play out over and over, in my own life and the lives of clients. Just when a teacher became necessary for forward progress, someone or something showed up to help.

In actual fact, Dante Alighieri first "met" Virgil by reading his poetry. Reading is the way I've met most of my life teachers, and clients often tell me that just when they felt most confused, the perfect book seemed to "throw itself off the shelf" and into their attention. Sometimes we meet our teachers because someone sees we need help and drags us to therapy, rehab, yoga, or some other environment where we can meet wise guides. Or maybe we catch a snippet of a podcast or an online lecture and become fascinated by the speaker.

Joseph Campbell, the famous professor of comparative mythology, noticed that in legends from around the world, some kind of mentor arrives shortly after a hero has accepted a call to adventure. Embarking on the way of integrity is just such a situation. We tend to meet teachers after we've realized we're wandering in a dark wood of error, after we've tried and failed to get out of it by climbing Mount Delectable, and while we're still being dogged by the wild beasts of our painful emotions.

At this point, our odds of finding the way back to wholeness all by ourselves are vanishingly small. After all, we wandered off course because of ideas and behaviors we've been learning since birth. Most of these errors lurk in our psychological blind spots. Without some outside assistance, we might never see them, no matter how earnestly we try. But someone with a different perspective can spot what we're missing and help set us right. And so we are primed to meet a very specific type of teacher: a *psychopomp*, or "guide of the soul."

Before going any further, I need to point out something absolutely crucial: no external teacher can ever be the answer to all your problems. The role of soul teachers is crucial but limited. They offer just enough feedback to help us find the wisdom at the core of our own consciousness. Ultimately (spoiler alert), Virgil won't be able to guide Dante all the way to paradise. No one can give us pure integrity: knowing our truth is something we can and must learn to do on our own. The role of the soul guide is simply to put us in touch with our innate ability to sense the truth.

That said, when we're still wandering around the dark wood of error, knowing we're lost but clueless about how to find ourselves, a teacher is essential. So stay alert for anyone that may offer help or guidance. The teacher may not look like what you expect.

HOW TO RECOGNIZE A
SOUL TEACHER

Soul teachers don't always fit our preconceptions. Some soul guides are actual schoolteachers, like the Robin Williams character in *Dead Poets Society*, whose wacky methods open his pupils' hearts and souls along with their minds. But as I've mentioned, your teacher may arrive via a book, a song, an animal. It may even show up as a time of intense experience, a phase when circumstances force you to gain a great deal of understanding, fast.

You may have had one or more of these oddly educational phases in your life. We've all seen them dramatized in movies: a bigot's life is saved by the very people he despises; a money-obsessed socialite loses her savings to a Ponzi scheme the same week her mansion burns to the ground; a narcissistic doctor develops the very illness he's been treating and is forced to experience his patients' point of view. When this kind of thing happens to us, we may feel as if we're being tutored by a subtle but powerful energy, far beyond our control. Any force that helps produce such situations is clearly a master soul teacher.

Most of our teachers, however, show up as individual humans. Usually rather odd ones. Meeting yours probably won't feel like sitting down with a loving nanny or wise, bespectacled professor. When we first encounter true soul teachers, they often appear anomalous, annoying, incomprehensible, or downright weird. I'm going to give you some general rules for identifying them. But first, let me tell you what a soul teacher is *not*, so you won't become enchanted with a fraudulent psychopomp.

There are plenty of people who are very excited to tell you exactly what you should do, think, and be: TV pundits, authority figures, opinionated relatives, friends who've just found religion, or strangers shouting at you from the internet. When you meet such a person, be very careful. Anyone who tries to force-feed you advice isn't likely to be a competent soul guide.

Other people promise to take you to the top of Mount Delectable, making you beautiful, rich, and famous, in exchange for absolute devotion and/or large sums of money. Again, these are rarely real soul teachers. If your heart *yearns* to follow such a person, go ahead. But beware of the craving that can arise in you when you're subjected to advertising. A real soul teacher will draw your attention in a way that makes you feel inwardly driven, not dazed by powerful marketing (if you need a review, you can repeat the exercise in Chapter 2).

These days, the term *soul teacher* is used by some spiritually minded folks to describe people they can't stand. "She's my most profound teacher," they'll say of the coworker with the hideous braying laugh, or of the stepchild who steals their credit cards to pay for sex. "He's the Buddha in my path." The danger of this is that it may lead people to stay in relationship dynamics that are actually unhealthy. Genuine soul teachers may perplex or disturb us, but they tend to be fascinating, not repulsive or unbearable.

With all that out of the way, here's what I *do* mean when I say "soul teacher."

Soul teachers capture our attention

When we meet a true guide, there's often something almost eerie about the encounter. Part of our attention gets inexplicably fixated on whoever or whatever has shown up to teach us. I call this the "R2-D2 effect," after the little droid in the first *Star Wars* movie. From the perspective of his friend C-3PO, everything is normal until the moment R2-D2 meets with Princess Leia. Then he zips off, abandoning his companion. Unbeknownst to C-3PO, the little droid has been given a mission by Princess Leia. That purpose overrides all other directives.

Sometimes our minds seem to buzz off in this unexpected way. We may find ourselves ruminating about a person we barely met at a dinner party, or an old friend we haven't seen for years, or a stranger whose name comes up in conversations with three different people. We don't know why these individuals command so much of our attention, but we can't stop thinking about them. We may even have the disconcerting sense that they've moved into our minds. We may find ourselves arguing with them, or explaining ourselves to them, all the time wondering why we care so much what they think.

Soul teachers come with a dash of magic

In Joseph Campbell's heroic saga, the hero's meeting with the teacher occurs by fate, magic, or divine assignment. When we meet a soul guide, there's often a series of coincidences or a touch of grace bringing teacher and student together. This bit of magic validates the R2-D2 effect, hinting that it's our destiny to cross paths with a particular teacher.

For instance, my client Michelle once received a certain self-help book as a gift from a friend, found another copy lying on an empty park bench, and ran into the author at a book signing, all in the same week. That book, she told me, was exactly what she needed.

Another client, Erin, met a fellow American at a coffee shop during a vacation in Paris. Later she told me, "I didn't go to France to meet other Americans, but for some reason I couldn't stop chatting with him." Erin's new acquaintance turned out to be a trauma counselor who lived a ten-minute drive from her home in Cleveland. Erin had survived a rape attempt in college. Once home from her vacation, she had a few sessions with her new friend that eased the suffering based on that trauma.

Still another client, Michael, was waiting tables at a restaurant when for some reason he felt compelled to trade one of his tables with another waiter. The next party to sit at his new table included an old friend of Michael's father. They struck up a conversation that eventually led to the older man offering Michael a job, then mentoring him until he learned enough to succeed on his own.

These stories may lull you into thinking that you don't need to look for a teacher, that the perfect soul guide will break into your apartment and offer salvation while you sit in your underwear eating Froot Loops out of the box. This could happen— I've seen weirder things—but it probably won't. As they say, the teacher appears when the student is ready. We make ourselves ready just by realizing we're lost and committing to the way of integrity. A teacher will eventually show up, often in unexpected ways. The dash of magic, if and when it happens, is like the cherry on the sundae.

Soul teachers offer genuine love

When we hear the term *soul teacher*, most of us initially picture a soothing, comforting presence, someone to sing us to sleep and then watch over us. But a real soul guide's job is to *wake us up* when we're somnambulating through the dark wood of error. This may involve jangling us, shocking us, contradicting what we deeply believe. In Asian traditions, spiritual teachers are known for dashing cold water in their students' faces or whacking them with bamboo sticks.

It may be years before we realize—often in hindsight—that this behavior is deeply loving. Many of us might use the word *love* to describe the kind of devotion spiders feel for flies. Spiders genuinely love flies (the way they taste, the way they crunch). They express that love by wrapping up any fly they can catch and keeping it close, slurping out its life force bit by bit. I've had many clients whose parents, friends, or lovers treated them this way. I call it "spider love," though of course it's really not love at all; it's a predator-prey relationship. And soul teachers never do it. Real love doesn't want anyone to be immobilized or attached, certainly not in the dark wood of error. It wants— always, always, always—to set us free.

That's why our truest guides don't help us get comfortable

in our illusions. Instead they rattle our cages, make us uneasy, confiscate our sedatives. When someone you feel drawn to upsets your patterns of thought, you may feel petulant and unloved, like a child whose parents refuse to serve candy for dinner. But pay close attention. As long as it liberates you, what looks like harshness or even cruelty may in fact be the purest love you could possibly receive.

Soul teachers don't share our culture's values

What? Not share our values? Aren't we supposed to spend our lives looking for teachers who *do* share our values?

Not when we're in the dark wood of error.

Remember, cultural value systems play a central role in leading us off our true paths and sending us up all those versions of Mount Delectable. Following cultural values, we exhaust ourselves chasing things that will never make us genuinely happy. To lead us away from such errors, soul teachers must be free from our particular brand of cultural delusion.

Because of this, real soul guides are the definition of "countercultural." Some of them are merely unpredictable, while others might live outside culture altogether, self-determined and wild, like John the Baptist before he ran into Jesus (or Jesus himself, with his obstinate refusal to throw rocks at sinners). Soul teachers often say and do things that just aren't said and done in our social circles—or any social circles. Their manners, their reactions, their advice may be different from anything we're used to.

Contrarian soul teachers are honored in many traditions.

The Lakota people have sacred clowns who deliberately defy social convention by riding their horses backward, going half-naked in winter, saying rude things at the worst possible moment. In medieval Europe, the court jesters were allowed to insult anyone, even the king. Teachers who flout convention and poke fun help us keep from getting lost in our social roles and taking ourselves too seriously.

Of course, not everyone who's strange, rude, or antisocial is a true soul guide. Such teachers are countercultural in a very particular way: they jolt us out of our assumptions and force us to see new perspectives. By contrast, mere gibberish may seem bizarre, but it won't feel compellingly interesting, and it won't expand your mind.

I felt the difference between cultural confusion and soul guidance after my adolescent crisis and my year of reading philosophy. Still curious about wisdom traditions, I read a lot of books I'd heard touted as soul guides. I'd been told that reading Mormon scripture was perhaps the most important way to ensure a happy life. I followed the rules but never found myself feeling deeply liberated by those particular books. Then I began studying Chinese and started reading things that made no sense to my American-made mind. Here's an example, from my favorite book, the *Tao te Ching*, written around 2500 BC: "All streams flow to the sea because it is lower than they are. Humility gives it its power."

This is a very un-Western way of thinking. At first blush, it may sound a little alien to you, a little strange. But see if it makes you want to stop and think. See if it knocks at the door of your mind, asking to come in. This is how real soul guidance affects us. It may be strange, but it isn't just bizarre. It's *potent*, like concentrated cleanser. It challenges our assumptions, but the challenge feels oddly compelling.

Soul teachers don't care about our hustle

Because they are outside culture, real soul guides couldn't give a damn about our hustles. They don't gush over us when we act sweet, or goggle at our street-smart toughness, or coo over our victim stories, or bow before our wealth and status. If you give a soul teacher a lavish gift, she may thank you and then immediately hand over your precious item to a passing stranger (that actually happened to me once). No flattery, manipulation, or temper tantrum will move soul teachers one millimeter from their own true paths.

This may be as frustrating to our egos as it is necessary for our liberation. I had a client I'll call Olivia, a classical pianist, whose music teacher drove her to distraction, dismissing all her impressive skills and giving her advice she couldn't follow.

"He never seems to approve of anything I do," she told me. "He never compliments me, just listens to my performance and says things like, 'Now play it as if you have no past.' What the hell does that even mean? Should I just sit on the piano bench without moving, and pretend I'm not really there?"

Despite her frustration, Olivia felt maddeningly intrigued

by her teacher, and continued to work with him. One day he gave her so many complicated, rapid-fire instructions that as she began playing, she lost track of them all.

"It wasn't that my mind went blank," Olivia told me. "It actually seemed to go *away*." At that moment she stopped feeling herself as being separate from the music.

"I stopped trying to impress him," she said. "I became those sounds as they made themselves happen with my fingers. It was so beautiful there were tears in my eyes, and when I looked at my teacher, there were tears in his, too. There was nothing to say about it. It was just . . . perfect."

Soul teachers help us think the unthinkable

Not only do soul teachers fail to fall in with our hustles, they may *actually talk about the fact that we're hustling.* Instead of praising our designer clothes or clever wordplay, they may mention that we seem to be trying to impress them. When we cover our existential despair with flippancy, they may skip the polite laughter and ask why we're acting happy when we seem so sad.

Yes, I know! Shocking!

This violates what psychiatrist Alice Miller calls the cardinal rule of all cultures: DON'T EVER MENTION THE RULES. In other words, never articulate that there's an unspoken code everyone in the room has been trained to follow. Even though you know everyone can see that the emperor has no clothes, don't mention that everyone's pretending he's dressed because everyone's afraid. Never say, "Mother takes too much laudanum," but more importantly, never articulate the family's unspoken rule against mentioning Mother's laudanum habit. Just lie when you're expected to lie, never mentioning that you all know you're lying. Soul teachers just run right over this rule and talk openly and honestly about what's actually going on, like savages.

Soul teachers know when to quit

"When you meet the Buddha on the road, kill him." This saying, attributed to the Zen master Linji, doesn't mean you should actually go after monks with chainsaws. It means that once you've recognized a real soul guide, you may be tempted to latch on to that person's teachings like a baby sloth. The problem is that reality is too vast and intricate to be fully represented by one person, one set of ideas, or indeed all people and ideas combined.

The idea of "killing the Buddha" means learning all you can from any given teacher, until you begin to transcend them. Then you can use both the truths you've learned and the falsehoods you've spotted to move on.

Every true guide will tell you this, repeatedly and insistently turning you back to your own discernment as the final arbiter of your beliefs. One of my favorite Indian sages, Nisargadatta Maharaj, put it this way, "The outer teacher is merely a milestone. It is only your inner teacher that will walk with you to the goal, for he [she] *is* the goal."

FINDING YOUR INNER GUIDANCE

Now that I've given you a few pointers for recognizing an outward soul teacher, I want to talk more about the inner teacher, the one who *is* your goal. This ultimate guide has been with you since before you were born, and will be available to you until the moment you draw your last breath (and who knows, maybe even after). Remember, when Dante wrote *The Divine Comedy*, he created the ghost of Virgil in his imagination. Dante's real guide was a projected teacher he made up—a part of himself. No external guide you'll meet will ever be as accurate as the teacher in your soul, and none can ever be as constant.

Your inner teacher has many names, but none of them really conveys the essence of this core wisdom. When spiritual traditions set out to describe it, they generate a lot of semantic confusion. This is because they're trying to describe something indescribable. Spiritual traditions have coined a whole lexicon of terms trying to label the inner teacher, the wisdom at our center, the essence of what we actually, intrinsically are.

In this book I've referred to your inner teacher primarily as your integrity. But I've also used the terms *true self, true nature,* and *essential self.* In another book I called it the *meta-self,* which means "beyond self," as opposed to your *meat-self* (your body and brain). Labels from other writers include the no-self, absolute awareness, Buddha-nature, Christ consciousness, enlightened mind, God-consciousness, the non-being, the I am, the absolute, the universe, fundamental consciousness, and many more.

The real essence of your inner teacher lies beyond labels. You can't experience it by thinking about it, only by *being* it.

Now, of course, having just told you that your inner teacher is indescribable, I'm going to try to describe it. When we think, hear, or understand something that's deeply true for us, our inner teachers rise in us as a delicious, lucid resonance. When we grasp truth—any truth, from the correct solution to a math problem to the capacity for love—all of our ways of knowing align. We recognize this alignment as our ideal state of being. It feels calm, clear, still, open. That feeling is the inner teacher saying yes.

The way of integrity is simply to listen to this voice, to sustain this feeling not just occasionally, but often—even continuously. Individuals who can do this are venerated as spiritual masters. If you despair of ever becoming so enlightened, remember that you've already done it once. You were a baby for a while, and babies who are too young to have any beliefs simply align with what they truly perceive. That's why spiritual teachers often point to little children as role models for enlightened living.

But even we grown-ups, lost in the dark wood of error, feel at one with our true selves again every time we brush away a cobweb of false belief and perceive something real. At these moments, when the inner teacher makes its presence known, we sometimes say we're experiencing the "ring of truth."

The last time you woke up from a dream, it may have taken you a few seconds to orient yourself. But you soon figured out that what had seemed to be reality, only moments before, was just a hallucination. How did you make this determination? How

cide which experience was real and which was illu-
~~.~.~: ny checking in with the inner teacher I've just described.

This isn't a complicated process: waking life is observably more resonant with truth than a dream once we've evaluated the two experiences. We do this with all our meaning-making systems: body, mind, heart, and soul. I'm going to spend some time breaking this down for you, using that four-part division (body/mind/heart/soul). I'm dwelling on this because *listening to our inner teacher is the most important skill we need to follow the way of integrity.* When we meet external soul teachers, we know to trust them only because we feel the ring of truth internally. And even when no external teacher is available, the inner teacher always is.

So another characteristic of the inner teacher—the most important one—is that you can feel it in all aspects of your being (body/mind/heart/soul) at once.

The **body's** reaction to recognizing truth is *relaxation*, a literal, involuntary release of muscle tension. When we surrender to the truth, even difficult truth, our bodies may go almost limp and we begin breathing more deeply. This may have happened to you when you read the statements at the end of Chapter 1, such as "I don't know what to do" or "I need help."

When our **minds** recognize truth, we experience that invisible cartoon light bulb going on in our heads, the feeling of a riddle being solved. "Aha!" we think, or "I get it!" or "Of course!" All the puzzle pieces fit. The math works. Everything makes *logical sense*.

To our **heart**, the ring of truth feels like a flower *opening up*. In total integrity, we're completely available to all emotion: overwhelming love, deep grief, terrible anger, sharp fear. This emotion may be painful, but it doesn't cause the intense, dull suffering we feel in the dark wood of error.

The emotional pain of a hard truth is eased by our **soul's** response to aligning with reality. Around and beyond mere emotion, we feel a sense of *freedom*, a vast openness that includes all aspects of our experience. We connect with an unalterable stillness around and within us. There's space for pain. There's space for joy. And the space in which all sensation happens is made up of absolute well-being. It is (we are) a perfect, fertile no-thing-ness in which everything, even pain, has a useful place.

All this mystical language may sound strange, but in fact your inner teacher is the part of you that feels most stable and ordinary. Because our secular culture denies the spiritual, some people think the "ring of truth" must feel unusual, like interior fireworks. In fact, it's the opposite. Our sense of truth, our ultimate inner teacher, is as familiar to us as the sun and the moon. We use it constantly in ordinary perception. As I've just noted, it's what allows us to distinguish our dreams from waking life every single morning.

Practices like fasting, taking psychedelic drugs, or spending years in silence can help us access the spiritual dimension of our being. But we're also responding to spiritual experiences every time we recognize any truth, even the most ordinary. Spiritual confirmation is present when we remember a phone number, laugh at a joke, or forgive ourselves for a mistake. It waves at us cheerfully from the most mundane things, like little Yoda scuttling after Luke Skywalker as Luke searches for the Jedi master he assumes must be huge and imposing.

Every external teacher you'll ever meet will be there only to help you connect with this sense of truth, this body-mind-heart-soul chime that is your ultimate inner teacher. For example, I hope this book is a helpful guide on your journey to integrity. But if you don't feel the ring of truth as you read something written here, disregard my words. Don't listen to me; listen to yourself. Do the same when the person "teaching" is your minister, your karate teacher, your mayor, or your spouse. Every real soul guide outside you will bow to the teacher inside you.

MY MOST UNEXPECTED SOUL TEACHER

As I've mentioned, when I was a teenager, the soul teacher who met me in the dark wood of error was Immanuel Kant, via his opus, *The Critique of Pure Reason*. Reading Kant's prose was like eating machine parts, but as he explained why pure reason can't know anything absolutely, I felt my whole being—body, mind, heart, and soul—come into alignment. I went limp with relief, with the logic of Kant's arguments, with the freedom they offered me.

I rested in Kant's worldview as I finished college, got married, went back to Harvard for my master's and doctoral degrees. I had my first child, a daughter, between undergraduate and graduate school. Then I got pregnant again. I didn't know it, but I was headed into one of those situations in which the whole world takes on a soul teacher's role. My world was about to turn upside down.

First of all, from the moment my son Adam was conceived, I became—I'll just say it—psychic. I could see what was happening to loved ones far away. I knew things would occur before they did. I felt myself being physically saved by people who weren't there (I was pulled from a burning building by someone no one saw, touched by invisible hands that stopped what should have been a fatal bleed-out). Then, almost six months into my pregnancy, I learned that Adam had Down syndrome.

Classic soul teacher move.

This extremely disturbing, culturally unacceptable, wild, unborn being shocked me clean out of my comfortable worldview. I had to either release my judgments about the value of intellect and fling my mind open to the possibility of some deeper reality, or hack myself apart from my own lived experience, totally destroying my integrity. It was time to kill the Buddha. I gave up Kant's pure reason, headed back down the slopes of the intellectual Mount Delectable, and accepted as my next soul teacher an unborn baby who would never in his life read philosophy.

All my doctors told me it was stupid and cruel to continue that pregnancy. I didn't disagree with their pro-choice politics. Those still made a lot more sense to me than the Mormon belief that I'd be cast into "outer darkness" if I had an abortion. But you know what? The Harvard doctors and the Mormon authorities all sounded weirdly alike. They were so certain, so absolute in their culture-based values. Nothing they said resonated with my inner teacher, my sense of truth. Instead it made me tense, confused, numb, and unable to access any kind of inner stillness.

Of course all the arguments I heard made sense from within each speaker's cultural value system. But the things that were happening to me—my physical misery, my weird psychic experiences, my baby's extra chromosome, my maternal love for him—didn't come from culture. They came from nature. And nature seemed determined to take me beyond all the beliefs and behaviors approved of by my society.

I suffered intensely during the next few months. But every now and then, when I was too tired to struggle, my body, mind, heart, and soul would fall into their natural alignment: integrity. It was like entering the eye of a hurricane. Right in the center of all that howling pain, bruised by the whirling debris of my shattered plans for life, I'd feel a moment of utter, silent, exquisite peace. *"Everything is okay,"* it would say without words. *"You're going to be fine."*

I had nothing in my vocabulary to describe this teacher. It definitely wasn't the bearded male God of my childhood, nor the trusty mental scalpel of pure reason. But in the rare moments I experienced it, the ring of truth chimed so intensely inside me I felt all my preconceptions dissolving.

EXERCISE:
Meeting your inner teacher

Maybe you've never had an experience of pure, sweet integrity. Do you want to have it? Or maybe you're remembering an experience of feeling briefly but totally aligned with your own truth. Do you want that feeling back? If so, one powerful step you can take right now is to acknowledge not only that you're feeling a bit lost, but that you would really like to have a soul teacher. Our society doesn't encourage you to admit this, but if it's true for you, your heart won't stop yearning for the mentor to arrive. Allow this feeling and keep your eyes open—your soul guide may show up any minute, from virtually anywhere. And if you'd like something to do while you're waiting for that to happen, here's a way you can access your inner teacher right now.

For this exercise you'll need five to ten minutes in a quiet place where you won't be interrupted. You'll also need something to write with. You can use your own paper for this exercise, or fill in the spaces provided here.

1. In the previous chapter you wrote down a few things you consistently make yourself do, even though you don't really want to do them. Now pick one of these things (or think of a brand new one) and write it here.

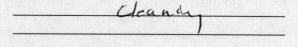

2. With this activity in mind, say to yourself, "I am meant to do [this thing]." For example, if your activity is "take out

the garbage," mentally repeat, over and over, "I am meant
to take out the garbage."

3. As you repeat "I am meant to [take out the garbage],"
notice any physical sensations. Scan your body, noting
the feelings in your muscles, joints, stomach, gut, skin
surface, and so on. Write down anything you notice:

_____

_____

_____

4. Now turn your attention to your emotions. As you repeat
"I am meant to [take out the garbage]," what emotional
reactions arise? Anxiety? Bliss? Apathy? Write them
down:

_____

_____

_____

5. Answer this question yes or no: As you mentally repeat
"I am meant to [take out the garbage]," do you feel free?
Circle one answer:

 YES   **NO**

6. Now let go of the thought "I am meant to [take out the
garbage]." Instead, mentally repeat this sentence: "I am
meant to live in peace." You don't have to believe this,
just repeat it in your mind over and over.

7. As you repeat "I am meant to live in peace," again notice
your physical sensations. Scan your whole body with your
attention and write down what you're feeling physically:

_____

_____

_____

8. Still repeating "I am meant to live in peace," notice any emotions arising. Write them down:

_____

_____

_____

9. Finally, answer this question yes or no: As you mentally repeat "I am meant to live in peace," do you feel free? Circle your answer

YES   **NO**

The takeaway from this exercise is simple. The voice of your inner teacher is not the one that tells you that the meaning of your life is to do something you think you're supposed to do. It's the sensation you get when you state that you are meant to live in peace.

I've tested this exercise on hundreds of people, checking to see what combination of words best connects us with our integrity. After trying many different statements, I found that "I am meant to live in peace" rings the chime of truth more loudly and reliably than anything else. It works for virtually everyone I've asked, including not only earnest do-gooders but also active addicts, extreme narcissists, and a couple of convicted murderers. These people weren't actually living in peace. But when they stated that they were *meant* to be at peace, all of them felt the physical and emotional release, the sense of freedom, that is the inner teacher saying "True."

You may have noticed that I didn't ask you to record what your *mind thought* when you said "I am meant to [take out the garbage]" and "I am meant to live in peace." If you're making yourself do something you don't like, it's because your mind believes you must. Ask it what's true, and it will just parrot whatever you've been taught to believe. Tell your mind that the only sure things in the world are death and taxes, and it will agree. Suggest that you're meant to live in peace, and your mind will probably raise one eyebrow and sneer.

In fact, right now you may be thinking, "But I *am* meant to take out the garbage! Nobody else in my family ever does it! If we all just stopped taking out the garbage, the world would go to hell in a handbasket! And who ever gets to live in complete peace? That's ridiculous."

Mm-hmm. And how does that make you feel?

The first neuroscientists who studied decision-making were surprised to find that people who'd damaged the logical, calculating areas of their brains had no trouble making good choices. On the other hand, when people had damaged parts of their brains that handled emotion, they became unable to make any kind of decision. They would weigh options endlessly, dithering and comparing, but never moving forward. They could reason all day, but they couldn't recognize a good decision if it bit them on both legs.

It turns out that the deeper, evolutionarily older, more subtle areas of the brain are much better at making decisions than the calculating neocortex. That's why, in order to "hear" our inner teachers, we have to tune in to physical and emotional sensations. No matter how hard our minds insist on something like "I am meant to take out the garbage," the body and emotions won't hop on that ride. They'll stiffen our muscles, clench our jaws, make our stomachs churn and our heads ache. It's not that there's anything wrong with taking out the garbage. You don't need to stop doing it. But taking out the garbage is not the meaning of your life.

On the other hand, you may never remember feeling complete peace. You may have been taught that such a thing is impossible. But your inner teacher will validate that this state—and whatever it takes for you to experience it—*is* the meaning of your life.

If you've done the exercises in this and the previous chapters, then you've already accepted the call to adventure that every hero hears at the outset of a great quest. I hope this book is an external teacher that can guide you through the steps to come. Remember what I've said about accepting my advice only if it resonates with your whole self. And, above all, please learn to trust your inner teacher, the burst of relaxation and freedom that rings through your whole body. However your sense of truth feels to you, it will never let you down. And so, with your teacher beside you—or rather, *inside* you—it's time to move on.

4.

The Only Way Out

Once we've met a teacher (again, this book counts if it rings your chimes), we're finally ready to leave the dark wood of error. Unfortunately, that process may not be as jolly and effortless as we'd like. As they say in therapy circles, "The only way out is through." Through what? Well, Dante calls it the inferno.

After meeting Virgil, the poet hopes to go immediately from the dark wood of error into an easier, more restful place. Instead, his teacher takes him to a damned gate. Literally damned. Above it is an inscription, like the signs at amusement parks that say "You must be *this tall* to ride!" only way gnarlier:

Through me to the city of sorrow, through me to eternal woe, through me to the way among the lost people. . . . Abandon all hope, ye who enter here.

"Dude," says Dante, "that sign is like, totally harshing my mellow." (I'm paraphrasing.) But Virgil, weirdly joyful, just pats him on the hand so lovingly that Dante agrees to follow him through the gate. And so, Dante tells us, "He led me in among the secret things."

To continue along the way of integrity, you must go in among the secret things—that is, the things you've been keeping from yourself. In Chapter 1, you admitted you were lost; now it's time to let yourself know why. In other words, now is the time when you emerge from specific areas of denial that are allowing you to live outside your integrity.

This step isn't complicated. It simply means accepting that certain parts of your life are as they are, even though you wish they weren't. It means looking squarely at truths you've been hiding from yourself, even though (paradoxically) you know they're in there. Ultimately, leaving denial is the most productive, grounding, calming thing we could possibly do. But for most of us, it's still terrifying. We live in the unarticulated but desperate hope that we'll never have to look at the secret things. That's one of the hopes we have to abandon to move forward.

After learning about my son's Down syndrome diagnosis, I was a veritable hope factory. I hoped so hard that on several occasions I probably ruptured something. Though I was grateful to have the choice about terminating the pregnancy, and never actually wanted that option, the reality of my situation terrified me. And so I set about hoping. I hoped the test was wrong. I hoped there had been a mistake with my medical records. I hoped a miracle would trim the extra twenty-third chromosome from every one of my unborn son's cells. Sometimes, late at night (though I knew it made no sense), I hoped the baby would take the whole decision factor out of my hands, and just spontaneously die. Sometimes I hoped I would.

At the core of all this hoping was the mega-hope that I wouldn't have to lose anything. Not my lifestyle, my goals, my self-image, my work, my place in society. I was twenty-five: old enough to imagine the losses ahead of me, but not old enough to realize that hope is a harsh, unstable master and that there are many benefits to abandoning it. This is the next step on your journey toward integrity.

ABANDONING DENIAL

In our culture, "Abandon hope" sounds horrible, almost sacrilegious. We are among the hopingest people in history. Manifest destiny! Continuous progress! Never give up on your dreams! YES, WE CAN! This is a good thing, mostly. High hopes really can usher in wonderful accomplishments. But when we hope for something that doesn't trigger the ring of truth inside us, we split from reality. We hope that things aren't as they already are. At that point, we've begun the cold war with reality that psychologists call "denial."

This isn't any kind of flaw or defect. Denial is a survival mechanism that keeps us from dying of shock by blocking our perception of things that are too frightening to face. We can use it half-deliberately, as I did after Adam's diagnosis. But usually, denial is involuntary. We can experience something, right out in clear daylight, and honestly not be conscious that it exists.

I've seen a lot of this in my work. Remember the Oxycontin junkie I worked with—the one who took two hundred pills a day? He was furious at anyone who hinted he might actually need rehab. He kept repeating that he was "not addicted, just getting through a rough time." He truly believed this, even as he rushed to resupply his habit.

On another occasion, a client I'll call Julia asked me to sit in as she confessed to her devoutly religious mother, Constance, that she'd been having an affair.

"Well," Constance said soothingly after Julia finished speaking, "at least you've never been unfaithful to your husband. You'd never cross that line."

When Julia tearfully clarified that yes, indeed, she had fully and enthusiastically crossed that line on multiple occasions, her mother repeated, "No, you'd never do that." Despite being told this truth repeatedly, Constance never let herself know it.

Another couple, two lovely men who'd been living, working, and sleeping together for over twenty years, told me they needed coaching because they were afraid people might start to think they were gay.

"Uh . . . well . . . aren't you?" I said.

"Oh, you're good," one of the clients replied. "You guessed! Ha ha! But no one else knows."

"My brother asked me about it once," said the other man,

"but I punched him in the gut for it, so I'm pretty sure he doesn't suspect anything."

I could go on telling similar stories all day—stories about intelligent, well-meaning people in mind-boggling denial. Their ability to keep secrets from themselves wasn't evidence of bad character or stupidity, but of the complexity inherent in every human mind. Without meaning to, we can wipe the slate of our awareness clean of everything we don't want to know.

Almost.

If it weren't for that damned gate.

APPROACHING THE GATES OF HELL

Buried in the half-light of every denial there's a mental gate labeled "Abandon all hope, ye who enter here." To find that gate, we simply have to acknowledge the things we don't want to acknowledge. We dread arriving at the gate, let alone passing through it, because even though we won't fully look at it, we sense that it's a portal to experiences we'd rather not have.

Beyond the gate we may have to stand up in front of other people and say, "I'm an alcoholic," while (shudder) not drinking at all. Beyond the gate we will absolutely know that we hate our jobs, and that nothing is stopping us from quitting. Beyond the gate we may have arguments with our loved ones. Beyond the gate, what we've been calling "love" may show itself to be nothing more than a spider-fly relationship.

Blundering through the dark wood of error, we can success-fully (though always uneasily) pretend that there is no gate, no "beyond." But once we meet our soul teachers, external or in-ternal, they pull us toward the gate like a team of mules. They point out, dwell on, insistently remind us of things we most emphatically do not want to think about.

Most of our minds have sensitive areas, like inflamed wounds that can't tolerate even the gentlest touch. I call these Do Not Mention Zones. Any topic related to these areas feels alarming. For example, we may avoid discussions about cancer, Alzhei-mer's, or other awful ailments because we don't want to acknowl-edge that they could happen to us. Or we may be so terrified of poverty that we avoid all discussions of taxes, salaries, sav-ings, money in general. Some of us can't look at photos of oil-covered pelicans or a clear-cut rain forest because we can't bear to think about the high probability that humans have irrepa-rably broken our home planet.

So, what are your flinch areas, your Do Not Mention Zones? Whatever you least want to know, whatever makes you most fidgety, uncomfortable, irritable, and anxious, is the general area of a gate to hell. Approaching that gate is the next step toward integrity. I wish I could say otherwise, but I can't. What I can do is tell you what Virgil said to Dante: Here, you have to find a way to kill your own cowardice. Be brave, my friend. You don't have to figure out your whole life right now. Just take one step toward the gate by identifying some things you *do not want to think about.*

EXERCISE:
My Do Not Mention Zones

Step one

Finish this sentence: Some topics, people, past experiences, or world events I do not want to think about are (list as many that come to mind)...

Affair

Hannah's criticism

Last ~~~~ face to face with Mother

Each troubling topic you just listed houses a gate to hell. We'll be working with one of them for the rest of this chapter. Since most of us have many sensitive zones, many gates, it may take several iterations of this process before we resolve every issue and come into total integrity. For now, we're just going to work on a single area. This will teach you the technique you can eventually use on other issues, ultimately bringing your whole life into harmonious alignment.

Step two

Now I'd like you to choose a workable Do Not Mention Zone for this moment. Some Do Not Mention Zones are truly devastating: a loved one's impending death, an overwhelming betrayal, a memory of being physically attacked. Whatever denial you may have about these issues won't dissolve easily, because it's a necessary coping device. I wouldn't recommend that you work with something so drastic right now.

As a veteran self-helper, I have to assume that you may be working through this book on your own, without a counselor or even a friend to stay present with you during the process. If so, it's even more important to choose a Do Not Mention Zone that feels uncomfortable but not terrifying. If you're harboring trauma you sense would totally unglue you, I beg you to get a trained therapist as a soul teacher to help you through that gate.

Right now I'd like you to choose a minor gate—something unnerving, but not shattering. For example, maybe you've learned about some far-away natural disaster on the news. Maybe your cat is losing some of his pep, and you haven't really faced the fact that he'll probably die much sooner than you will. Maybe no one you love is in danger, but you can't stop worrying about the possibility of freak accidents at amusement parks. Poke around your brain and find a problem like this right now. Write it here:

My troubling but not devastating Do Not Mention topic:

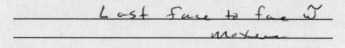

Last face to face w/
mother

There's only one way out of the discomfort you feel about this topic: you have to stop avoiding your thoughts and feelings. You have to admit the truths that make this issue so uncomfortable to face. Those truths are hellgates. If walking right up to them sounds like bad advice, remember that a hellgate is the only way out of the dark wood of error. Even so, it's usually hard to approach disagreeable truths at a solid stride. What with denial fogging up the landscape, the best way to find our hellgates is by groping.

Step three

After reading the last few paragraphs, you may have suddenly realized you need to alphabetize all your cleaning products, or learn to play the banjo, or visit Norway. That kind of distraction and avoidance is part of denial. If you want to stay in the dark wood of error, then fair play to you—go plink away among the fjords, and I'll catch you later. But if you're interested in attaining inner peace, think of the "Do Not Mention" topic you just wrote down and move on to the next step.

Step four

Complete the sentences below with whatever comes to mind. Try not to overthink; just write down anything that pops into your head. Remember, this is all in relation to the topic you identified above.

In regard to this topic, what I'm most afraid to know is. . .

how much it hurt mother

In regard to this topic, what I'm pretending not to see is...

Is that it did hurt her

In regard to this topic, what I don't want anyone else to know is...

What took place — my cruelty

If other people knew about this topic, I'm afraid that...

_____ They will think _____

_____ badly of me _____

Okay, that's enough for now. Stop. Breathe. Go get a drink. Of water.

Also, give yourself a congratulatory pat on the back. You just did something so difficult many people never manage it. You've taken a huge step toward freedom, because *the reason you've been wandering in the dark wood of error is precisely to avoid the thoughts and feelings you've just stopped avoiding.* Thinking about them deliberately, asking these hard questions, brings you straight up against your own personal hellgate. This is always a bit scary, so please, go easy on yourself. But keep reading. The next part won't be as bad as you might expect.

WHAT TO DO WHEN YOU REACH A HELLGATE

Even taking a quick peek at a secret we've been keeping from ourselves (as you did by finishing the sentences above) sends most people into a mental spin, if not a panic attack. As we approach hellgates, our minds generate catastrophic fantasies. We visualize all sorts of horrendous outcomes. We fret over

What People Will Think if our worst fears are realized. We may feel desperate to control every possible outcome, prepare for every contingency, prevent every calamity. But beneath this effort to control the universe, we feel a dreadful deeper truth: the universe is not ours to control.

I gradually reached this point—the point of abandoning all hope—after Adam's diagnosis. Seeking advice from various experts didn't soothe me; it just kept pushing me closer and closer to the damned gate. No matter how much I learned, the bottom line was that I couldn't control my son's future. I couldn't control my own. In fact, I realized to my complete horror, *I couldn't control anything*. My baby could be born genetically "normal" and still get snatched by dingoes or hit by a meteorite. I couldn't know what would happen to him, me, or anyone else, except that we will all eventually die.

This was a central fear for me, a true gateway into hell. But my circumstances wouldn't let me avoid it. After a while I stopped my frenzied research into Down syndrome and all its complications—research that had been helping me avoid my feelings by masquerading as the possibility of control. At that point I went into a sustained state of absolute, unbearable fear. It felt as if I were spinning in an infinite cold vacuum where only suffering was real.

Whatever hellgate you wrote down in the last exercise, you may need to repeat that advice Virgil gave Dante as they approached the gate in that long-ago dark wood—this is the place where all cowardice has to die. There's no way you can make it through the next steps without being brave. But I'm delighted to tell you that after smashing right into several of my own hellgates, generating so much fear and misery, I found a better way—the way of integrity. And it is surprisingly gentle.

HOW TO KILL YOUR COWARDICE

One day, as I sat terrified and nauseated in the very shadow of the hellgate labeled "You Have No Control," a soul teacher managed to connect with me. That teacher, who brought me my first measure of comfort since Adam's diagnosis, was a singing snake.

At the time, my "parenting" (I use the term loosely) involved playing many, many Disney videos for my two-year-old daughter Kat. That day I had plugged in *The Jungle Book* and then lain down on the couch, ostensibly working on a term paper but actually just roasting in my familiar, intolerable blend of hope and fear.

As I lay there, something odd happened. One particular song from the Disney movie threaded itself into my attention and wouldn't let go. I'd been completely oblivious to all the previous songs, but for some reason I couldn't ignore this one; it filled up my mind even as I tried to concentrate on something else. The singer was Kaa, a python, who tries to hypnotize the little boy Mowgli in order to eat him. The lyrics go like this:

Trust in me, just in me
Shut your eyes and trust in me
You can sleep safe and sound

Knowing I am around

Trust in me, just in me
Shut your eyes and trust in me

These words seemed to have some sort of muscular power to push their way into my head and force everything else out. The moment they filled up my entire mind, I felt what I've been describing as my inner teacher, the ring of truth. My body went limp. My mind stopped its panicky fantasies. My fear and sadness felt suspended in a clear space that seemed generative and warm, not desolate.

This was a completely new sensation for me. I desperately wanted to hang on to it, but I expected it to melt like a snowflake on my tongue. When the song ended, I found the remote control, rewound, and played it again, lying back on the couch to listen. I did this many times. Kat didn't mind. Whatever we may say about the "terrible twos," children that age have a truly spectacular tolerance for song repetition.

It's ironic but fitting that my first adult experience of mindful presence came from a literal murder song. If I had believed in any sort of god at that point, it would have been the kind who sings you to sleep so he can kill you. I felt ridiculous, playing and replaying a children's ditty, but the calm it gave me was like a miracle drug. I kept my brain focused on those lyrics until nothing else remained. As the song played for perhaps the twentieth time, I fell into a deep, healing sleep.

This was how I discovered the most powerful way I know to

kill our own cowardice as we approach a gate to hell. We must pull our minds away from situations that exist only in our hopes and fears, and rivet our attention—all of it—on the present moment. Then we do something so simple it sounds almost nonsensical: we trust that in this moment, everything is all right, just as it is. We don't have to trust that we'll be okay in ten minutes or ten seconds, only in this razor-thin instant called NOW.

If we do this repeatedly, we discover something remarkable: by dropping resistance to whatever is happening *right now*, we are always able to cope. Even when we're not coping, allowing ourselves to not-cope gets us through this moment, over and over and over. Presence is the sanctuary integrity offers us as denial comes to its dreaded end. You can try it as you read this paragraph. Just notice that right now, you're basically okay. You can trust that gravity will keep holding you in place. You can trust the air you're breathing. You can trust everything in the entire universe to be as it is. You are already coping with it right now, and right now is the only thing you'll ever have to cope with.

In the years that followed my *Jungle Book* experience, mindful presence would become quite trendy. People would sell books about it, teach it at clinics. My clients, many of them enthusiastic readers of books like Eckhart Tolle's *The Power of Now*, benefitted greatly from it. And I'd later discover that the "disabled" baby I feared so much was a genius at it.

For example, when Adam was twenty he had a job bussing tables at an elder care facility in Phoenix. One day I got so busy worrying about gum disease that I forgot to pick him up from work. When I realized my mistake, I drove to the center like a bat out of hell, arriving ninety minutes late to find Adam fast asleep in a rocking chair on the building's shaded porch.

"Adam!" I said, shaking him awake. "I'm so sorry I'm late! Why didn't you call me?"

Adam rubbed his eyes, sighed peacefully, and said, "I wasn't worried. I was just tired." He hadn't spent one second of that day being a tragically disabled young man forgotten by his loopy mother, wondering if and when help would come. He was just a tired guy in a comfortable chair on a sunny day, ideally situated to take a nap.

Twenty years earlier, thanks to Kaa the python, I took my first faltering step toward Adam's mastery of presence. Listening to the words "Trust in me" over and over, I forgot to be a suffering woman faced with the loss of all I held dear. I was just a person on a comfortable couch, watching a video with my adorable daughter. I wasn't worried. I was just tired. And then I was asleep, and there was literally no suffering at all.

EXERCISE:
The surrender-allow meditation

When we feel most helpless and mute, says the poet Rumi, "a stretcher will come from grace to gather us up." Whatever gate of hell you may be facing, you can drop into the stretcher from grace, the present moment. You can handle the entire universe being as it is in this precise moment. Look, you just handled it. There, you did it again. And again. You are crushing this! To get even better at this, try the exercise below.

1. Reread what you wrote as your "Do Not Mention" topics in step two of the previous exercise. Whatever thought made you most uncomfortable, allow it to remain in your mind. For now.

2. However you're feeling—edgy, irritable, depressed—just let yourself feel that way. For now.

3. Sit in a comfortable chair or lie down. Make sure you're warm. Put a fuzzy blanket around you if need be. Get cozy. For now.

4. As you sit or lie there, notice how your breath goes in and out. The first thing you did when you entered this world was breathe in. The last thing you'll ever do is breathe out. Watch your breath reliably keeping you alive, without any effort on your part. For now.

5. On an inhale, think the words, *I allow everything in the universe to be as it is in this moment.* After all, you can't make it different *in this moment*, so just stop trying. For now.

6. As you exhale, think, *I surrender all resistance to the universe being as it is in this moment.* For now.

7. Continue to think *I allow* on every in-breath, and *I surrender* on every out-breath. You don't have to surrender and allow any moment but this present one. But in this instant, let it all be. Accept every out-breath as a death to *this* fleeting moment, every in-breath a rebirth to *this* new one. Relax into the rhythm of letting go and opening up, for now.

> 8. Consider the uncomfortable thing you wrote down in step two your "Do Not Mention" exercise. Allow everything about that situation to be as it is, for now. Surrender all resistance to its being as it is, for now.

If you keep this up for a while, allowing and surrendering to everything inside you and everything around you *at this exact time and place*, you'll eventually notice that part of you is fine. It isn't even afraid of that damned gate, that scary thing you've been avoiding by staying in denial. This unworried part of you, which never denied reality and never divided against itself, is pure integrity. It's your inner teacher, putting a comforting hand on yours, telling you everything's okay.

I awoke from that epic, python-induced nap and recommenced hoping. I hoped through the final weeks of pregnancy, through several hours of labor. But as a team of specialists delivered Adam and wrapped him in a hospital blanket, I got a glimpse of his tiny right foot, and saw that the big toe was a bit further away from the others than one might expect.

Abandon all hope, ye who enter here.

My denial collapsed. There had been no mistake. My baby had Down syndrome. But weirdly, I found that I could cope. I didn't have to do much about it right at that moment; just let my body finish delivering the placenta, which lord knows I wasn't doing deliberately. Once more I let go of hope, and came home to what was happening now. Here's what was happening: a young mother lying on a delivery table. A beautiful baby, drawing his first breaths and waving his tiny arms j͟ every other person ever born. A small squadron of people devoted to keeping both of us hale and hearty.

I could handle that.

In fact, as I watched all these people caring for me and for Adam, I found the situation quite wonderful. Astonishing, in fact. This reality was more sustaining than any of my desperate hopes. The path to that particular gate of hell had been awful, but one step past the gate, one step beyond hope, everything was fine. I didn't even need hope anymore, because I wasn't worried. I was just tired.

Stage Two

INFERNO

5.

Into the Inferno

As he passes through the damned gate, Dante leaves the dark wood of error and arrives somewhere much more dramatic: the inferno. Hell turns out to be a vast cone-shaped pit, divided into circular terraces. Each circle is a little smaller and a lot nastier than the one above it. Also, Dante sees dead people: the inferno is chock-full of deceased sinners undergoing various ghastly punishments. And the noise! Dante can barely stand the cacophony of "sighs, complaints, wailing, words of agony" bashing against his tender mortal eardrums.

There are as many ways to interpret this hellscape as there are readers. Some religious folks may believe it's literal. Others might read *The Divine Comedy* as a work of medieval theology, or a political manifesto, or simply as fiction, since most of Dante's images actually weren't official Catholic doctrine (he just made them up). But in this book, we're using the poet's magnum opus as a metaphor for our personal journeys from misalignment to integrity. From this perspective, every one of us has a personal hell, an internal inferno.

I don't happen to believe there's a geographical place where awful things happen to dead people. But I do believe in hell. I've been there. As I see it, hell is suffering—particularly any suffering that feels inescapable. You may remember that I make a distinction between the words *pain* and *suffering*: Pain comes from events, while suffering comes from the way we handle events—what we do about them and, especially, what we think about them. As Epictetus wrote in the second century AD, "What upsets people is not what happens to them, but their *thoughts* about what happens."

For example, if you punched me in the head because you were trying to do a fist-bump and missed, it could hurt. The pain might send me to the freezer for an ice pack, but it wouldn't cause inescapable suffering—unless my thoughts got involved. Depending on my predilections, I could spend years fussing about that punch, thinking "You meant to hurt me!" or "I must have my revenge!" or "You can't trust anyone in this rotten world." I might stay in a perpetual snit for the rest of my days.

I'm exaggerating to make a point, but I've had dozens of clients who lived in hell—that is, constant suffering—because of thoughts almost this absurd.

For instance, Helen, a sixty-year-old millionaire, spent her whole adult life brooding about the fact that her grandfather, who died when Helen was five, left all his money to charity instead of to Helen's already-wealthy parents. The thought "That man robbed us," and the bitterness that arose from it, dogged Helen every day.

Another client, Louis, came unglued when his younger brother married a woman much more beautiful than Louis's own wife. "He's shaming me," Louis fumed. "He only did this to make me look like a failure." His mental competition with his brother almost ruined Louis's marriage. Then there was Rhoda, whose best friend had a baby and stopped initiating lunch dates. Rhoda went into despair, remembering every moment of rejection and loneliness she'd ever experienced, thinking over and over, "I've been left out in the cold—again."

If you're in a relatively comfortable place right now, with no one physically attacking you, the vast majority of any suffering you feel is coming from your thoughts. (This is true even if you're in physical pain. During my own years of chronic pain, I suffered much more from my thoughts—"I can't bear this!" "It will last forever!" "I'll never have a normal life!"—than from the actual physical sensations.)

If it makes sense to you that suffering can come from your thinking, you're ready for another concept—the one crucial insight that can free you from hell. Here it is: your thoughts, *even thoughts you absolutely believe*, may not always be true.

THE LIES WE BELIEVE

Remember Keith, the client who called me from a party to say that the two hundred million dollars he'd just pocketed WASN'T

F*ING ENOUGH? Well, that wasn't Keith's only bad night. He always felt restless and unsatisfied, desperate for inner peace—and he thought he knew how to get it. Keith lived and breathed one thought: "More money will make me happy."

Actual evidence didn't support this belief. Keith's happiest memories were of a teenage backpacking trip when he had virtually no money or possessions. In later years, despite being worth more than some small countries, he could never regain that state of carefree joy.

"So," I'd say to him, "you were happy with almost no money, and you're unhappy with hundreds of millions of dollars. Are you *sure* more money will make you happy?"

Whenever I went into this line of reasoning, Keith would react like one of the androids in the TV drama *Westworld*, where lifelike robots are programmed to think they're cowboys living in the Old West. If the robots ever see evidence that their worldview may not be true—for example, a photograph of a modern city—their programming causes them to go blank and say that the evidence in question "doesn't look like anything to me."

Whenever I pointed out that Keith had been happier without money than with it, he'd squint at me and say, "What are you talking about? You're not making any sense." Then he'd change the subject. It didn't look like anything to him.

I got a similar response from Helen when I first asked if her obsessive thought, "That man robbed us," might not be literally true. I don't think Louis even heard me when I said, "Are you sure your brother got married just to spite you? Could there be any other reason?" And when I suggested to Rhoda that her friend may not have deliberately left her "out in the cold," she fussed, "Now you're doing it, too! You're just like everyone else!"

These cases are extreme, but everyone I've ever coached had an inner inferno filled with tormenting thoughts. In fact, many had the same thoughts—the favorites of our culture. You may share some of these. For example, there's Keith's classic "I don't have enough money." Other popular hits include "I'm not good enough," "No one loves me," "I don't deserve to be happy," "You can't just have what you want," "I have to do work I hate," and so on. And on. And on and on and . . .

Now, if you noticed one of your own beliefs in the paragraph above, you may be thinking, "Wait, that one *is* true! Everybody knows it!" Here's what I have to say about that: if you believe a thought is true *and it also makes you happy*, terrific. This chapter isn't about challenging your every belief, only the ones that cause suffering. Which brings us to another crucial idea. This one is a mind-pretzel, but bear with me. Our worst psychological suffering comes from thoughts that we *genuinely believe, while simultaneously knowing they aren't true.*

This may sound ridiculous. How can anyone believe something if they know it's not true? It flies in the face of logic! Yes, indeed. But we do it anyway. We do it because we've been taught to do it.

When I'm speaking in public, I often stop mid-speech and ask the audience, "Is everyone comfortable?" They nod, smile, murmur that they are. "Really?" I insist. "Are you *sure* you're comfortable?" They nod again. I press them: "You're *completely* comfortable?" By this time people are starting to get annoyed. Yes, they insist, they are *absolutely certain* that they are *absolutely comfortable.*

Then I ask, "If you were at home alone right now, how many of you would be sitting in the position you're in at this moment?"

Virtually no one raises a hand.

"Why not?"

There's a long pause before a few audience members begin to realize why they'd be doing something different at home: the position they're in at the moment is mildly uncomfortable.

Now, the problem here isn't the discomfort itself—humans are as tough as junkyard dogs; they'll be fine. The problem is that these people are *simultaneously feeling uncomfortable and swearing that they're completely comfortable.*

What they really mean is something like this: "Given that I've been taught since childhood to sit in chairs for long periods, my present discomfort is easy to tolerate." Their brains put this filter on their experience automatically, so that they can look me straight in the eyes and lie, repeatedly, without even realizing it. Their culture says they're comfortable. Their nature knows they're not.

✓ Believing things that aren't true for us at the deepest level is the commonest way in which we lose our integrity. Then suffering arises—not as punishment, but as a signal that we're being torn apart. The purpose of suffering is to help us locate our internal divisions, reclaim our reality, and heal these inner rifts.

Many of my clients, having dipped a toe in popular psychology, believe that "positive" thoughts, like "I love my job," make us happy, while negative thoughts, like "I hate my job," make us unhappy. But a cheerful statement can feel like soul murder if you know it isn't true, while a supposedly "negative" thought can set you free to experience joy.

For example, I've had several clients who found themselves in terrible relationships, enduring abuse, infidelity, and all sorts of cruelty, while valiantly insisting "I can make this work." But despite all this "positive thinking," their hearts remained broken, their suffering terrible. I've seen these folks brighten up, often dramatically, when they allowed themselves to think "negative" things like "This marriage has never really worked" or "I think my partner is keeping secrets from me" or "I'm exhausted by this relationship; I need some space."

You may have experienced versions of paradoxical relief. Maybe you finally relaxed it when you admitted that something (jogging, hobnobbing with coworkers, medical school) felt bad to you even though you'd previously believed it was good for you. Or that someone you admired was wrong, even though you'd once thought they were always right. I've seen people go from torment to peace by voicing "negative" things like "My mother just hates men" or "I'm dyslexic" or "There was no real love in the house where I grew up."

So it's not the positivity or negativity of a thought that makes us feel happy or sad, trapped or free. The operative variable is whether the thoughts we believe match what we deeply feel to be the truth. Being split from ourselves is hell. Reclaiming integrity is the way out of it.

I must remind you here that being out of integrity isn't a sign you're bad—only that you've internalized false assumptions, usually in an effort to be good. The most moral, well-meaning people often have the biggest infernal landscapes, filled with the most frightening demons. For example, when the shy, gentle British author C. S. Lewis first began observing his own mind, he wrote, "There I found what appalled me; a zoo of lusts, a bedlam of ambitions, a nursery of fears, a harem of fondled hatreds. My name was legion." He hadn't been cast down to hell because he was an awful person; he'd just inadvertently created a lot of suppressed suffering.

HOW TO UNCHAIN YOURSELF FROM THE INFERNO

The process that frees us from our inner hell is very simple, though not necessarily easy. Dante models it in *The Divine Comedy*. Horrified by the anguish of the tormented souls, the poet often wants to give up or turn back. But his soul teacher won't let him. Throughout the inferno, Virgil keeps urging Dante to do three things: observe the demons, ask questions about them, and move on.

These are the same steps we need to end our own psychological suffering. First, we must become the observers of our suffering, instead of drowning in it like swimmers sucked into a maelstrom. Second, we must question each belief that traps us in misery until we figure out where it diverts us from our sense of truth. At that point, our infernal chains break, and step three—moving on—is almost automatic.

In the last chapter I asked you to identify a hellgate, an issue that troubles you without being truly overwhelming. Write it (or a comparable topic) in the space below. We'll work with it as we walk through the process of liberating your mind, thought by thought, from its suffering.

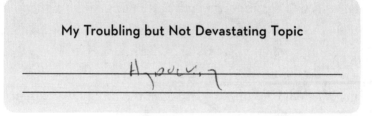

My Troubling but Not Devastating Topic

In Chapter 4 I asked you to cope with this topic by dropping all thoughts of past and future and taking sanctuary in the present moment. Now I want you to do the opposite. Contemplating the topic above, deliberately allow your mind to create its usual bedlam of frightening thoughts. Recall the fears about it that mar your days and keep you awake at night. This may feel awful—but also familiar. I wouldn't ask you to do something so distressing if I didn't suspect you've done it countless times already.

You'll probably find clusters of painful thoughts surrounding your chosen topic. For example, if your issue is loneliness and you allow your mind to go into its usual soliloquy on the subject, your mind may rattle off, "No one really loves me. No one ever will. I'm just not a lovable person. I'm going to die alone."

Or perhaps your anguish may not use actual words, just random screaming, along with generalized panic, rage, or despair. Don't push these feelings away (they've been there all along anyway, under everything you've done to cover them up). Instead, pay attention to the cacophony until you begin to discern the specific fears or regrets that underlie your misery.

For example, if you have vague relationship worries that appear as a wordless mass of dread, letting yourself go *into* that fear might bring up visual images of people yelling at you or storming out of your life. Gradually, the images will coalesce into a thought like "Everyone is angry at me!" Thinking this will trigger the usual cluster of related thoughts. "I'm in serious trouble. People hate me. They want to hurt me. I have to defend myself!"

If you immediately "hear" concrete statements about your troubling topic, write them below. If you only feel terrible emotions, let them whirl until they begin to tell you their scary thoughts (there will always be at least one). If you're in physical pain, examine your *thoughts* about that pain. Whatever your "hell thoughts" are, write them below. Try to put down at least three.

List of Hell Thoughts Related to
My Troubling Topic

H. won't love me
H. will cut off

Be very gentle with yourself at this point, especially if you're currently living in a difficult situation. Many people who consult me during periods of trauma or trouble have especially horrible—and convincing—hell thoughts. Just voicing them can be excruciating.

I've been through this myself several times. My hell thoughts were never worse than the day my son was born. The doctor pulled him out, mopped him up, ascertained that he was healthy (aside from his "problem"), and put him in my arms. Like my first child, Adam was a miniature miracle: same array of limbs and features, same utter vulnerability, same itty-bitty fingernails. But he felt floppier than I thought a baby should be. His eyes were shaped strangely. His ears were unusually small.

My own little hellgate.

As I finally dropped denial and walked through that gate, the infernal chorus howled inside me. "He'll always be a burden." "He'll never succeed at anything." "People will be disgusted by him." "People will be disgusted by me." I kissed and cuddled my brand-new baby. I loved him with my whole heart. And my name was legion.

So I understand if you can't hear anything but your hell thoughts right now. Go easy. Be kind. Wrap yourself in a warm blanket, get a bowl of chicken soup, don't push yourself. But when your longing to be free from suffering outweighs your fear of moving ahead, follow the way of integrity through the steps below.

EXERCISE:
Dissolving your hell thoughts

Step one: Observe your own suffering demons.

Look over the list of hell thoughts you just wrote down. Now imagine that each thought is being screamed by a fragment of yourself, a demon trapped in hell. This creature looks like you, but its entire consciousness is devoted to proclaiming this one terrible thought. Maybe it's moaning "No one respects me, no one respects me, no one respects me ..." Another demon, standing next to it, constantly mutters "I'm so stupid, I'm so stupid, I'm so stupid ..." A third shrieks "Everyone's out to get me, everyone's out to get me, everyone's out to get me ..." There's a separate demon for every thought that hurts or scares you.

Now imagine yourself standing right in front of the demon that's shouting a thought about your troubling topic. Resist the impulse to run, blot out the noise with food or drugs, call your best friend for comfort, or pick a fight with your partner. Listen to the advice Virgil gives Dante when the poet faces horrors in the inferno: "Here all cowardice must die." Don't avoid your frightening thought. Don't push it away. Just observe it.

Now, while remaining aware of your internal demon, look around you. Where are you right now—in a room, a subway car, a park? What colors can you see? What's the temperature of the air? What can you smell and hear? Notice what you're wearing, how your clothes feel against your skin. Are there any other living creatures around—people, animals, plants? What are they doing? Write a brief description here.

Description of My Present Location:

_____

_____

_____

_____

This exercise may not seem life-changing, but it can be. In fact, it can actually restructure your brain, making you less vulnerable to suffering and more prone to joy, permanently (more about that later). Whenever I'm with clients who go from observing only their suffering to noticing their surroundings as well, I feel an almost tangible shift of energy.

For instance, I've had many clients who, like Keith, thought money and happiness were the same thing. But, unlike Keith, they broke free. Just by putting their attention on their environment, part of them began to notice and enjoy things like sunlight, air, friendship. Their lives became richer, instantly. Of course, not every demon story falls apart this easily. At this stage, most people still believe their awful thoughts, and continue to hurt. But their observing selves can watch their suffering while also noticing that they're wearing a soft blue shirt, that a cardinal is singing outside, that there's a light rain falling. That small shift is a ticket out of the inferno.

This happened to me spontaneously a few weeks after Adam was born. My demons were in full voice, constantly shouting frightening thoughts about my ruined future, and my son's. I believed everything they said. Fortunately, this was unbearable.

One night, as I rocked Adam to sleep after a two a.m. feeding, I became so tired of my own fearful thoughts that part of my attention slipped off them. I clearly remember that moment. Suddenly I noticed the pattern of city lights shining on the ceiling, the comforting sway of the rocking chair. For the first time since Adam's birth, a bit of my mind separated from my inner demons and began to simply observe.

From that moment, everything in my life slowly, subtly started changing. When you observe your suffering, yours will change, too.

Step two: Question the "absolute truth" of your painful thoughts.

Dante picks his way through the inferno, gaping at damned souls who are battered by wind and filthy rain, or immersed in mud, or condemned to roll massive boulders. All the while, he questions Virgil and sometimes the damned souls. When they tell Dante about how horribly they're suffering, he gets "utterly confused with sadness." This is how we usually respond to our own painful thoughts—we simply believe them, then go into overwhelmed despair. Our misery feels endless. And it is, unless we go on to step two: questioning the beliefs that cause our suffering.

If we're committed to integrity, we have to act like detectives on a case, testing every bit of evidence, seeing if it makes sense. Organizational behaviorist Chris Argyris calls this "seeking disconfirmation." In other words, we have to deliberately search for reasons that whatever we believe might not be accurate.

Here's a challenge: in the space below, write as many reasons as you can imagine why your Troubling Topic—the one you've been working with—might not be true. This won't be easy, because as we've seen, you believe this thought. But you have a good mind and a working imagination. Use them to put a bit of doubt between you and your tormenting story.

Virtually all my clients feel a bit stumped by this step at first. I'll never forget watching a man go into five minutes of furious thought, trying to come up with a single exception to his belief, "All women want me to rescue them." I sat right in front of him thinking, "Hello, what am I, chopped liver?" Eventually, I said it out loud. At first his face went blank. Then we both burst out laughing.

If you're having trouble coming up with anything that might contradict your hell thought, ask a friend, coach, therapist, or twelve-step buddy to help you see what might be in plain sight to them but hidden from you by your beliefs.

Reasons I can't be absolutely sure my hell thought is true:

_____

_____

_____

_____

_____

_____

With a bit of priming, even Helen—the woman who believed she'd been "robbed" by her grandfather—eventually came up with a list of ways old Grandad contributed to her family's fortunes: setting up her father's business, teaching each of his grandchildren how to manage money. Louis grudgingly realized that although he constantly compared himself to his brother, the competitiveness was one-way—his brother actually showed no signs of caring how he compared to Louis. And after Rhoda and I talked about how busy and tired new parents almost always are, she stopped fearing that her friend was deliberately shunning her.

You don't have to believe any of your own new ideas. Just keep working on this exercise until you find the part of yourself that is capable of doubting your demons. Notice how, as you pull back just a little from your hellish thought, you feel slightly more relaxed. The relief will increase as you get better at contradicting any belief that makes you suffer.

This happened to me spontaneously the night I lost my grip on terror, as I rocked Adam to sleep. After part of me began to simply observe the scene, memories began rising into my attention. I thought of the strange psychic experiences I'd had during my pregnancy. I remembered Kant's assertion that all reality is subjective. I still believed my fearful thoughts, but not quite so completely.

Then I began to hear another inner voice. Not a demon-scream, but a barely audible whisper. It didn't say anything earthshaking—or so I thought at the time. As I sat there believing "My life is ruined!" this voice asked me one small question.

Are you sure?

My initial reaction was anger. *Of course* I was sure! My child had a *birth defect!* All my experiences, all my doctors, all of science itself were telling me my life was ruined!

Are you sure?

Well, I thought, settling down a bit, I guess I can't be totally sure of anything. I mean, Kant and all that. And nobody is sure of the future.

That was the first moment since Adam's diagnosis that I felt relief. After that, whenever I'd fall into despair, that soft voice would show up again, just asking, *Are you sure?*

As the months and then years went by, I began to hold my tormenting beliefs more lightly. I questioned them. I doubted them. And gradually, because they felt so horrible and I was no longer certain they were true, the hell thoughts faded away. Yours will, too. Once you begin to question the truth of an inner demon, its days are numbered.

I've watched this happen to the vast majority of my clients, including even hard cases like Helen, Louis, and Rhoda. Gradually, they all shifted from obsessing over the same torturous thoughts to noticing that the world around them was full of ideas and experiences that brought them joy. Without much fanfare, they moved on to happier lives.

Step three: Move on.

Beliefs—especially scary ones—act like blinders. Once we believe a thought, we selectively pay attention to anything that seems to support it. If evidence contradicts a belief, our attention slides away.

It doesn't look like anything to us. Doubting and contradicting our painful thoughts removes our blinders. We begin to see evidence—most of which was in plain sight all along—that our terrible beliefs aren't true.

You've done this already if you've ever outgrown a childhood fear. You may have lost your conviction that you'll be sucked down the bathtub drain, that zombies will burst from your closet, or that stepping on a crack will break your mother's back. Write down a fear that bothered you in the past but doesn't bother you now.

One of my former fears:

_____

_____

Now for a little time travel. Remember being truly scared of the thought above. When you can recall that old terror, imagine going back in time to meet your younger self. Sit down with that child and say, "I am from your future. I can tell you with one hundred percent certainty that this thing you fear won't happen, and you won't always be afraid of it." Feel the ring of truth that comes with this statement, the sign that you are connected to your inner teacher. Let your inner child be comforted.

Next, call to mind one of the hell thoughts you've been using in this chapter. Imagine you can hear your own voice from a future version of yourself. It's saying, in a confident, comforting voice, "I am from your future. I can tell you with one hundred percent certainty that this thing you fear won't happen, and you won't always be afraid of it."

You don't have to believe this. Just notice what happens. See whether your future self's reassurance chimes the ring of truth in your body and heart.

Looking back from a distance of thirty years, I can tell you that none of my terrible thoughts about Adam ruining my life turned out to be true. Instead of bringing me shame, he has made me immensely proud. Instead of destroying my career, Adam became the subject of the memoir that launched me as a writer. From babyhood, his calm, balanced personality has anchored me when I feel anxious or upset. And strangely benevolent events often occur around him, some so improbable they feel like magic.

Sometimes, after Adam does or says something I find particularly delightful, I imagine going back in time to that dark bedroom in Cambridge, where my suffering younger self began, ever so tentatively, to doubt her way out of hell. I try to tell that twenty-five-year-old how much Adam has improved my life. Generally she can't hear me—she's too busy listening to her terror and despair. So I just sit beside her, on the floor next to the rocking chair, and keep asking over and over, *Are you sure?*

When I talk to a client or an audience about the material in this chapter, they often just stare into the middle distance: it doesn't look like anything to them. Questioning one's own beliefs is a paradoxical business, and our culture doesn't usually acknowledge that it's possible, let alone advisable. We aren't trained to nurture doubt and seek disconfirmation—quite the opposite. We like to strongly affirm our beliefs and prove that we're *right*, dammit!

But suffering is a dauntless ally. Because of it, most of the people I've coached ultimately learned to observe, question, and free the parts of themselves stuck in their inner infernos. If this fundamental step toward integrity feels strange to you, or it isn't working yet, don't worry. We'll be practicing variations of inferno-busting skills throughout the next three chapters. If you fear you can't make sense of the process, it's okay. That's a fear you'll outgrow.

Whatever your terrors are right now, whatever your inner demons are screaming at you, notice that they don't feel like your inner teacher, that clear chime of truth. They aren't just unnecessary, they're toxic. Your true self is showing you that. It's trying to get your attention, to help you question, doubt, and drop the beliefs that are trapping you in hell. If you can feel that, congratulations. Your trip through the inferno isn't over yet, but you've rejoined the way of integrity. You've learned enough to go all the way through your suffering, and out the other side.

6.

Innocent Mistakes

No one sets out to suffer. In fact, most of us unconsciously put "Avoid Suffering" at the very top of our lifetime to-do lists. We spend almost all our time diligently avoiding pain and pursuing pleasure. And yet, after all our efforts, one of the few certainties of human life is that we all suffer. Every damned one of us. Why?

Dante asks this question as he hikes deeper into the inferno, chatting with Virgil and querying some of the condemned souls. They confess to doing all sorts of things: lusting after other people's spouses, wasting all their money, getting into political arguments that turned violent, and so on. But though they can all say *what* they did wrong, the majority aren't really sure *why*. In fact, six of the nine levels of hell—two-thirds of the inferno—are reserved for what Dante calls "sins of incontinence." This has nothing to do with adult diapers. By "incontinence," Dante means any inability to control an aspect of one's own behavior.

Most of hell's residents, in Dante's view, never meant to commit sins. They were just moseying along, avoiding pain and pursuing pleasure as one does, when they got swept up by inner forces (desire, grasping, rage) that they didn't ask for and couldn't control. They might as well have tripped on a toddler's Lego and fallen into hell.

WHY WE MAKE INNOCENT ERRORS

Most of us end up in psychological suffering in this completely innocent way. We know we're hurting, so it seems logical that we did something unwise, but we're not sure what. This confusion isn't pleasant—it's a mild form of suffering. Like all suffering, it stems from believing things that aren't true. But these are insidious lies, aspects of our cultural training and assumptions so deeply entrenched we don't even realize they exist. In this chapter, we're going to go looking for them.

As we do, I'll use a phrase slightly different from Dante's "sins of incontinence," because in modern times, the word *sin* and the word *incontinence* both have connotations that I think may be a bit off. I believe it's closer to Dante's meaning to call these problems "errors of innocence." I'm betting the lion's share of your own inferno (that is, your unhappiness) can be traced back to such innocent errors. In the next few pages I'll help you identify yours, examine them, and scour them out of your life.

From infancy onward, we soak up incredible amounts of

information—not only explicit concepts, but the entire set of cultural attitudes and beliefs around us. Our parents and siblings, our religious and political leaders, the books we read, the television shows and YouTube videos we watch, are all filled with assumptions that enter our belief systems as we grow. We can't see these assumptions for the same reason we can't see our own eyes: they aren't just thoughts, they're the way we think.

Some cultural beliefs, like "Puppies are adorable," may jibe completely with our deepest sense of truth. Others, like "Beautiful people are better than ugly people" or "I can't be happy unless I'm in a relationship," may not match our inner truth at all. Believing them may affect us like swallowing poison. But we believe them anyway—often without even clearly articulating them in our own minds.

Many "inexplicable" feelings of depression, rage, and anxiety are actually reactions to hidden false beliefs. For example, I once had a client I'll call Irene who took virtually everything I said as an attack or an insult. Once I commented that she looked quite fit, and asked if she liked sports. She teared up and said, "I can't believe you're criticizing me for not being more athletic!" We eventually figured out that Irene had a death grip on the belief "Everyone thinks I should be perfect at everything." It had never even crossed my mind to judge Irene. But in a culture where we're all ranked against one another from preschool on, it's easy to see where she got her fear of being judged.

Another client, Jeff, was so burnt out by his advertising job that he couldn't even speak during sessions. He just sat there clenching his jaw, trying not to cry. His worried wife, who had a decent job herself, had begged him to leave advertising and figure out what would make him happy. But Jeff had a bone-deep belief that a husband and father had to keep working at whatever paid best. He'd learned this by watching his father slowly fade away into a job he'd hated. No one ever explicitly told Jeff "A real man never leaves a steady job," but it chained him in hell all the same.

At times, cultural assumptions send millions of people to hell all at once. Anyone who has suffered race- or class-based oppression knows that all too well. But even more innocuous-looking discrimination can cause enormous suffering. For example, in the 1950s American society idealized women as demure, sweet-natured, intellectually dim creatures specializing in the production of children and the care of suburban houses. By 1963, when Betty Friedan published *The Feminine Mystique*, huge numbers of women were suffering from something Friedan called "the problem that has no name." They were unhappy, unfulfilled, and baffled about how they could feel so awful despite having lovely families and all the gelatin-based dessert recipes a girl could want.

The problem, as most of us now see it, is that the *Leave It to Beaver* feminine role doesn't fit most women's true, full expression of self. Moreover, the presumption that females are less capable and valuable than males tends to rankle. So does the idea that people's worth depends on the color of their skin, or that the poor are lazy, or that mental illness is a punishment from God. "Rankling" is literally the pain of an unhealed wound getting worse. It's how false cultural assumptions make themselves known to us as we unwittingly cart them around in our belief systems. They hurt.

Once someone like Betty Friedan starts analyzing cultural assumptions, the reasons they rankle may seem obvious. But they almost always start out as vague irritants, "problems that have no name." I guarantee you have a few such beliefs—perhaps many—in your own worldview. Maybe in your family, even though no one ever said it out loud, you were "the dumb one" or "the drama queen," and you might still unconsciously hold that self-definition near the very core of your self-concept. You might have a wordless assumption that you're defective because you can't make your body match your culture's standard of perfection. Maybe you've absorbed the idea that the only way to succeed is to become a bully, because you see bullies succeeding all around you, at all levels of society.

Whatever our uninvestigated false beliefs, they cause pain. And we often try to cope with that pain by doing things we don't want, don't understand, and can't control. These actions—these errors of innocence—may break every promise we've made to ourselves. Yet, bafflingly, we can't stop. Welcome to the inferno!

SUFFERING AND SELF-SABOTAGE

When we're internally divided, believing a lie we've been trained to accept, the result is often a tendency to self-sabotage. Like the souls Dante questions, we may find ourselves swept up by the Seven Deadly Sins, or perhaps we just make the Four Million Unfortunate Choices.

For instance, maybe you repeatedly carve out time to write that novel, then fall down a rabbit hole by watching YouTube videos of, say, rabbit holes (google them—they're adorable!). Or perhaps you keep pledging to avoid all political discussions with your in-laws, only to find yourself blurting out unsolicited, unpopular opinions during the family grouse hunt. Or you set five alarms to wake up for an appointment with your tax advisor, then lie down for just a minute before leaving the house, and sleep blissfully through the entire event.

Doing things that so blatantly contradict our own intentions is a sign that somewhere inside us, a civil war is in progress. My clients often tell me they feel as if they have an alter ego working against them. The conscientious Dr. Jekyll self makes the rules, and the heinous Mr. Hyde self breaks them—over and over and over again. This sense of being split in two is a clear experience of duplicity, and the way to stop the self-sabotage, obviously, is a return to integrity. Most people try to do this by dominating Mr. Hyde with Dr. Jekyll's willpower, which is a great idea—except that it doesn't work. It can't stop the pain that drives most self-sabotage, because the duplicity comes from an *unrecognized* split in our belief system.

The best way I know to deal with self-sabotage is to treat it as a signal that somewhere, deep in the murk of our internal inferno, is a belief that's hurting us. Taking this as a starting point allows us to use instances of self-sabotage as signals, revealing our false assumptions. Finding an error of innocence, seeing it clearly, allows us to regain integrity we may not have experienced since we learned to talk. Here's a method for doing it.

HOW TO WALK BACK THE CAT

In order to show you how this exercise works, I'm going to focus on a form of self-sabotage I'm currently battling in my own life. The problem, which I will now confess to you, is as follows: I have been told by my doctor that my immune system reacts badly to eggs. For most people they're great, but for me they're dangerous. I should not eat them. But sometimes I do.

Truth to tell, I ate an egg this very morning. No, full confession: I ate two. I went into a diner, surveyed the myriad choices on the Sunday brunch menu, ordered "Avocado Eggs Benedict," and fell upon them like a wolf.

Please note that I'm using a *recent* incident of self-sabotage. When you apply this exercise to yourself, you should do the same. A recent incident will be fresh in your memory, and the better you can recall it, the more effective the exercise will be. Clear memory helps a great deal for the next step, which is called "walking back the cat."

The phrase "walk back the cat" comes from the world of espionage. Intelligence specialists use this technique to analyze what went wrong in everything from a bungled undercover operation to a failed coup. To do it, you reconstruct an event chronologically moving *backward*, starting with the most recent events and moving further and further into the past.

As I walk back the cat on my act of self-sabotage, the Eating of the Eggs, I'll replay the scenario like a reel of film running very, very slowly in reverse. As I picture a "snapshot" of each moment, I'll try to remember: (1) what was happening around me at that precise time, (2) what I was doing, (3) what I was feeling, and (4) what I was thinking. Here's how it goes in my case:

For my starting point, I'll go to the actual act of egg-eating. I remember it well. There I was in the diner, silverware clinking and people talking all around me. I recall eating too fast, with almost reckless abandon, thinking, "I shouldn't do this, BUT I WANT TO!"

Now I'll move to a moment a few minutes before the actual Eating, say the moment I ordered the eggs. I recall the server standing there, smiling. I'd planned to order something doctor-approved. But suddenly I felt a flash of grumpiness, of confinement. I decided on the eggs in that instant, and as I ordered them I felt a kind of savage triumph.

Now I'll walk the cat back to a few minutes before that: to the moment I entered that diner. I remember how cool it was. I, on the other hand, felt tired and overheated. I was thinking that I'd done a good job cleaning a friend's apartment.

Move a few more minutes back, to the moment I finished cleaning the apartment. My friend had let me use the place while she was gone, and I'd spent the morning making it spick-and-span for her return. That involved walking a few blocks back and forth to the laundromat, carrying towels and bed linens. I remember wanting to rest. But I didn't. Instead I told myself, "No. I can't stop."

AHA!

Now I recognize that the moment in the apartment when I didn't take a rest as the point where I left my integrity. I can feel it. And feeling it, really zooming in on the moment we split from our truth, is the third step in our exercise.

If I walk back the cat to earlier in the morning, say, when I went to pick up the laundry, I remember feeling happy and peaceful. If you'd offered me Avocado Eggs Benedict just then, I'd have declined without a twinge of temptation. But the moment my need to rest crashed into the belief "I can't stop," I abandoned myself. My body, heart, and soul all reacted to the thought "I can't stop" the way they do to any lie. I've described this in previous chapters, but I'll summarize it here:

Physically, I felt an overall tension and a drop in my physical energy—in fact, my throat began to feel a bit sore, and my head started aching.

Emotionally, I began to feel sulky, and then angrily attacked myself for sulking, telling myself to *cheer up, dammit!*

Spiritually, instead of freedom, the thought "I can't stop" brought a sense of heaviness and captivity.

The reason I ignored all these signals and kept working was that I'm strongly attached to a belief that's very common in our culture: continuing to work is always more virtuous than stopping to rest. Now, I'm not saying that tenacious persistence isn't a good idea *sometimes.* I've often prospered by following all those don't-stop slogans: "Quitters never win, winners never quit." "When the going gets tough, the tough get going." "No pain, no gain."

The problem is that today, in my friend's apartment, *I believed these thoughts when my sense of truth was saying they were wrong at that moment, for me.* Even as I write this, I can retroactively feel the loss of peace, the slight uptick in stress. The sensation was partly fatigue, but mostly the anxiety of believing something that didn't feel true. A few minutes later, I tried to soothe myself by ordering and inhaling the Eggs of Error.

This might seem like a teeny-tiny incident to you. It was. But I've learned that the whole trajectory of our lives can turn on the hinges of such minuscule events as they accumulate over time. Each choice against our sense of truth, no matter how trivial, makes us more likely to self-sabotage. It's as if, by splitting ourselves, we launch the alter ego that destroys our best intentions.

In my case, today, the error of innocence was egg-eating. But my real, unwitting mistake was following a cultural assumption away from my sense of truth. I've done this enough to know that if I can release the lie, my psyche will relax back into integrity, and the urge to eat food my body can't tolerate will disappear. But we'll get to that process in a minute. Right now, let's see if you can identify one of your own innocent errors, starting with an instance of your own self-sabotage.

EXERCISE:
Your errors of innocence

Step one: Pick a recurrent unwanted pattern that you can't quit.

Think of a pattern of behavior you keep repeating, despite the fact that you really wish you could stop. We'll call this your act of self-sabotage. It may involve procrastinating, purchasing bizarre objects from craft stores, driving by your ex's house several times a day despite the restraining order, etc. Write it here:

_____

_____

_____

Remember the last time you indulged in this particular kind of self-sabotage, and write a few specific details below to remind you of the incident (for example, "Yesterday I yelled at my kids again" or "Three nights ago I sneaked over to Pat's house and hid in a tree until dawn"):

_____

_____

_____

Step two: Walk back the cat.

You've recalled your self-sabotaging behavior. Now you're going to remember what was happening, what you were doing, what you were feeling, and what you were thinking at the time. Then you're going to examine the moment before that, and the moment before that, and the moment before that... all the way back to the moment discomfort appeared and set you up for self-sabotage.

In the moment you self-sabotaged:

What was happening around you?

_____

What were you doing?

_____

What were you feeling?

_____

What were you thinking?

_____

Now go to the moment right before that.

What was happening around you?

_____

What were you doing?

_____

What were you feeling?

_____

What were you thinking?

_____

And the moment right before that?

What was happening around you?

_____

What were you doing?

_____

What were you feeling?

_____

What were you thinking?

_____

If you need to, grab another piece of paper and keep moving backward, answering the "cat-walking" questions moment by moment. Keep noticing your actions, feelings, and thoughts until you arrive at the moment in your past when something shifted. Before that moment, you felt good. Then you didn't. This is the moment you left your truth.

Step three: Zero in on the moment you left integrity.

Really dwell on the moment your mood shifted. What was happening? What were you doing? What were you feeling in your body, your heart, your soul? And most important, **what were you thinking**? Write the thought here:

_____

_____

The thought you just wrote down is a false belief, even if it sounds true. It's the chain that's binding part of your psyche to a wretched spot in your internal inferno. Having identified it, you are now very close to freeing yourself from something that may have caused years of suffering.

SHATTERING FALSE ASSUMPTIONS

It's quite likely that the thought you wrote down just above sounds virtuous and right. Many of us get trapped in hell by thoughts like "I must always be nice" or "I shouldn't complain." The more your culture emphasizes such thoughts, the more likely you are to assume they're true. As my daughter Kat once wrote, "Belief is just someone saying something near you enough times." Our miraculous minds can take strings of sounds, attach them to images and emotions, and honestly conclude that the abstract ideas they convey are Universal Truths.

Happily, the same tool that forges our chains—the mind—can be used to break them. Once you've observed the beliefs that caused your self-sabotage, the next step is to question them. In the previous chapter I asked you to pick one of your loudest "hell thoughts" and introduce a note of doubt: *Are you sure?* Now I want you to take a more deliberate, assertive approach to a thought that fuels your self-sabotage.

My favorite way of freeing myself from my own inferno comes from a spiritual teacher named Byron Katie, whose books and online videos I strongly recommend. Katie (the name she uses) encourages us to locate beliefs that cause suffering, then break their hold on us using a method she calls "Inquiry." First, Katie asks the simple question "Is that thought true?" Then she follows up with slightly different wording: "Can you absolutely know that thought is true?"

This simple one-two punch of questions is more powerful than it may initially appear. The phrase "absolutely know" is strong language. It snaps the mind to attention, urges it to observe its own beliefs like a scientist. Can you absolutely know that you must *always* be nice, even when, say, someone physically attacks you? Should you *never* complain, even, for instance, when you see an act of horrific injustice?

Katie recommends that we really dwell on this second question, getting in touch with the deep sense of truth that I've been calling the inner teacher. Even when everyone around us agrees on a belief, our inner teachers will still tell us it's false. In my case, as I tidied my friend's apartment, the thought "I can't stop" felt true enough to keep me in motion when I wanted to rest. But when I look back on that moment and access the clear sight of my inner teacher, it's obvious that the thought "I can't stop" was a lie.

As I ponder this topic, I can see plenty of situations where "Quitters never win!" is blatantly false. I recall people who died on Everest because they wouldn't stop climbing when the weather turned ugly. I remember clients who stayed in abusive relationships because they refused to be "quitters." I think of all the people I know who would do well to stop smoking, or gambling, or cutting their own hair.

Once grounded in the truth-seeking mind of my inner teacher, I can reimagine the moment in the apartment when I noticed I was tired. I picture myself thinking "A little rest would do me good," then getting a glass of cold water and sitting down to catch my breath. Immediately, the slight clenching and irritability I felt in the diner disappear. I feel much calmer, less prone to compulsively seeking comfort. I become a person who can quit working—and quit eating eggs—when that is the wisest course of action.

Once you've seen through a false assumption, you don't need another belief to replace it. Getting out of hell doesn't mean picking up a new set of chains, a new set of absolute beliefs. It means replacing rigid convictions with curious openness, to your own sense of truth in every moment.

For example, when Irene (my perfectionistic client) broke through the thought "Everyone wants me to be perfect," she didn't decide on some other thing that everyone wanted. She focused on knowing what felt right to her at any given time. When Jeff questioned the thought "A real man never leaves a steady job," he didn't start disparaging people with jobs. He began brainstorming about making money in more original ways (Jeff ultimately quit his job and started a business helping troubled teenagers by teaching them martial arts—something he'd been passionate about for years).

ESCAPING MY ERRORS OF INNOCENCE

Not long after giving birth to Adam, I walked with my eyes wide open into an error of innocence that almost destroyed me. I talked my then-husband into returning to our hometown in Utah, where we could both teach as assistant professors while I finished my doctoral dissertation. Tired and heartsore, I just wanted to be around people who wouldn't disagree with my decision not to abort. John and I settled in and had a third child, a daughter we named Elizabeth.

I had so much: a supportive community, a teaching job, three kids I adored. But I could never keep pace with everything I thought I should do. As I raced around town before work, dropping off each child at different locations (Lizzy at daycare, Adam at a special preschool program, Kat at regular preschool), I felt like a substandard, abandoning mother. When I picked up the kids and put Adam through his physical therapy while trying to entertain the girls, part of me heard my dissertation advisors telling me I should be working. When I stayed up all night doing research and grading papers, I felt guilty for exhausting myself too much to really show up for any of my tasks or relationships.

During this time, my dark wood of error symptoms reached an all-time high. I suffered persistent pain that defied diagnosis, contracted every contagious illness short of bubonic plague, and was forever landing in the hospital with problems requiring massive antibiotics, minor surgeries, or both. My outward life was overwhelmingly busy, my inner narrative a storm of self-criticism. I was intensely confused. I didn't realize that I had picked up two sets of cultural beliefs that contradicted each other. My error of innocence lay in not seeing this contradiction, and trying to fulfill both sides of two mutually exclusive codes for living.

I figured this out by "walking back the cat" not only through my own life, but through American culture in general. At the time (the 1990s), conventional wisdom expected women to be devoted caretakers for the young the old, and the ill—while also succeeding in jobs designed for men with free full-time domestic support. We were expected to give up the pursuit of professional success by caring for others, *and* give up traditional caretaking roles to succeed as individuals. It was like being caught in one of those paper finger traps, where the harder you struggle to free yourself, the tighter the it holds on.

By trying to be both a devoted Mormon mother and a successful Harvard scholar, I'd ended up in an extreme version of this innocent error. The harder I tried to fulfill one set of requirements, the more I felt I was failing at the other. The more

I tried to "balance" contradictory roles, the more off-center and miserable I felt. My research showed there were a lot of women in the same boat. Most of us never even saw that we were trying to fulfill irreconcilable demands, because they were deeply rooted cultural assumptions. It was a genuinely innocent error, but it still landed us in hell.

After walking back the cat until I understood all this intellectually, I completely despaired. It never occurred to me that I could drop my belief in *all* the cultural demands that were making my life so conflicted. I knew it was impossible to do everything society told me I should do. But that didn't mean I stopped feeling social pressure. I was a person, after all, and people orient their lives by obeying social standards. I saw no escape from my miserable condition—that is, until I met a soul teacher.

It came, as my teachers usually do, in a book—specifically Stephen Mitchell's translation of an ancient Chinese volume, the *Tao te Ching*. I'd bought it as an undergraduate but never got around to reading it. One day, I came across the book, opened it at random, and read:

> *In the pursuit of knowledge,*
> *every day something is added.*
> *In the practice of the Tao [Way],*
> *every day something is dropped.*
> *Less and less do you need to force things,*
> *until finally you arrive at non-action.*
> *When nothing is done,*
> *nothing is left undone.*

These words hit me like a mallet striking a gong. They made no sense to my mind, but I felt a physical sensation like a jolt of electricity. I began pacing rapidly around the room, shaking my hands to discharge some of the energy. This was odd, because my right hip and knee had been almost unusable for months. Usually I had a pronounced limp, and felt completely exhausted. Now I wanted to move. *Fast.*

I thought a drive might help, so I got into my car and headed up into the mountains. By then I felt as if I'd switched into autopilot. I stopped at the head of a trail I'd often hiked as a child, jumped out of the car, and ran—*ran*—up that trail. I waited for fatigue and pain to stop me. They didn't. I kept speeding up for two steep, mountainous miles, when I reached a massive waterfall. I ran straight into the water, to a spot at one side where the water wouldn't flay me alive. As the ice-cold torrent pounded down on my head, it felt as if the fire rising from inside me had finally found an equal and opposite force.

My usual mind felt thunderstruck, completely unable to understand what was happening. Years later, I would learn that in Asian traditions, my outburst of energy might be seen as a typical response to sudden freedom from mental concepts, from delusions. Pondering the *Tao te Ching* from a place of deep inner conflict shocked my mind right out of its cultural framework. The energy I felt was my body's response to dropping away from a toxic belief system and connecting with my integrity. That's how dramatic this process can be.

At the time, though, I had no idea what was happening. I simply felt astonished. I seemed to watch from a short distance as all my tormenting thoughts about what it meant to be a woman disintegrated. Could I absolutely know *any* social demand was true for me? No, no, no, no, no.

After a few minutes, my mind had fallen silent, and my body had undergone a healing that seemed miraculous. Unfortunately, the physical effect didn't stay long. By the time I got back to my car I was limping again. But all those contradictory ideas about what women must be and do? They had virtually no control over me anymore. I could still *think* them, but I could no longer *believe* them. I've never believed them since. Those particular inferno-chains were broken.

As you walk back the cat on your own errors of innocence, you too may find that many of your untrue beliefs are built into your culture. It can be frightening to let go of such beliefs. Won't people think you're wrong? Won't they judge you?

Yes, dear reader, they will.

As you spot the innocent errors that have been damaging your life, as you dissolve them with observation and inquiry, you'll soon end up breaking the rules. Which rules? I don't know. But the people around you who believe in those rules may find your behavior dubious or even wicked. You'll feel a thousand times freer—and they won't like it. Don't worry. This can actually be evidence you're on the right track. You're entering the part of the inferno where you'll learn to cope with judgment— yours, and other people's. Things are about to get radical.

7.

When Righteousness
Goes Wrong

The day I ran to the waterfall I left part of my inferno behind, but not all of it. Not by a long shot. I was still living in that toy finger trap of contradiction between two radically different cultures. While I wrote my dissertation, John and I stayed afloat financially by teaching at Brigham Young University, where both our fathers had been professors. I found myself simultaneously working at one of the most conservative colleges in the country and finishing a degree from Harvard, one of the most liberal. Given my live-and-let-live philosophy, I didn't expect this to be a problem.

Ha!

In hindsight, my naivete is hilarious. Every day I spent working for BYU brought head-spinning contradictions. For example, I was told that the university needed to hire more women to keep its accreditation—but on the other hand, I mustn't encourage female students to pursue careers, since Mormonism frowned on women having jobs. In fact, some female students filed complaints saying I was setting a bad example of womanhood just by teaching them. And though I was assigned to teach "sociology of gender," I was warned never to speak the incendiary word *feminism.*

I soon realized that I'd retreated to Utah just in time to get whirled up in an ideological tempest. Mormon leaders had begun "disciplining" academics for writing or teaching anything that contradicted church doctrine. For example, an anthropologist was asked to leave the church when his DNA research showed Native Americans to be descended from Siberian ancestors, not, as Mormons believe, from Middle Eastern Jews. Every professor at BYU, from geologists to historians to artists, risked expulsion from their jobs and community if they contradicted the church's doctrines. Few people outside Utah even noticed all this—I hadn't noticed it from Massachusetts—but trust me: in my home state it was huge news.

My inner social-science nerd was fascinated by the conflict between religion and academia in Mormon country. It was like watching Galileo being tried for heresy after figuring out that Earth travels around the sun, not vice versa. But to my people-pleaser personality, the intense controversy I ran into everywhere I went felt like hell. Specifically, the seventh circle of Dante's inferno, a region occupied by "the violent."

ERRORS OF RIGHTEOUSNESS

After Dante trudges past the six circles of hell where "incontinent" sinners are punished, he finally encounters souls who caused trouble on purpose. Unlike the incontinent, who weren't sure why they had sinned and never meant any harm, the people in Circle Seven set out to wreak all manner of mayhem, and they bloody well liked it.

Blood looms large in Dante's seventh circle. Many of "the violent" are condemned to swim in a boiling-hot river of it while being shot at by centaurs. Others have become trees that are continuously torn at by harpies. Still others run around on burning sand, tormented by a rain of fire. All these horrors, like everything else going on in Dante's inferno, are *contrapasso*—tortures designed to resemble the sins they punish. Everyone in the seventh circle is being continuously attacked, because the act of attack, with the sole purpose of causing suffering and destruction, is the essence of all violence.

At this point I want to make it very clear that violence and anger are very different things. Anger is a normal, healthy response to injustice or ill-treatment. Violence, according to the Oxford Dictionary, is intended to "hurt, damage, or kill someone or something." There are many points in *The Divine Comedy* at which Dante, Virgil, or various holy beings express anger. But their reaction is to create justice, rather than merely destroy whatever is bothering them.

Anger at inequity or ill-treatment seems to be embedded in

our biology. We react with anger when something essential is withheld from anyone who needs it, or something intolerable is being imposed. The high energy of anger helps correct unfair situations, the way a fever fires up the body to kill an invading virus. Without it, no one would leave abusive relationships, question the systemic oppression of certain populations, or work toward fairness in the world.

Arun Gandhi, the grandson of one of history's most powerful proponents of nonviolence, wrote that Mahatma Gandhi "saw anger as a good thing, as the fuel for change." But when we become violent, intending solely to hurt or damage, we've joined the forces of destruction. It takes wisdom and maturity to use anger for positive change without becoming mindlessly violent. It's much easier—and in the short term, more gratifying— to go into a psychological mode of blind attack.

Even if you've never raised your hand against a living thing, you've almost certainly been violent. We all have. We've attacked other people, ourselves, or frustrating situations, if only in the privacy of our own minds. If you've ever felt a surge of rage at another driver in traffic, or checked a mirror and genuinely hated the way you look, or cheered through your popcorn when an action-adventure movie hero killed the villain, you've participated in the energy of violence. And chances are, you liked it.

This is because part of our hardwiring makes us *enjoy* destroying anything that threatens us. That's just good evolutionary policy. Any creature that lacked the will to fight when threatened would soon be dead and gone. But unlike animals, humans don't just attack clear and present physical threats. In fact, we may feel threatened by people we're dominating, simply because they want to be treated better, like a dictator raging at his subjects or a racist reacting to people of color who ask for fair treatment.

We're also unique in that we're frightened not only by powerful creatures that want to eat us, but by anyone or anything that may potentially *change* us. We're especially leery of people or ideas that might shake us out of our cultural assumptions and preconceptions. Such things feel *morally* threatening, and we react to them by becoming almost reflexively resistant and oppositional. This is the mindset from which all violence is born.

A lot of what we may call our "ideals" is actually this kind of knee-jerk combative reaction against change. Again, this reflex is different from perceiving an injustice, articulating places where that injustice causes inequality or suffering, and agitating for change. (For example, Martin Luther King Jr. based his civil-rights agitation on an appeal to equal rights. James Earl Ray, who killed Dr. King, was under no actual threat; his actions were based on fear of change and reflexive self-righteousness.)

People in the grip of their righteous minds generally believe that their personal moral codes are logical, rational, and universally true. But research shows that such judgments actually come from emotional reactions, shaped by specific cultures. This means that the violent mind literally can't hear reason. It shuts down our ability to make thoughtful judgments. People who are emotionally attached to a political leader may observe that leader flagrantly violating their own values—and simply not care. In fact, when people learn that their political beliefs are based on inaccurate information, they don't change their minds—instead, they cling to their belief systems more tightly than ever.

This sounds irrational because it is. The part of the brain that causes us to feel that familiar ways are right, *no matter what*, is older, bigger, and stronger than the rational mind. One psychologist, Jonathan Haidt, compares the logical brain to a human rider sitting on the back of an illogical elephant. We assume the rider is in charge, making fair, just decisions and directing the elephant. But it's usually the elephant who's calling the shots. In Haidt's words, "The rider acts as spokesman for the elephant, even though it doesn't necessarily know what the elephant is really thinking."

The elephants in our heads—our reflexive reactions—perceive anything unfamiliar as just plain wrong. Familiar things feel right, right, RIGHT! This is the sensation comedian Stephen Colbert famously dubbed "truthiness." It's like being drunk or high: delicious in the short term, ultimately toxic. The righteous mind can temporarily overwhelm our sense of truth, including our allegiance to justice and fairness.

When our righteous mind is in control, we lose the way of integrity and become weirdly, obviously self-contradictory, like proponents of world peace who advocate war against anyone who disagrees with them. Because violence and the righteous mind are closely linked, I don't call destructive actions sins of violence, as Dante does. I think of them as "errors of righteousness." They are psychological mistakes we make when our irrational rejection of the unfamiliar takes over our thinking.

WHY ERRORS OF RIGHTEOUSNESS ARE DELICIOUS (AT FIRST)

Humans depend for survival on belonging to close-knit groups of cooperating individuals. Because of that, we're biologically programmed to identify with the people who look, act, dress, talk, and think the way we do. The downside of this is a universal human tendency to mistrust anyone who seems different from our in-groups. Many tribal groups, from the South African Khoikhoi to the Siberian Yupiit, call themselves by names that in their languages mean "the real people." This implies, of course, that folks from outside the group are *not* real people.

This is called "othering," and everyone does it. From early childhood, we see anything unfamiliar as weird and unnerving. The eighteenth-century social reformer Robert Owen pointed this out in his famously ironic statement, "All the world is queer save thee and me, and even thou art a little queer."

Once we've "othered" someone, we may unconsciously define them as inhuman, inferior, even abhorrent. Why, the very existence of such anomalous creatures is a threat to our way of being! When we band together with our in-groups to complain about the "others," our adrenaline and other "fight" hormones spike, giving us an intoxicating, artificial sense of purpose and belonging. The more violently we speak and act, the more righteous we feel.

Again, this is different from the anger we feel when we experience injustice or oppression. Healthy anger motivates discernment. It focuses on specific problems. It works toward changing conditions, and when those conditions change, it subsides. Righteous error attacks for vague, ill-defined, or contradictory reasons, and doesn't change with circumstances. It *passes* judgment, often without evidence. Healthy anger *makes* judgments, discerning what is fair and what isn't. Here's a chart to help you tell them apart.

Healthy Discernment	Righteous Error
(Making judgments)	*(Passing judgment)*
Compels actions that reduce anger	Compels actions that increase anger
Sees all people as connected	Sees all people as "us versus them"
Seeks new information	Avoids new information
Learns about many topics	Focuses obsessively on a few topics
Is able to imagine other perspectives	Imagines only its own perspective
Sees shades of gray	Sees everything as black and white
Acknowledges it is fallible	Insists on its own infallibility

If we're serious about integrity, we need to take a close look at that right-hand column. When we see ourselves described there, we're not connecting with our sense of truth; in fact, we're dividing ourselves from our innate desire to live in peace. The emotional high we may get from righteousness can blot out our genuine values, blind us to the facts about who's being harmed and who's doing the harming, and deafen us to the clear voice of integrity. If we don't question it, we may end up in a mental state of continuous attack: the inferno's seventh circle.

THE VICIOUS CYCLE OF VIOLENCE

Dante divides this level of the inferno into three rings: one for people who were violent against others, another for those who turned violent against themselves, and a third for souls who were violent against God, art, and nature—the forces of creation. This metaphor reflects the three most common ways we can get stuck in errors of righteousness: by attacking other people, ourselves, or the way things are.

I've seen all three types of psychological violence in my practice. I once had a client I'll call Edna who looked like a sweet granny but sustained continuous, simmering mental violence. She thought constantly about the ways she wanted to hurt everyone from her neighbors, whom she envied, to world leaders, whom she despised, to entire cultures, whose customs she found subhuman. She spent hours each day writing blog posts about this to her three online followers, all of whom were bots.

Another client, Brian, directed his violence at himself. Ordinarily, he was so shut down he barely seemed to be conscious, but once he started attacking himself ("I'm nothing but a worthless, stupid piece of crap!"), you could see where all his energy was going.

Amelia never stopped complaining about her "bad luck," by which she apparently meant everything that ever happened to her. A rainstorm, a flat tire, the fact that her cat avoided her—all of these felt to Amelia like deliberate violations aimed straight at her. She spent most of her mental energy striking back.

All these people were using an obsession with judgment to avoid various hellgate issues. Most of us do this. The surge of pleasure our egos get from attacking others is a great emotional painkiller. When I met Edna she'd just lost her husband, and her constant angry blogging kept her from feeling her grief. Brian had always felt isolated, and his self-loathing helped him numb his loneliness. Amelia was carrying a lot of childhood trauma she didn't know how to process. Constantly fussing about everything absorbed her attention so she never had to.

I doubt you hang out in Circle Seven as persistently as these folks, but you may well spend some of your time in the realm of violence. You may engage in a constant inner monologue, stating and restating your moral positions, revving up a payload of destructive rage against your enemies. You may spend all night tweeting to tell the world how bad those enemies really are. Maybe you get together with like-minded people to voice your hatred, and notice that the energy climbs even though nothing in the environment has changed. People sharing a session of righteousness may go from grumbling to lashing out viciously, like a war party of chimpanzees or a clique of middle-school girls. Joking aside, the fury that rises when groups share righteous rage leads directly to mob frenzies, hate crimes, and genocides.

The righteous mind at its full tilt is completely insane. Herman Melville wrote a brilliant description of it in *Moby-Dick*, a heartwarming story about an ordinary guy and the whale who bit off his leg. After spending his whole life hunting the great white whale, Captain Ahab dies screaming the ultimate slogan of all righteous minds: "To the last I grapple with thee; from hell's heart I stab at thee; for hate's sake I spit my last breath at thee."

If this is how you feel about, say, the people who keep changing the software on your smartphone, consider the possibility that you may be stuck in errors of righteousness. Allowing yourself to stand up against unfairness is healthy. Staying in constant righteous attack mode isn't. It will give you dark wood of error symptoms just like any other departure from integrity.

For example, Edna's sustained anger probably contributed to her chronic stomach ulcers. Brian's obsessive self-hatred made him so hard to be around that his wife, after hanging in for twenty years, finally left him. Amelia, constantly preoccupied with her bad luck, couldn't sustain a friendship or a steady job.

When errors of righteousness run into each other, they lead to vicious cycles of mutual destruction. Throughout history, people who feel attacked by "others" ignore the perspective of their opponents, rev up their righteous minds, and set out to cause harm. This can trigger similar righteous-mind destructiveness in others, who stop acting creatively and fight back in their own righteous rage, which makes the other side even angrier, and so on. There's a reason Dante's river of blood runs in a circle: there's no end to this madness.

Notice how different this is from the clarity of people who voice their anger from a place of integrity. For example, in his bestseller *How to Be an Antiracist*, Ibram X. Kendi freely expresses his anger at racial oppression. But he also methodically, logically, and consistently requires of himself the same fair-mindedness and wisdom he wishes to see in all people. He cautions against the righteous high that "avoids the mirror." He uses the impartiality necessary to avoid errors of righteousness, even while trying to change injustice:

> What if antiracists constantly self-critiqued our own ideas? What if we blamed our ideologies and methods, refined our ideologies and methods again and again until they worked? When will we finally stop the insanity of doing the same thing repeatedly and expecting a different result? Self-critique allows change.

This kind of self-scrutiny brings us back into harmony with our sense of truth. It means we apply one standard in all cases, replacing duplicity with integrity. To go from "righteous mind" to genuine fairness, we actually have to change brain states, go from the intoxication of violence to a clear, calm mind. Here's an exercise that can help you sober up.

EXERCISE:
Fighting monsters

Step one: Pick your issue.

Start by thinking of a controversial social issue you really care about. It might be gun control, immigration, capital punishment, animal rights—any issue will do, as long as you have a strong opinion about it, and you know there are people who strongly hold the opposite opinion. Write it here:

_____

_____

Step two: Name the "others."

Focus for a moment on the people who disagree with you. Imagine them en masse, marching in the streets, posting on Twitter, denouncing things you care about. Maybe you already have a phrase to describe them, like "less-informed voters" or "misguided children of God" or "knuckle-dragging, scum-sucking, pea-brained morons." But here and now, let's just call them "monsters."

Step three: Let your blood boil.

Think for a moment about the way your monsters behave, the damage they do. Really feel all the anger and outrage this creates. Once your blood is boiling, fill in the following blanks as if you were writing your monsters an anonymous letter. This is for your eyes only, so don't hold back. Write what you think in your most politically incorrect moments. Don't try to make your words pretty or polite. Use a separate sheet of paper if you need more space.

To My Monsters:

Let me be frank.

Here's what I don't like about you:

_____

_____

Here's what you do that's just plain wrong:

_____

_____

Here's what would happen to the world if you and your kind had control of it:

_____

_____

Here's what I hope happens to limit your power and influence:

_____

_____

Here's what you should do, and I am serious:

_____

_____

Sincerely,
Me

Step four: Go get the mail.

Now imagine that you go to your mailbox and find an envelope addressed to you. Picture opening the envelope and finding a letter inside. Quelle coincidence! It's identical to the letter you just wrote to your monsters.

Right now, go back and reread the letter above—the one you just wrote—as if someone you've never heard of has written it to you. Really imagine it.

As you read, notice how your mind, body, and heart react. What happens inside you as you take in the stranger's words?

- Do you want to agree or cooperate with this person?

- Do you feel that the stranger knows, understands, and cares about you?

- Do you feel like opening your heart, or closing down hard?

You don't have to write down your answers. Just feel them.

If you found your letter reasonable and uplifting, congratulations. You may be acting for justice, but you're not stuck in an error of righteousness. If you're like most people, though, this exercise may have helped you see that while delivering righteous judgment feels fabulous, receiving it feels awful. When we're attacked—*even with the very words we use to attack others*—we feel confused, scared, misjudged, angry, rigid, and intensely inclined to lash back. As Friedrich Nietzsche wrote, "Beware that, when fighting monsters, you yourself do not become a monster." When we go to war on something that we see as a war on us, the ultimate winner isn't either side of the conflict, but war itself.

Living in errors of righteousness wears us out and drags us down. I wish I could show you how exhausted and sick Edna felt after years of continuous anger. Brian's continuous self-attack was another tar pit of paralysis and despair. Amelia felt utterly dejected, friendless, and alone. Once we get stuck in an error of righteousness, we suffer big time.

The only path that leads away from all this misery is the way of integrity. To follow it out of the seventh circle, we'll use the same steps you learned in the last chapter: (1) observe thoughts that cause suffering, (2) question them, and (3) move on. In the next section we'll see how this works when we confront our own errors of righteousness.

THE CENTRAL LIE OF RIGHTEOUSNESS

I think there's a good reason Dante only imagined one level of hell for the violent instead of six, as for the incontinent. There are many beliefs that cause innocent mistakes, like "Everyone hates me" or "Happiness comes from hard work" or "Charles Manson is the source of all wisdom!" But there's only one massive lie that turns us toward violence. It is the fundamental belief of the righteous brain. It says, "I can fix everything that upsets me by destroying my enemies."

Again, this doesn't mean you shouldn't react when someone tries to hurt you. If a mugger jumps you in an alley, by all means fight back. If you see unfairness in society, speak out, put your views in writing, march for justice. But while you do these things, maintain a discerning mind that's open to new information and new ideas. When I studied martial arts, I learned over and over that we can fight most effectively when we aren't locked into a mental position of blind attack. Fighting has its place, but by itself violence never fixes, heals, or mends anything. Its essence is destruction, never creation.

Think about the previous exercise, your letter to your monsters. Recall the issue you chose for that exercise. Go into your righteous mind and feel what it does to you. Watch your body tense, your anger rise, your mind start circling like an MMA fighter in a cage. Notice that while the adrenaline surge might be intoxicating, this state of body and mind quickly is dominated by fury and discontent. Is this really the place from which anyone can increase justice, love, or peace?

Now consider this thought: "I can fix everything that upsets me by destroying my enemies." Write the thought down, if you like. Then put it under the microscope. Ask the questions you learned in the last chapter for puncturing any mental error:

Are you sure you can fix this situation by destroying your enemies?

Can you absolutely know that thought ("I can fix this by destroying my enemies") is true?

If you remember how defensive you felt about receiving

your very own letter to your "monsters," you'll see that just attacking, with no other intention, can only escalate mental and perhaps physical violence. You may notice the irony of attack, of your hope that people will end up agreeing with you because you're trying to hurt them. The desire to destroy others is fundamentally hypocritical, because no one, especially an attacker, wants to be destroyed. Juicy as violence feels to the righteous mind, it's internally divisive, incompatible with integrity.

VALUES WITHOUT VIOLENCE

Many of my clients worry that if they lose their inner violence, they won't be motivated to resist unfairness in the world. But when we clear our minds of that righteous urge to destroy, our perceptions of wrongdoing remain clear. We can see evil, recognize it for what it is, and address it without falling back into errors of righteousness. How? By turning our attention away from arguing and moralizing, and focusing instead on our integrity, our deepest inner truth.

Psychologist Steven Hayes calls this connecting with our "core values." His research shows that focusing on values has an almost magical ability to accomplish the very things we think we'll get by attacking our enemies. Simply shifting our attention from attacking our enemies to defining our values can "reduce physiological stress responses, buffer the impact from negative judgments of others, reduce our defensiveness, and help us be more receptive to information that may be hard to accept."

Here's an exercise based on a technique Hayes uses to help clients escape destructive anger. Start by thinking of a verb and an adverb that combine to describe the way you want to live your life. It will be a phrase like "teaching compassionately," "loving courageously," or "serving honorably." Think for a few minutes about what verb-adverb combination best sums up your core values. If you could always live this way, you'd feel that you'd lived an honest and meaningful life. Got it? Write your value here:

> *The verb-adverb phrase that best describes my core value is:*
>
> _____
>
> _____
>
> _____

Just focusing on this phrase ("learning joyfully," "caring generously," "creating unabashedly," or whatever) will change your internal state. Feel how different it is from moral outrage, how it settles and relaxes your body, mind, heart, soul. Now, with your core value in focus, you're ready for a next step on the way of integrity. Try this one:

EXERCISE:
Going to the mountain

Step one: Imagine yourself in a peaceful natural landscape.

You may be on a beach, in a forest, or in a meadow (I like to imagine going to the mountains). You're alone, but everything is beautiful, calm, and completely safe.

Step two: Connect with your inner teacher.

You can use the "Meeting Your Inner Teacher" exercise in Chapter 3, meditate on the thought "I am meant to live in peace," or simply focus on the word *peace* as you breathe in and out. When you feel the quiet, calm place at your center, continue.

Step three: Recall your core values.

You can write your verb-adverb combination here as a reminder:

_____

_____

Step four: Think of an issue that upsets you.

You can use the same topic you wrote about in your "monster" letter or think of a different issue. Write it here:

_____

_____

Step five: Answer this question:

In regard to the issue I've just cited, acting in accordance with the core values I just defined, *what positive thing can I create?*

_____

_____

Step six: Whatever step you wrote down in the blank above, take it.

I know this sounds blunt, and that working toward a better world by following your values could take a lifetime. But it's really that simple.

Each time I do the exercise above, I find myself giving different answers, thinking up different creative steps. Some are obviously related to solving a troubling issue, but sometimes they seem unrelated. Yours may surprise you. Maybe you'll feel motivated to read a book, plant a tree, make a bold statement online, or back off an argument. Maybe the action step that occurs to you will seem too small, or too odd. Take it anyway. *The moment you begin any creative activity, you leave the realm of violence, which knows only destruction.*

Shifting from righteous self-defense into creativity can catalyze life-changing, even world-changing action. I think that's why famous moral leaders are often creative in small ways as well as large. Gandhi not only modeled civil disobedience but also made his own clothes, right down to weaving the cloth. Harriet Tubman, a multitalented genius, not only helped people escape slavery but also started her own restaurant, where she taught freed women to get paying jobs providing goods and services for the Union Army. Eunice Kennedy Shriver, heartsick about the lack of opportunities for people with intellectual disabilities, started a sports camp for children at her home that later grew into the Special Olympics. These people stood up against injustice without violence, and they were always creating things, even small things: cotton clothes, delicious food, a foot race.

A closed mind is like a weapon whose only function is to harm. It grips the thought "I exist in continuous violent reaction to whatever is threatening." By addressing problems with core values and creativity, we choose a different *mode de vie*: "I exist in continuous creative response to whatever is present." Sacrificing our reflexive tendency toward destruction gives us access to a much greater power: creation.

Back when my job and education sent me in opposite directions, I spent many sleepless nights consumed by errors of righteousness. It felt like my blood was literally boiling with controversy. I didn't like the Harvard ideals that said my son's life wasn't worth living because he could never be an intellectual. But I also disagreed with Mormon leaders who were firing, shaming, excommunicating, and isolating my colleagues for knowing the wrong facts.

Because these were the cultures that had shaped me, the conflict tied my mind in knots. On the one hand I was wrestling with intellectualism; on the other, I struggled against a religion that designated intellectuals as one of the "enemies of truth in the latter days."

Drowning in that gory river, I grabbed for anything solid that might help me drag myself out. The truth, I thought. I need to know the truth. And so I launched my first "integrity cleanse." On New Year's Eve, I made a resolution not to tell a single lie, of any kind, for the next full calendar year. This turned out to be a quick trip out of self-righteousness and into a clearer mind. If you ever want to try it, you can count on freeing yourself from innumerable errors. But you should also expect it to change every single part of your life.

8.

The End of Self-Betrayal

In Dante's inferno, after picking their way through the ghastly realm of "the violent," the poet and his teacher Virgil finally reach the inferno's lowest depths. Imprisoned here are the worst of all sinners, those whose crimes exceed even those of the most vicious atrocities, like war crimes and murders. Approaching circles eight and nine, Dante braces himself to encounter the worst sinners of all: liars.

Wait, what? Liars? Shouldn't they be up in some comparatively mellow white-collar circle at the very top of the inferno? After all, everybody lies. We do it to be *nice*, for heaven's sake! Research shows that the majority of people lie multiple times in a typical ten-minute conversation, tossing out fibs like "I'm doing great, thanks" and "I was just going to call you" and "I love your shoes." Is this really worse than, say, plotting terrorism?

Well, just remember that the wild creature most likely to kill a human being is the mosquito. Lying, like a ubiquitous bloodsucking insect, is insidious partly because it's so small, so common, so nearly invisible. And lying enables every other type of evil.

Maya Angelou wrote, "Courage is the most important of all the virtues, because without courage you can't practice any other virtue consistently." Lying is the dark counterpart to courage: it's the most important of all the vices, because without lying you can't practice any other vice consistently (if you never lie, your terrorist plots just won't pan out). Conversely, if you can't *stop* lying—at least to yourself—you'll never make it out of the inferno.

We've seen that all our errors of innocence and righteousness come from false beliefs—either "lies" that we truly believe or, more commonly, assumptions we don't even know are there. We've gone through your inferno spotting these errors and assumptions, then questioning them. All this truth-telling makes you a kind of archeologist, digging into your own psyche. As you release yourself from the lies that trap you in errors of innocence or righteousness, you lay bare what I call "foundational lies," falsehoods that drive and support all the others.

Sometimes we lie with full awareness and intent, usually to hide some kind of unethical behavior. Dante labels such falsehoods "fraud," and puts those who perpetrate it in the eighth circle of hell. There, flatterers are covered in excrement (after talking bullcrap all their lives), crooked politicians are mired in tar as sticky as their fingers, and priests who sold religious favors are buried head-down in baptismal fonts, with their feet on fire.

There's a lot of hellfire in Dante's inferno. In fact, today English speakers use the word *inferno* as a synonym for fire. But in *The Divine Comedy*, hell's deepest circle isn't hot. It's terribly, terribly cold. The floor of the inferno is a lake of ice. Frozen into it are "the treacherous," people who in life perpetrated some kind of betrayal.

This chapter is about how we perpetrate fraud and betrayal in our own lives. Remember, we still aren't talking about changing your external behaviors. The "inferno" stage of our trek to integrity is about our *inner* lives. The time will come to shift your actions—later. This chapter is meant to help you simply notice occasions when you cheat, lie, and betray. It's important to know that you may be doing these things to others. But it's absolutely crucial to see where you're doing them to yourself.

THREE KINDS OF LIES

We tend to categorize lies as black, white, or gray. I've seen all of them in my practice. Here are some examples.

Black lies: Deliberate, premeditated deception

A participant in one of my seminars—I'll call him Ernest—once accosted me during a lunch break. He seemed quite eager to talk. He was a defense attorney, and during his career he'd represented several murderers. Many of these people had told him they were guilty. Ernest had spent years thinking about them.

"I used to wonder what was different about them," he said. "What makes them capable of killing? Then I figured it out. You know what it is?"

I shook my head.

"Lying," said Ernest. "Once you decide to lie—I mean *really* lie—you have a kind of hiding place in your life, like a secret room. You can put anything in there. It's all invisible. It all disappears."

I wasn't sure what he wanted me to do with this information, but it seemed important to him. The seminar ended, and I forgot all about Ernest until years later when he called me out of the blue. "I guess you've probably seen my name in the news lately," he said. I hadn't. I barely recalled who he was. But my memory of our conversation came back in a rush when he told me why he'd contacted me. Ernest had been convicted of murder, and he wanted some coaching to help deal with prison life.

I still wonder if I failed Ernest, if he was reaching out during our previous conversation. But he hadn't come across that way. He seemed, if anything, quite proud that he'd worked out a simple way to do absolutely anything without feeling troubled. In contrast to other incarcerated people I've worked with, Ernest seems more like a true sociopath, someone I could never have "fixed" no matter how hard I tried. At least I comfort myself by thinking that, and my sense of truth doesn't disagree.

At any rate, despite seeming proud of his "accomplishment," Ernest didn't have the air of someone who was at peace with himself. In fact, after our phone conversation, it occurred to me that I'd never seen any client become completely happy without a direct commitment to honesty. Though Ernest's crime was especially awful, I'd seen similar dynamics play out in many other people, including myself. We don't exactly think lying is right, but we do it anyway, and then excuse ourselves. Research reveals that though most of us consider ourselves honest, we don't mind fudging here and there, and sometimes everywhere.

Once I asked a woman I'll call Bernice how she managed to work in law enforcement while also selling the illegal drugs she'd confiscated from dealers. Didn't the irony make her head explode? Wasn't she overwhelmed with guilt? She answered, "Everything is easy once you believe your own lies." But things were easy for Bernice only in the outer world. Her inner life was an inferno of isolation and paranoia. When we deliberately leave our own truth, we live in a foggy world where nothing we experience feels trustworthy or reliable, because we ourselves aren't trustworthy and reliable.

White lies: The social contract leads to social fibs

Maybe you've never told a dark lie. So, just to make sure you feel included, let me swing the pendulum all the way over to little white ones. In Chapter 5 I mentioned that audiences predictably lie to reassure me they're comfortable in uncomfortable chairs. Most of us engage in a lot of such unconscious self-deception. We use it to ignore anything from slight discomforts to flat-out torture.

For example, if we're raised hearing our drunken parents smash furniture, if we're sexually or physically abused, or if we get stuck in disasters like war or wildfire, our conscious awareness of the unbearable events can get fuzzy, even disappear. We may repress conscious knowledge of the trauma, or drastically minimize it to make it less painful.

These responses are automatic, often involuntary. But they can cause us to suffer as much as deliberate deception. Going blind and deaf to our own pain means we don't realize that we must leave dangerous situations or people. It puts us, or keeps us, directly in harm's way. We endure one horrible experience after another. Is this fair? No. Fairness doesn't enter into it. Any lie, even an unconscious one, splits us from integrity. Remember the reason planes crash. Not God's punishment. Just physics.

Then there's the more typical type of white lie: the things we say, knowing they aren't true, in order to maintain social equilibrium. When friends ask how they look in ridiculous pants, we may say, "Great!" When a seven-year-old cooks us a nearly inedible birthday cake, we tell them it's delicious. Many social situations work a bit better because of our collective agreement to tell such fibs. But be careful: little white lies can easily turn gray.

Gray lies: The fudge factor

"I went to a marriage counselor with Ed last week," said a client I'll call Cindy. "And I was radically honest. I talked about how emotionally distant Ed is, how we don't share any interests, how I've lost my attraction to him. I put everything right out there."

"That's great!" I said. "So you told him you're having an affair?"

Cindy looked shocked. "What? That's none of his business!" she said. "Besides, it would only hurt Ed if he knew. I may not be perfect, but I'm certainly moral enough to spare him that."

This wasn't the first time, or even the fifth time, I'd heard an unfaithful spouse use this argument. Economist Dan Ariely has found that while it's rare for people to commit huge crimes and tell wholesale lies, it's quite typical to cheat *a little* and then tell stories that preserve our concept of ourselves as upstanding citizens. This is what I call a gray lie.

There are two questions that will help you differentiate between a white lie and a gray one. First, could you be blackmailed by someone threatening to tell the truth you're hiding? If so, that lie ain't white; it's gray. Second, are you following the Golden Rule ("Do unto others as you would have them do to you")?

For instance, Cindy said she was being "moral" when she lied to Ed. But when I asked her whether she thought it would be moral for Ed to lie to her, she said, "Absolutely not!" She lived in duplicity: one set of moral rules for herself, a contradictory set for others.

A lot of my clients try to follow the Golden Rule to a fault: they are continually accepting, even apologetic, toward people who treat them badly. "Well," they reason, "I'm treating others the way I want them to treat me." These people are telling as many lies as Cindy, though a very different kind. They're violating the opposite of the Golden Rule (I call this the Elur Nedlog, which is Golden Rule spelled backward). This version says, "Never allow others to treat you in ways you would never treat someone else."

I had one client, Josie, whose former boyfriend kidnapped her and chained her up in an abandoned house for days. "But he didn't really mean any harm," Josie said, basting in a brew of white lies known as Stockholm Syndrome (a condition in which captives involuntarily develop an emotional connection to their captors). It was only when I asked Josie if she would ever chain up another person that she finally realized her ex had committed a serious crime.

If someone in your life consistently hurts you, ask yourself if you would treat anyone else the way you're letting yourself be treated. If the answer is no, then to stay in integrity you must start thinking of ways to change the situation. This may take courage, ingenuity, civil disobedience, and time. But to accept your own mistreatment is to participate in a lie.

Obviously, the moral differences between and among black, white, and gray lies are enormous. The darkest lies are evil; a white lie may be unconscious or kind; a gray lie is a tool almost all of us use to calm the waters of life. You'd think that actions with such disparate origins would have very different effects on our bodies and minds. But this isn't the case.

All lies, whatever their origin, wreak similar kinds of inner havoc.

THE HIGH PRICE OF LYING

We sometimes say that deception traps us in a "tangled web," but Dante's metaphor of being frozen into ice may be even more apt. Lies tend to proliferate: tell one, and we often end up needing several more to support it. The more deceitful we get, the more we feel forced into actions that uphold our stories. We can't talk freely, can't do things that would break the narrative, can't relax. We begin to lose emotional connection with the people we've lied to. Our lives become increasingly cold, lonely, and numb. We may end up feeling completely frozen, able to see the world but not touch or feel it.

This separation from life and love makes everything seem pointless. It's also exhausting. Hiding our crimes, acting cheerful despite hidden anguish, or lying to impress people requires a constant, sustained effort. It ties up large areas of the brain, so that all our thinking becomes foggier and slower. Lying is so hard that most animals can't even attempt it. (The few who try don't do it well. Koko, the famous gorilla who could communicate in sign language, once pulled a sink off the wall during a temper tantrum. When humans asked her what had happened, Koko pointed at her kitten and signed, "Cat did it." Nice try, friend, but no cigar.)

It isn't just our brains that struggle when we lie; our bodies weaken and falter as well. One study showed that people who present "an idealized image of themselves" had higher blood pressure and heart rates; greater hormonal reactions to stress; elevated cortisol, glucose, and cholesterol levels; and reduced immune-system functioning. Lying and keeping secrets have been linked to heart disease, certain cancers, and a host of emotional symptoms like depression, anxiety, and free-floating hostility.

Deciding not to lie can lessen such symptoms almost immediately. In one study, researchers asked a group of subjects to stop lying for ten weeks. There's no way to tell whether they actually stopped telling *any* lies, but even making an effort significantly improved their physical and mental health. Those who told just three fewer lies a week reported noticeable drops in negative emotions like tension and sadness, and fewer physical symptoms such as sore throats or headaches. Their relationships benefitted as well: the participants said their personal lives were smoother and happier during the weeks they reduced their lying.

TRUTH ROCKS THE BOAT

Since lying is so stressful and makes us so miserable, why would anyone ever do it? I found out, in spades, during my Year of Not Lying at All.

At first everything was great. I realized that I rarely lied anyhow, and when I did it was by saying "I'm fine!" when I wasn't or "No problem!" when it was. When I stopped telling such fibs, my chronic pain and autoimmune symptoms almost instantly improved. I had fewer cold sores and stomach aches. My memory felt sharper. It was fabulous!

But then I began watching my righteous mind, which spent a lot of time fussing about Mormonism. I realized that, as Aleksandr Solzhenitsyn put it, "There are times when silence is a lie." As church authorities kept punishing scholars for knowing too much, I realized that my remaining silent wasn't in integrity.

Nowadays, when I get a client who's angry and fed up about a certain person or institution, I suggest that they take the challenge I gave myself: stop lying to the person or institution that bothers you, and tell the whole truth instead.

Often, just thinking about this makes the heat of anger transmogrify into an icy blast of fear. Most people stop talking, then back away from the whole subject as if it's a cobra they've discovered in the bathroom.

These people aren't cowards: they're often facing real consequences if they stop lying. I knew I could get pilloried if I spoke openly about my thoughts on Mormonism. You see, my father happened to be a famous religious "apologist," or defender of the faith—possibly the most famous in the church's history. As his daughter I'd draw a lot of attention if I said publicly what I actually believed.

Nevertheless, I'd made that New Year's resolution. So I began talking at work about things I discussed at home. Newspaper and television reporters started calling. My name made the papers. My friends and coworkers were either strongly supportive of my openness or intensely worried about the consequences—which weren't long in coming.

What happened next in my own life is the reason I recommend caution as you erase lying from yours. Don't go public immediately. Just notice *for yourself* where, why, and to whom you lie. If you're stuck in a society where people are oppressing you, or you're trapped by a psychopath, go ahead and keep lying to these dangerous people, at least for now. *But stop lying to yourself.*

THE SHOCK OF TRUTH

Every lie you stop telling is like a layer of soil in your archeological dig toward your core truth, your full inner integrity. As it continues, you may unearth fake pretenses of happiness and dishonest excuses for people who've treated you badly. I've watched people discover many common truths, like "I just realized that I'm complicit with a racist system," or unusual ones, like "I think all my uncles were in the Mafia."

Once, a client in one of my seminars told the group how she'd once read in her daughter's biology textbook that two blue-eyed parents can't have a brown-eyed child (this isn't 100 percent true, but the phenomenon is rare). "My eyes are brown," she pointed out, "and both my parents have light blue eyes. I'd always had this secret thought I didn't dare let myself know:

that my dad couldn't be my dad. After reading that book I confronted my mom. Sure enough, she'd had an affair." Across the room, another woman said, "Wait, could you repeat that?" The second woman also had brown eyes, unlike her blue-eyed parents, but *exactly* like her father's best friend.

Some of the truths you'll uncover will ping the clear chime of truth that is your inner teacher saying yes. Some will set your whole mind ringing like a gong. Seeing a really deep truth, something that's been locked away in semi-consciousness or even unconsciousness, can make sudden sense of a million troubling shadows, of other people's behavior, of your own feelings. This truth will make sense to your body, mind, heart, and soul. It will feel wildly liberating. And it may very well terrify you.

At this point I must repeat the caveat I offered earlier: *if you feel that you're approaching an unbearable truth or trauma, don't go forward without enlisting professional help.* Hire a therapist, call a crisis hotline, join a group of people who are excavating their truth together. The lies that are hardest to cope with are frozen and buried because they're literally unbearable. You can't carry them alone. *Get help.*

That said, unless you've experienced profound trauma, your deepest lies probably aren't devastating enough to need this kind of support. Maybe you're just reluctant to face the fact that you're getting farsighted, or that you actually do have a favorite child, or that some of your friendships just don't work. But whatever your lies are, digging through them will eventually take you to the center of your inferno. There you'll encounter three major aspects of your own psyche: the monster, the betrayer, and the betrayed.

THE HELL OF SELF-BLAME

At the dead center of Dante's frozen lake, locked in ice up to his waist, stands the immense monster Lucifer. He has three horrible faces, a couple of which are gnashing away at the two Roman leaders who betrayed Julius Caesar. The middle face, the nastiest one of all, perpetually chomps on Judas Iscariot—in Dante's eyes, history's worst traitor.

Remember, I'm not taking this literally. I'm interpreting each aspect of *The Divine Comedy* as an allegory for our own lives. If we break it down, what might hell's center symbolize? Julius Caesar may be the part of us that's just and noble (that's how Dante saw him, anyway). Jesus may represent the part of us that's unconditionally loving. These aspects of ourselves—the noble and the loving—are the qualities we betray when we leave our integrity. This leads to deep, wordless suffering, a frozen-in anguish that continuously punishes us.

Almost always, our deepest self-betrayals have their roots in our childhood. Jesus, so the Bible says, hated it when people hurt children. Most folks agree with him. But we've all betrayed and hurt at least one child: our young selves. Each time you obediently kissed scary Aunt Ethel, each time you forced a laugh while being taunted by other ten-year-olds, each time you pretended to feel fine when your parents fought, you abandoned and betrayed yourself. You had no other option.

As this happened, you may have sensed that something truly monstrous was going on. It was: a child was being hurt or ignored, and someone (you, if no one else) was pretending this whole awful situation was just fine. In fact, you probably unconsciously blamed the child (you). Psychologists call this the "just-world hypothesis." To feel safe, children must believe that the world is fair, that good things happen to good people and bad things happen to bad people. So when something bad happened to your childhood self, you likely decided it was because *you* were bad. Almost all of us have this kind self-blaming lie stored deep in our unspoken childhood assumptions: "If I weren't so stupid . . ." "If I took better care of my mom . . ." "If I just worked harder . . ."

Accepting responsibility is honest, but blaming ourselves when we did nothing wrong is cruel, deceptive, and devastating. Even as children, we sense that there's something off about it, something horrendous. We know deep down that we've betrayed ourselves, and (here's where the lies really are a tangled web) we hate ourselves for our own self-betrayal. Locked in ice like Dante's Lucifer, we demonically attack our traitor selves for abandoning and betraying our innocent and noble selves. The more suffering we've encountered, the more viciously we loathe and punish ourselves. The part of us that hates most gnashes relentlessly on the part of us that hurts most.

If you stop lying, you'll eventually uncover such deep, confusing, tormenting untruths. Therapists, coaches, and other allies can help you pick your way toward them. In addition, you can use the following exercise to find the frozen anguish deep in your own inferno. Get honest, get help, kill all cowardice, and keep moving.

EXERCISE:
Journey to the frozen lake

What was the last lie you told?

_____

_____

_____

What were you hiding with this lie?

_____

_____

From whom were you hiding it?

_____

_____

What do you fear this person/these people would **do** to you if they knew the truth you were hiding?

_____

_____

What do you fear this person/these people would **think** of you if they knew the truth you were hiding?

_____

_____

What do you fear this person/these people would **feel** about you if they knew the truth you were hiding?

_____

_____

What do you need or want from this person/these people you lied to?

_____

_____

Whose respect, love, admiration, inclusion, or esteem would you lose if you revealed your lie?

_____

_____

Remember telling the lie. Feel what you were feeling when you did it. Zero in on the part of you that decided not to tell the truth. How old does that part of you feel?

_____

Become the part of yourself that lied. It might be younger than you are, even a small child. What is the thought that upsets or frightens **that part of yourself** the most?

_____

_____

What does the thought above mean about your capacity to be loved and accepted?

_____

_____

When you identify with this part of yourself, do you feel connected or alone?

_____

According to the part of you that lied (who might feel very young and childlike) what's the worst thing that would happen if the whole truth about you were known to everyone?

_____

_____

I've sat with countless people as they've done versions of this exercise, drilling through trivial surface lies to scarier, deeper truths. And here's something that happens virtually every time. All their cheating, all their fudging, all their repressing, all their fraud and betrayal, is driven by some version of one single lie:

I am not loved.

You may phrase this thought a little differently. Maybe for you, the deepest lie is "I'm defective," "No one wants me," "I have no community," "I don't fit in anywhere," or any of a thousand other variations. But the bottom line is that we humans cannot survive without belonging. The most awful thing we can believe is that we are doomed to solitary confinement. However this worst fear shows up for you, write it here.

My frozen-lake fear:

_____

_____

_____

HOW I HIT ROCK BOTTOM

During my Year of Not Lying at All, I found myself feeling more and more free—and more and more terrified. I began having nightmares so troubling I was afraid to sleep. I began reading books or writing in my journal constantly, locking my mind into streams of words so that it couldn't wander. I had a hunch that if it did, I'd end up finding something really monstrous inside me—something frozen, numb, trapped.

One day I was supervising a psychology class discussion when several female students began talking about being sexually assaulted. Suddenly I felt as if fire ants were biting every millimeter of my skin. Without giving any warning to my students, I ran out of the room and collapsed in the hallway. I couldn't breathe right, couldn't think or talk clearly, and felt intense pain between my legs. My husband drove me to a doctor, who examined me and became alarmed that I might have had a tumor growing in my pelvic region. He sent me to a hospital, where I was rushed into surgery.

It turned out that there were no tumors, just a lot of blood. I was bleeding internally from an inner mess of poorly healed scar tissue. This tissue had spontaneously ruptured, for no reason anyone could figure out.

I knew all that scarring was there; an obstetrician once mentioned it, assuming I'd had an unattended childbirth that had caused significant tearing. He told me that the tissue had healed raggedly, and asked if I wanted him to "clean it up." I declined, never wondering how those scars got there. I didn't give it a second thought, or even a first one. *Why yes, doctor, I'm completely comfortable.*

The day after my emergency surgery, I began having intense, recurrent flashbacks of being sexually abused by my father when I was five years old. Each flashback felt like a nuclear explosion, physically and emotionally. But horrific as they were, the memories explained all sorts of things that had tormented me for as long as I could remember. The lie my brain told me to get me through childhood ("Well, *that* never happened!") had also created years of depression, anxiety, overachievement, insomnia, compulsive behaviors, suicidal ideation, and a host of other miserable adventures in the dark wood of error.

My first verbal thought when I remembered the abuse was "No one will believe me." It wasn't quite true. My husband believed me. A high school friend asked me about it when he came to visit; apparently, I'd told him all about the abuse. I felt my skin crawl: I didn't remember that conversation at all. It wasn't just vague, it was *absent*. It was strange enough having remembered something I'd repressed at age five; the thought that some part of me had apparently known the truth all along felt even more bizarre. But my high school friend repeated what I'd told him in detail. This both convinced me that repression is a real phenomenon, and devastatingly confirmed the intrusive memories that suddenly wouldn't leave me alone.

For days I didn't go anywhere but work. I closed myself up in my house, where I could deal better with unexpected, horrific, intrusive flashbacks. After a week or so, my mother called to ask why I hadn't been in contact. I hemmed and hawed about dealing with some bad feelings. Then she calmly asked if my father had molested me. When I said yes, she seemed unsurprised. "You actually believe me?" I gasped in astonishment.

"Of course I believe you," she said. "I know him better than you do." Later she would claim she'd been joking.

So, yes, some people believed me. But very few of them were willing to admit it. My mother immediately backpedaled when I told her I thought I needed therapy—she'd assumed, she said, that I would keep the secret. Ironically, when I told her I was going to look for a therapist she spread the word herself by calling people and telling them not to believe anything I said. As a result, many people soon knew what was happening. But bad things happening to powerless people are uncomfortable for everyone. It's always easier to go along with the system— white privilege, domestic violence, animal abuse, as well as child molestation—than to stand up for those it has harmed.

Because all of this happened during my Year of Not Lying at All, I kept telling the truth at the specific times when silence felt like a lie. Within a couple of months, I lost virtually every close relationship I'd ever had. I found a therapist who championed me in our private sessions but asked me not to talk about my situation when I joined one of her therapy groups. She didn't have to explain why. We both knew that if another client gossiped about my situation and it got back to Mormon authorities, it could cost my therapist her career.

I'm telling you this story to confirm your suspicions that absolute honesty really might end some of your relationships. If that happens, the fear of being alone may feel very, very true. Unbearably true. But it's still worth telling, I promise. Keep reading.

THROUGH THE CENTER OF HELL

As Dante gazes at Lucifer, almost fainting with terror, Virgil does that thing he does: he tells Dante to keep heading down. But *how?* There's no "down" left to go. Undaunted, Virgil carries Dante directly onto Lucifer's huge body and, gripping the beast's moldy hair, lowers himself and Dante right through the surface of the ice lake. As Virgil reaches the monster's hip, he laboriously turns around and keeps going in the same direction—toward Lucifer's feet—but now he's *climbing*. He's gone past the center of Earth, so what was down has become up. Dante follows, expecting annihilation. Instead, the pair traverse Lucifer's body and reach a dry, clear path that slopes upward. They're out of the inferno.

Whenever we inquire deeply enough into the truth about our suffering, we arrive at the place where, without changing direction, we stop descending and start ascending. Sometimes it happens slowly—for example, when we grieve a loved one until all the sadness is gone, then wake up one day feeling okay (not great, but okay). It often happens in therapy or coaching, when troubled people find enough safety and guidance to acknowledge truths they've been afraid to see. It's what happened to me each time I told myself the truth about anything, from slight discomfort to the worst thing I could imagine.

For all of us, passing the center of Earth means connecting very directly with that core lie: I'm alone. This is the chain that

binds you to your deepest suffering. Fortunately, you've practiced the method for breaking such chains all the way through
your inferno. This works as well on core lies as on surface ones.
Here's how to use it on a frozen-lake fear.

First get still, right there in the presence of your most tormenting thought. Ask yourself, *Am I sure this thought is true?*
Can I absolutely know it's true? Feel how your inner teacher
reacts. Does your most painful thought ring a sweet, resonant
chime through your body/mind/heart/soul? Does it make you
feel as if you're being set free? Or does it feel like a set of chains
and lead weights that trap you in your personal inferno? See
who you become when you believe the thought, and who you
become when you stop believing it.

When I finally hit the core lie *I am not loved*, down became
up in a very dramatic way. It was the last thing I expected—a
bolt of magic that arrived when I felt absolutely frozen, utterly
without options. It happened during that emergency surgery,
after I'd passed out in the hallway. As the doctors literally re-
opened my old childhood wounds, I became fully conscious—
oddly, since I was still under anesthesia and felt no pain. Though
my eyes were closed, I could see everything in the room. I "sat
up," though my body was still lying down, and watched the
surgeons work on me. Then, bewildered, I lay back down.

That was the moment when an extraordinarily bright light
appeared between the surgical lamps, directly above my head.
It was small at first, a sphere about the size of a golf ball, but
so dazzlingly brilliant that the huge surgical lamps seemed fee-
ble by comparison.

What can I say about that light? It sounds so ordinary—I mean, we've all seen sunsets and Christmas displays. This was not like that. It was far and away the most beautiful thing I'd ever seen. It was exquisite, cosmic, full of colors I didn't know existed. As I stared at it, the sphere of light grew larger, suffusing objects rather than bouncing off them. Then it touched me, and the way it felt was even more gorgeous than the way it looked. It bathed me in an inexpressibly sweet warmth, a love beyond anything I'd ever imagined. I began to weep, tears sliding down the sides of my face as I lay on the table.

The light seemed to merge with me, and as it did all my worries and sorrows vanished. The light and I, which now felt like the same thing, were made of pure, unutterable joy. I realized that we could communicate, though we didn't need words. The light "spoke" to me in direct downloads of information. *You're about to go through some hard times,* it told me. *But I am always with you. I've always been with you.* Then it added, *Don't think you have to die to feel this way. The whole point of being human is learning to feel like this while you're still alive.*

I awoke from that surgery sobbing with happiness. Then I asked to see the anesthesiologist. I wanted to know if I'd had a drug-induced hallucination (and if so, to request more medication). When the doctor showed up I peppered him with questions: Had he given me a hallucinogen? How did people usually respond to the chemicals he'd used on me? He told me there was nothing psychedelic about my anesthesia, and that most patients just blacked out, then woke up remembering nothing.

At this point, the doctor said, "Look, could you please tell me what happened in there?" Then he told me his side of the story. He said the surgeons had noticed I was crying during the surgery, and everyone had become extremely worried that I was in pain. The anesthesiologist was about to increase the medication when he heard a voice say, "Don't do that. She's fine. She's crying because she's happy." The doctor told me he had obeyed the voice—this seemed crazy to him later—and left the medication as it was. Now he was terrified that he'd made the wrong decision.

I gave this lovely man a brief account of what I'd experienced—just that a warm and comforting light had connected with me during the surgery. "I've been practicing over thirty years," he said. "Do you know how many times this has happened? Once. Just this once." Then he kissed me on the forehead and walked away.

This experience left me so full of bliss I didn't think anything could ever make me feel bad again. Uh, wrong. I had a lot of integrity cleansing left to do. In the years that followed I would chisel my way through thousands of lies, large and small, that were chaining parts of me to my internal inferno. The light was a blessed preview of the way I *could* feel, once I'd released myself from the countless errors I'd picked up during my sojourn on Earth.

Brief though it was, that communion with the light was a watershed. It showed me the single, simple truth I desperately needed to know. You need to know it, too—we all do. Here it is: *You are infinitely worthy. You are infinitely precious. You have always been enough. You will always be enough. There is no place you don't belong. You are lovable. You are loved. You are love.*

I can't convince you of this, but you can know it for yourself. That knowledge is waiting for you just beyond the center of your own frozen soul.

OUT OF THE INFERNO

Considering how much trouble it was for Dante to claw his way through hell, the last few lines of the *Inferno* are stunningly brief and simple. Virgil guides Dante up a path that goes straight to the surface of Earth. Without even needing to stop for rest, they climb up to a circular opening through which they see "the beautiful things that heaven bears."

Something similar happens in our hearts when we finally acknowledge every place we've been lying. The relief that comes when we're fully honest with ourselves can take us from seemingly intransigent suffering to calm and peace, even before we've changed a thing in our outer lives. From here on, everything gets better. "So we came forth," as Dante says, "and again beheld the stars."

Stage Three

PURGATORY

9.

Beginning the Cleanse

Dante and Virgil emerge from the inferno into the first light of a dawn as soft and sweet as the inferno was ghastly. They're at the base of a huge mountain. It's shaped like an upside-down ice cream cone, but terraced—the exact inverse of the inferno. This is no coincidence: the mountain is made of the rubble that was displaced when Lucifer fell from heaven to Earth, smashing down with tremendous force, blasting out the crater that would become the inferno, and killing the dinosaurs. Okay, I made up the dinosaur part. But Dante made up all the rest, including the concept that this mountain is "purgatory," the place where repentant souls cleanse themselves of error and, ultimately, attain perfection.

There are a lot of dead people in purgatory, just as there were in the inferno. Refreshingly, not one of them is screaming. Quite the contrary. Dante hears joyful singing from the souls climbing the mountain. Everyone here is happy because they all know they're headed for paradise. They just have to purify themselves by summiting the mountain, doing various strenuous tasks along the way. It's a kind of paradise training camp. Even though the climb is strenuous, Dante sees that Saint Catherine of Siena was right: all the way to heaven really is heaven.

Once you've made it all the way through the inferno segment of your quest for integrity, you too should be feeling very pleased with yourself. The skills you've learned so far in this book have shown you where you've abandoned your true nature to serve some aspect of your culture. You've dissolved some false thoughts based on socialization or trauma. You can go a long way toward happiness just by reading and thinking in these new ways. Good job, you! Congratulations for talking the talk of integrity!

Now it's time to walk the walk.

CLIMB EVERY MOUNTAIN

To Dante, the first few terraces of purgatory look impossible to climb: high, steep, craggy, and trackless. For a while he and Virgil wander around asking deceased souls for directions, but no one is able to give them much help. Virgil consoles Dante by telling him this mountain is hardest to climb at the beginning, but gets easier as you go.

Dante's metaphor is right on track. Our own purgatory requires leaving duplicity behind, adjusting our outward behavior to match new inner truths. This is hardest as we begin. We entered the inferno at a comparatively mellow spot, where the sinners were sad but not savage. Things got harder and scarier as we moved down. In purgatory the pattern is reversed: learning to walk the walk of integrity is arduous at first, effortless by the end.

The inferno ended at the place of self-betrayal and fraud, so our first steps up purgatory, the mirror image of hell, address those same errors. The instruction for your next step is the ultimate self-help strategy, the one practice that could end all your suffering and get you all the way to happiness:

Stop lying.

Sounds so simple, doesn't it? And it is, from a logistical standpoint. We've already seen that lying is hard and toxic, while truth-telling is relaxing and healthy. Here's the rub: if you stop lying, you'll eventually, inevitably violate the rules of a culture that matters to you.

Remember, a "culture" is any set of social rules that guide behavior for any assortment of people. Every couple creates a little culture of its own. Ditto for families and friendships. Then there are the big cultural entities: religious, ethnic, national, and so on. Pressure from one or more of these social groups is what convinced you to act against your own sense of truth in the first place.

Cultures need our cooperation to survive, so they're designed to control our behavior. All cultures do this by threatening or inflicting what psychiatrist Mario Martinez calls the three archetypal wounds: abandonment, betrayal, and shame. You may recognize these from your recent visit to the core of the inferno.

They immobilize us, freezing us in place at the center of our inner hell—which is why the threat of any of them is such an effective tool of social control. To be whole and free, we must move forward anyway. But when we're facing cultural pressure, following the way of integrity can feel almost impossible.

STEEPEST AT THE START

Gina had reached her wits' end. Her forty-year-old son, Cody, a drug addict since his teens, never really moved out of her house (though her husband, sick of domestic drama, had done so years ago). Gina had exhausted herself—financially, emotionally, and physically—by trying to control Cody. She'd paid for three stints in rehab, none of which worked. "I have to make him leave," Gina told me, her face gray with weariness. "But if I do, he may never speak to me again. He may overdose. He may die." She thought for a moment and added, "On the other hand, if he stays, I'm going to die."

Janice was the only Black partner in a prestigious law firm. Whip-smart and seemingly tireless, she'd pulled straight A's in college, served on the law review, and climbed the ladder to partnership faster than almost anyone in the firm's history. But when I met her, she was exhausted. "I have to do perfect work to be judged half as good as a white partner," she said. "And white lawyers keep telling me my race is an 'advantage.' I have to be nicer and funnier and calmer than anyone in the room because the old stereotypes are everywhere. If I slip up once—

get tired or misspeak in any way—then I'm lazy, I'm a bitch, I'm that Black woman who took some white person's job. I'm tired of keeping it all in. I'm tired of pretending it's okay."

I've watched many clients like Gina and Janice contemplate what might happen if they began speaking and acting with complete integrity. It's always terrifying. In the last chapter, I asked you to think about the times, places, and relationships where you noticed yourself lying or behaving inauthentically. What would happen in these situations if you began saying exactly what you really think and doing exactly what you really want? Take a guess. If you suspect things could blow up in your face, you may be wrong. Then again, you may be right.

Maybe you're stuck in an unhappy relationship or a miserable job, terrified to rock the boat and lose what little security you have. Maybe you're trying to sell a product that doesn't work, knowing that if you blow the whistle, your company will go belly-up. Or maybe you're having intrusive flashbacks of being sexually abused by a beloved religious authority figure who is also your father.

BEGINNING MY OWN CLIMB

Like everyone whose life journey brings them to the base of purgatory, I found that my no-lie vow took me directly to a spot where I had no idea what to do next. I might as well have been staring up a sheer cliff face at the foot of Everest. Forward movement of any kind seemed impossible. The one thing I kept doing, because of that encounter with the light (and because at some level I knew it was the only thing that could ultimately help me) was Not Lying at All. Of course I didn't just blurt out my uncomfortable truths in public. But I often responded to the question "How are you?" by changing the subject or saying pleasantly, "I'm a hot mess. How are you?"

The way I dealt with my situation is a long story, which I've told in another book (*Leaving the Saints*). Here I'll just say that trying to deal with posttraumatic stress disorder in a culture that doesn't want to know your truth is no joyride.

Constant intrusive flashbacks plagued me as I tried to raise my kids and teach my classes and write my dissertation. After an initial burst of openness, my mother and siblings reverted to claiming that I either had "false memories" or was simply lying. I confided in a couple of my closest friends, both Mormon. They were sympathetic but told me I absolutely had to keep my secrets to protect the church. Not long afterward, one of them committed suicide.

I spent a lot of time driving through the mountains, listening to music and crying, with my kids strapped in their car seats behind me. I worried they might be scarred by all that time in the minivan, watching their mother disintegrate in the driver's seat. (Fortunately, they grew into extraordinarily loving adults who know a vast medley of bittersweet ballads from the 1990s.)

Meanwhile, the controversy over "heretical" scholars at BYU kept heating up. I continued to get calls from reporters. I was also working at the Women's Resource Center, supposedly helping counsel female students adjust to things like term papers and roommate disputes. Instead, young women came in almost daily, depressed and weeping, to tell me they'd been sexually abused, usually as children. It was like a preview of the #MeToo movement, but with less variety.

In short, I began to see my old-time religion as a hotbed of dysfunction. My whole life, strangers had approached me to say, "Your father is the reason I'm still Mormon." This still happened, but now graciously accepting compliments on my father's behalf seemed corrupt. Going to work felt like a darker and darker lie. But telling the truth would be social and financial suicide. For money, John and I depended on our BYU jobs. Our huge extended families were true-blue Latter-Day Saints. To oppose the church, let alone leave it, would shatter everything.

So if you're standing at the base of a difficult purgatory right now, wanting desperately to live your truth but terrified of what will happen if you do, I really, really get it. And I repeat: even here, integrity is the way to happiness.

WINGS OF DESIRE

Dante begins to creep up the first level of purgatory, sometimes inching along, panting and exhausted, sometimes dragging himself on hands and knees. Still, there are places where the way is so steep that he says, "I had to fly; I mean with rapid wings

and pinions of immense desire." In other words, the only reason
Dante gets past the lowest reaches of purgatory is that he just
wants it so damn much. That intense wanting propels him forward over terrain he doesn't believe he can cover.

If your purgatory is a difficult one, you'll need your own
"pinions of immense desire." Many times, I've doubted that clients like Gina or Janice would ever find the courage to speak
and act in total integrity. But more often than I would have
thought possible, I've watched them grow wings right there in
front of me. Their longing to be whole became steadily more
intense until it overwhelmed every inner obstacle, all their worst
fears.

EXERCISE:
Wings of desire

You may recall that back in Chapter 2 I asked you to think of
something you want because you've seen it advertised. Then
I asked you to write down something for which you *yearned*.
Almost everyone who does that exercise tells me they yearn for
similar, very simple things: Freedom. Joy. Peace.

At that point on your way of integrity, I just wanted you to
see that the cultural trappings of success, like wealth or power,
don't bring those deep rewards. We didn't even discuss how to
get the things you yearn for. But now you've come so far, there's
not much distance left between you and the things your heart
and soul most prize. Your longing for those things is what you
need to move forward. Here is an exercise to help you grow and
strengthen your own "pinions of immense desire."

Step one

Think of a situation in your life in which you don't feel you can safely be your real self. Write a few words below to identify the situation. For example, you might write, "Any day at work" or "Family dinner" or "Whenever I'm around white people." You can work with literally any situation, but I suggest you choose the one that feels most frustrating to you right now.

Situation where I don't feel I can be my real self:

_____

_____

Vividly imagine being in this situation. Do an internal scan of your body, noticing all your physical and emotional sensations. Describe these sensations here:

Physical sensations:

_____

_____

_____

Emotional sensations:

_____

_____

_____

Step two

Now imagine that you're in the same situation, but this time the following things have magically changed:

1. You've drunk a magic potion that makes you feel completely unconcerned about anyone else's opinions or actions. You care less about human indignation than an alley cat.

2. Everyone else has drunk a potion that makes them completely, joyfully accepting of anything you do or say as long as it's your deepest truth. These people are now unconditionally supportive when you feel what you feel, know what you know, say what you mean, and do what you want.

Picture yourself speaking your truth in this situation and feeling deeply, sympathetically heard. Picture the other person or people validating and supporting your truth. Breathe in the air of complete acceptance, the total absence of any need to guard or conceal your real self.

Again, slowly scan your internal sensations, noticing what you feel physically and emotionally. Describe the sensations here:

Physical sensations:

_____

_____

_____

Emotional sensations:

_____

_____

_____

Step three

The most important part of this exercise is to move back and forth several times between the sensation of not being free to live your truth and being absolutely free to live your truth.

Think of this as shifting between two fields of energy. The first is the energy field of a particular culture. It drains you. The second is the energy field of your true nature. It nourishes you. Notice how different they feel.

Step four

Each time you go back and forth, notice how good it feels to leave culture and move into truth. Notice how bad it feels to hide or contract your truth in order to go along with culture. **Let these feelings grow stronger and stronger each time you go back and forth.**

This exercise is a bit like those tire-rippers placed on the road to keep drivers from backing up. When you move forward into your longing for truth, you'll feel yourself gaining momentum. When you try to reverse back into the situation where you don't feel free, everything will fight you. Another analogy: moving into integrity is like petting a cat front to back, while moving away from your truth to please your culture feels like petting the same cat back to front. The more you imagine freedom and let yourself feel it, the stronger your yearning to stay in truth becomes.

This longing can be so intense it's painful, but your inner teacher will still tell you it's good for you. It's the desire that helps us overcome the fear of telling the truth in even the most difficult situations. *Until you feel an actual desire to move forward in real life,* don't make any behavioral changes. Just focus completely on the yearning to belong, to feel completely safe, and to know you are unconditionally accepted. This is your true self longing for total integrity. The more you focus on it, the stronger your wings.

In my case, it took months to develop enough strength to move upward. I thought about truth obsessively, but in my culture the whole concept seemed mushy and elusive. My father had spent his career doing what Mormons call "lying for the Lord," to prove their religion was "the one true church"—a bit of head-spinning doublespeak. In a culture where "truth" was whatever the authorities said it was, I often felt it was impossible to stay a true course for myself.

The only thing that rang unquestionably true to me was the light I'd encountered during my surgery. My body, mind, heart, and soul experienced it as the most real thing that had ever happened to me. When I thought about it, the yearning to stop guarding secrets and simply live my truth grew so strong nothing else mattered. I was still terrified, but I decided to keep moving toward my truth. Damn the torpedoes.

HOW TRUTH SETS US FREE

I've seen the same thing happen to clients once they fall in love with the truth. When they stop lying, these people often experience some chaotic life changes. But they also feel the benefits of truth-telling that I mentioned in the last chapter: they become physically and emotionally stronger, healthier, more peaceful. Even if the people around them raise merry hell, they find themselves coping—more than that, *thriving*—more easily than they'd imagined.

Gina, for example, finally told Cody he had to get out of her house if he didn't stop using drugs. Things looked bad for a long time. Gina heard that Cody was living on the streets, staying high, telling people she'd exiled him. "It's awful," she told me. "The only thing I can think of that would be worse is the way I was living before."

To no one's surprise, Cody ended up in prison. While there he joined a twelve-step group and a program that gave puppies to convicts, who trained them as seeing-eye dogs. The combination worked wonders. One day Gina came to my office in tears, holding a letter Cody had written to her as part of making amends. "He says he understands I was always trying to help him," Gina told me. "He actually thanked me for taking care of him, *and* for kicking him out." Gina began to flourish after that. She said she felt twenty years younger—and she looked it, too.

Janice finally decided that cautiously navigating the racism at her job was worse than losing it. She began to respond when other lawyers made casually racist assumptions and comments. Most of them responded coldly, and for a while Janice thought she'd have to quit to live in peace. But a minority of her white colleagues were listening. They began to take Janice seriously when she pointed out racist practices or behaviors at the firm. It was touch and go for a long time, but slowly, especially when the

#BlackLivesMatter movement began gaining cultural momentum, the company culture began to change for the better. This was still worlds away from fair; it shouldn't have been Janice's job to teach basic human respect to an entire company of white people, and she had plenty of experiences where her honesty was met with racism. But in the end, Janice's immense courage, strength, and persistence created major social change toward justice.

Most of my clients don't face situations as dire as these. Alistair stopped "lending" money to a sister who never paid him back. Leah broke up with a boyfriend who simply assumed that even though they lived separately, she'd cook and clean for him. Lars appalled his parents by dropping out of dental school, which he hated, to study filmmaking, which he loved. In all these cases, as well as my own, not lying turned out to be transformative in all the right ways. The old saying is right: the truth sets us free. All of us.

See for yourself. Try this.

EXERCISE:
The no-lie challenge

Step one

Decide on a time period for your no-lie challenge. I'd suggest a week minimum. There is no maximum. Write it here:

I commit to Not Lying at All for the following period of time:

_____

Step two

Don't lie at all for that period of time.

Step three

Keep a journal where you can write about what happens once you stop lying. You may see health benefits and improved relationships—most people do. On the other hand, if things get tough, expressing your truth on the page is a safe way to keep telling the truth.

Step four

If you do lie, don't stop your challenge. Forgive yourself. Then recommit to not lying until the challenge is over.

TRUTH AND CONSEQUENCES

As your no-lie challenge moves along, you'll find yourself making a lot of judgment calls. Are there times when you feel you're lying with silence, or by performing actions that feel wrong even though you're not speaking? What truths must you tell to feel completely honest, and when? No one else can answer these questions—it's up to you and your inner teacher. Do and say whatever feels like harmony in your body/mind/heart/soul. You'll know the truth by the sense of solid alignment that comes with it.

During my own first Year of Not Lying at All, as things

got weirder and scarier, I wondered constantly how to be honest without destroying my life, or the lives of loved ones. I kept speaking out in support of scholars condemned for heresy, and also started joining forces with survivors of sexual abuse (though, for a long time, I kept my own story under wraps). With one friend, I gave a presentation to Mormon authorities about the high frequency of child sexual abuse reported by students. With another, I wrote a paper on "sanctuary trauma," the double damage that resulted when Mormon girls and women reported their abuse to church authorities, who dismissed them and protected the perpetrators.

Predictably, my culture of origin did not respond to this behavior with open arms. I was just glad they didn't use open firearms. My colleagues and I were "called in" by our various department chairmen, warned against disputing religious doctrine or suggesting that sexual abuse was common in Mormon communities. I started receiving threats—a note pushed under my office door calling me the "anti-Christ," an anonymous phone call telling me "The Lord will punish you."

Eventually, it felt like a lie to stay Mormon at all. To end my membership, I wrote a letter to the proper authorities asking them to take my name off the church's records.

Now, for Mormons, the worst possible sin anyone could commit—the only *unforgivable* sin—is to leave the religion. It's considered worse than murder. Cold-blooded serial killers have a chance at redemption and an eventual place in heaven, but apostates are consigned to "outer darkness," condemned to drift in space forever, utterly alone.

This belief is drilled into children barely old enough to talk. The few friends I had left in Provo turned pale and wept when I told them I'd left the church, as if I'd said I had a terminal illness. "Don't do it," one friend begged, weeping. "Make them excommunicate you. Then it won't be your fault." I hugged her and said that for one thing, it most definitely was my fault—my choice—and for another, I was fine with the consequences of my actions. Because while my culture said I was headed for outer darkness, everything inside me felt the opposite: I was moving toward inner light. I could feel myself knitting together inside, like a wound healing. I had the strangest, most beautiful sense of *lifting*.

No question, the road ahead of me—as much as I could even see it—looked impossibly steep. Unclimbable. It didn't matter. For the first time I could remember, everything inside me felt connected, harmonious, true. If the way grew so difficult I could no longer climb it on foot, or even on hands and knees, I'd just have to use my wings.

10.

No Turning Back

If you've spent much of your life among people who couldn't or wouldn't support the expression of your true nature, taking a no-lie challenge may have created an unprecedented sense of peace and relaxation within you.

Or maybe you're freaking out.

Probably you're freaking out.

Radical truth-telling rocks a lot of boats, so other people may be reacting badly to your no-lie challenge. This isn't fun, but it's actually a good sign. If you've really stopped lying, with both words and actions, resistance from others is often evidence you're on the right track.

People around you are probably unnerved by your new behavior because it challenges their own cultural compliance. In other words, they're all telling polite or mandated lies in order to keep peace with others, and the way you're following integrity may involve the very things they're repressing in themselves. Cultures rely on consensus—if everyone agrees, there's no pressure on the system. Any dissent, like the child shouting that the emperor has no clothes, could bring down the whole social order. People who want their culture to stay as it is (remember, *everyone* is socialized to feel that way) may react to honesty by trying to push you back to your inferno of self-betrayal and self-abandonment. They may push *hard*.

After your no-lie challenge comes a choice point. You can go back to the way things were, or commit to continue living your truth—even if others disapprove. If you choose integrity, your no-lie challenge will extend into the future. Instead of visiting integrity as a tourist, you'll adopt it as your path through life. You'll dissolve the beliefs that split you from your nature, then change your behavior to reflect your deepest truth. And for this you'll need the skills of a social ninja.

CHANGING HABITS AND HANDLING PUSHBACK

Remember the inferno's first six circles, where people had gone to hell for reasons they didn't understand? In *The Divine Comedy*, souls in the lower-middle range of purgatory are working out that kind of error. They're changing errant behavior that came from pressures they didn't understand and couldn't control. Dante describes this as "bad" or "disordered" love. It emerges when people are well-meaning but mistaken—for example, when we feel loyal to people and ideas that don't match our inner truth.

When we begin dropping all "disordered" love, following nothing but integrity, our lives may change dramatically, and *fast*. Inwardly, this feels incredibly good. But the pushback from outside can be intense. If just speaking the truth bothers your culture, you can imagine what happens when you start *acting* with integrity. You might stop laughing at your coworker's crude jokes. You may come out as gay or trans. You may start posting things on social media that shock your loved ones. You may turn into some version of Rosa Parks, refusing to give up her bus seat to a white person.

Some people will applaud your new behaviors. Others—often the ones closest to you—will not. In fact, if you're entrenched in political or racial oppression, you may even face violent resistance. This chapter is designed to help you through whatever pushback you encounter on your way toward integrity. This requires becoming a kind of mental martial artist, able to turn the energy of opposition in your favor. It's the most heroic adventure you could undertake. And like so many heroic adventures, it begins with a wave of reluctance.

NOSTALGIA FOR THE KNOWN MISERY

As Dante struggles up the steep, trackless slopes of purgatory, he gets a little wistful. He thinks about travelers yearning for their homes. Still moving forward, he feels the gravitational pull of the life he led before starting his surreal journey. He's getting very close to a fundamental shift in identity. Sensing this impending transformation brings on a spasm of nostalgia for the life he's known so far.

Contemplating integrity as a way of life is like deciding to leave your homeland and become a citizen of a new country: it involves a major identity shift. Even if we deeply feel that this transition will bring us happiness, health, and purpose, it can be almost too huge to contemplate. Studies in psychoneuroimmunology show that if we plunge too quickly into any major change, even a good one, our bodies and minds can't absorb the shock. We must give our psychological and physiological systems time to adjust. We do this by allowing something that neuroscientist and cultural anthropologist Mario Martinez calls "mourning the known misery."

Every time I've seen a client make substantial moves toward integrity, I've also watched them mourn their known misery. When Matt's wife had a baby, he finally managed to quit smoking. He was very proud that he'd managed to do for his little daughter what he'd never been able to do for himself. But he also felt strangely sad. Most of his friends at work were other smokers, who'd bonded standing outside to share cigarettes on freezing winter days. "Plus," Matt told me sadly, "smoking felt like the friend that was always there for me."

Zoey and her best friend, Laura, worked in the same high-stress tech company. Almost every day, they'd go for coffee and spin daydreams about leaving the firm and heading out on their own. Eventually, Zoey decided to act on those dreams. She quit her job and became a successful freelance web designer. "Everything is better now," she told me. "But I get these waves of sadness. I miss coffee talks with Laura. I miss complaining and joking about my job. I miss it all."

After I resigned from my religion, I mourned my known misery for months. I could tell that my psyche was healing, but living in Utah as an apostate from Mormonism made me feel like a treasonous freak. I desperately missed the sense of fitting in with the people around me. Even though I was grateful and relieved to be out of the church, I felt paradoxical waves of intense sorrow for my old familiar ways of behaving.

If you start honoring your true nature and find yourself missing your old culture, don't panic. Be kind to yourself. Allow yourself time and space to grieve. Confide in loved ones. If they don't understand, find a coach or therapist. *But don't think that missing your old life means you should go back to it.* Everyone who decides to embrace integrity must mourn the known misery, the familiar patterns and dysfunctional relationships they've left behind. I promise: if you give your grief space and time, it will eventually bring you to a level of joy you may never have imagined. And as it does, you'll arrive at yet another gate.

COMMITTING TO TRUTH

Dante and Virgil struggle up the first daunting steeps of the great mountain only to find out *they haven't even reached purgatory yet.* They've been in what some commentators call "ante-purgatory," a kind of final proving ground that qualifies them for the *real* purgatory. Climbing this mountain is like going to the DMV; it takes forever just to get started. And at the end of ante-purgatory, after already hiking a long way, Dante and Virgil find themselves facing—you guessed it—a gate.

This gate, unlike the one in the dark wood of error, is guarded by an angel. He tells Dante that no one gets to pass through this portal unless they agree never to look back. Where the gate to the inferno said, "Abandon all hope," this one basically says, "Abandon all intention to backslide." It's when we make this major commitment that we begin shifting not just our thoughts, but every word and action, to align with integrity.

As I've mentioned, your no-lie challenge leads to a choice point. Once you've experimented with telling and acting on your truth for a limited period of time, you may choose to do one of three things: continue moving into more integrity; keep wandering around purgatory by staying at exactly the level of self-disclosure you've reached; or go back to whatever secrets, lies, and habits you've abandoned. The first choice—committing to complete integrity—may sound radical. It is. But endlessly circling purgatory at one level gets dull, and reverting to old lies is like repairing an airplane with parts that dissolve in the rain. So at this point, ask yourself if it's time to follow your own way of integrity, at whatever speed you like, *indefinitely*. Ponder this as long as you want, but know that this is the choice you now face.

I've had many clients who couldn't go through this gate. During our sessions, as they connected with their true thoughts and feelings, integrity reaped all its promised rewards. Truth-telling brought joy, relief, and healing. But they never dared speak honestly, much less change their behavior, outside our protected coach-client relationship. Counseling sessions of all kinds are confidential precisely so that clients can access their truth without alerting the people in their "real lives." They can blow off enough steam to feel a little better without encountering cultural pressure. Some people become therapy or seminar addicts, constantly seeking environments where they can be themselves without upsetting any apple carts. They may wander around ante-purgatory for years, not really in hell anymore, but definitely not in heaven.

This is not a criticism! As I continued my Year of Not Lying at All, my own new truths often felt too vulnerable to disclose outside therapy and a few confidential relationships. People who live under repressive regimes, people who are gay or trans, and any nonwhite person in America may risk physical harm or death for offending the power structure. Take your time, and listen to your inner teacher about how much of your truth to reveal in any given setting.

If you reach the point at which you're terrified to be really honest but determined not to return to your known misery, proceed with caution. Find safe people to confide in about next steps. Keep toggling back and forth between the feeling of self-protective lying and the feelings you might have if you could live as your truest self. Gradually, your yearning for wholeness will grow stronger. At some point, scared though you are, you'll no longer *want* to look back. You'll feel the pull to go forward— not as the same person doing different things, but as a different person.

CHANGE-BACK ATTACKS

When you first commit to following the way of integrity indefinitely, you'll feel that ring of truth, your inner teacher saying, *Yes!* But something about the power of the decision seems to send a shockwave through the people who socialized you. Julia Cameron, author, creativity guide, and so-called Queen of Change puts it this way: "When you're going to leave, they know."

The imminent threat of someone abandoning group norms foments social resistance at its strongest level. Almost every time I've seen a client announce that they're quitting a job or a relationship, the people around them begin to cajole and bargain, trying to keep them where they are. Many clients tell me, "If they'd been this nice to me all along, I wouldn't have needed to leave."

If carrots of praise and sweetness don't work, people will use sticks—long, sharp sticks—to keep others inside cultural boundaries. This happened to Matt after he stopped smoking. His nicotine pals at work took him off their group text thread and stopped answering his emails with anything but cold, work-related information. When Zoey got her first client, she invited Laura out to lunch and paid the bill happily, saying, "That's the first lunch I've bought with money I made on my own!" After a pause, Laura said in a clipped, tight voice, "Just be careful. You can't do whatever you want and not expect some serious consequences." Zoey felt as if she'd been slapped. "Laura seemed really angry at me," she said. "I can't figure out what I did wrong."

Your loved ones may shame and blame you for disobeying the cultural rules of your relationship. They may try to manipulate you with displays of neediness, anger, or straight-up aggression. If you're in an oppressive system, you could get arrested or physically threatened. When someone embarks on integrity and refuses to look back, culture pulls out its whole arsenal of control strategies to make them drop their stupid obsession with integrity and go back to acting *normal*!

My Utah therapist used to call reactions like these "change-back attacks." After leaving Mormonism, I got all kinds. A few people begged me to repent and return to the fold. Some of my neighbors literally turned their backs whenever I walked past. Late one night my fax machine (remember fax machines?) printed out a message that read: "I've heard you've made certain accusations against your father. I feel you owe me an explanation." Bizarrely, there was no name, just a return fax number. During that period, I spent a lot of time curled up in a ball, listening to my inner people-pleaser shriek that I'd made a terrible, terrible mistake.

So maybe you want to pass the gate of no looking back, but you're afraid your parents will scold you, or your colleagues will gossip about you, or your spouse will give you a dose of the silent treatment. You're probably right. When you commit to honoring your true nature over every false habit, change-back attacks may come from anywhere. But don't despair. This is all going to turn out better than you expect.

THE ATTACK ZONE: PRIDE, ENVY, AND WRATH

You may recall the way sinners were arranged in Dante's inferno: first the souls who'd committed innocent errors, then "the violent," and then the liars. Since purgatory is the mirror image of the inferno, the order is reversed here. The first and hardest step is to stop lying to ourselves. You started that in the last chapter. Now we encounter errors of righteousness. It's time to deal with people (and aspects of ourselves) who are violent in thought and action.

My Catholic-school-educated readers may recall there are seven "deadly sins": sloth, gluttony, greed, lust, pride, envy, and wrath. In Dante's theology, the first four don't hurt anyone but the sinner, but the last three are violent. They make people attack each other. Pride doesn't just say "I am good," it says "I'm better than *someone else*." Envy doesn't just make us want stuff, it makes us want at least as much stuff as *someone else*. Wrath isn't random; it's targeted at *someone else*. When we lock into errors of righteousness, we invariably point at *someone else* and turn them into what therapist Bill Eddy calls "targets of blame."

Want to see an example? Turn on any cable news show, or log on to an online political forum. Much of our political discourse consists of people attacking targets of blame. They choose a side, stop looking for truth (if they ever even started), become rigid in their positions, and whip themselves up to higher and higher levels of emotional and verbal violence.

You'll often hear such people claim that their targets of blame are "attacking our way of life." A woman who decides not to have children, a kindergarten teacher who decorates his classroom with menorahs as well as Christmas trees, a seven-year-old who looks like a boy but feels like a girl—all may be accused by complete strangers of "attacking our way of life." Without a single hurtful thought in their heads, these individuals are seen as dangerous to entire cultures.

Because they are.

Whenever we follow our true nature away from a cultural norm, we're demonstrating that social consensus is arbitrary and fragile. The lurking fear of people who follow the culture is that if one childless woman, kindergarten teacher, or seven-year-old can abandon their society's rules for living, *anyone could!*

Now, just the fact that you're reading this book means you're less likely to blame others, and more likely to seek understanding, than political opinionistas. But you probably still have traces of pride, envy, and wrath deep inside. We all do. The problem is that these errors of righteousness lurk in our perceptual blind spots (remember all those unseen errors that stranded you in the dark wood?). In order to cleanse away mistaken beliefs, we must get them into the foreground of our minds where you can observe and question them.

So how do you get a clear view of something you can't see?

You don't. You have people who do that for you.

HOW CHANGE-BACK ATTACKS CAN HELP YOU UP THE MOUNTAIN

Ironically, change-back attacks—especially the ones that hurt most—can be some of our most powerful helpers on our way to integrity. When we're trying to be good and someone attacks us for it, we feel hurt. Usually angry. Sometimes furious. There's nothing wrong with that if we follow the steps in Chapter 7: instead of raging, define our values and get creative about responding to our attackers. For examples, contemplate how people like Gandhi and American civil rights leaders dealt with the horrific, baseless violence directed against their people.

Reacting to injustice and hatred with justice and compassion is hard. It goes against the "righteous mind" that makes every attacked person want to fight back. But it's possible. Even when we're feeling hurt and angry, we can follow the basic integrity process: (1) observe what's happening inside us, then (2) question our thoughts. This will show us if we're stuck in the same violent, righteous mindset others are using to attack us. Our own blind rage will rise into clear view. Then choose to either stay on the path of violence or (3) move away from the ranting righteous mind and follow the way of integrity.

For example, say that you playfully decide to dye your hair blue. Then someone—maybe your grandmother or a stranger on the street—launches a change-back attack ("Your hair color is threatening our way of life!"). You'll probably have an automatic "fight, flight, freeze" reaction: argue with your attacker, try to get away, or go numb and mute. Because this portion of your brain is activated, you'll also perceive your attacker as huge and powerful, and yourself as vulnerable. This is as true of presidents and dictators ("I'm being attacked by the press!") as it is of people who favor unusual fashion statements. It's a natural, reflexive response—but that doesn't mean it agrees with what you most deeply know to be true. *When you feel like a victim, always suspect that you may be caught in your own errors of righteousness.*

When Matt quit smoking, Zoey became an entrepreneur, and I left my religion, it's a safe bet that the people around us felt that we were judging them for their choices. Feeling that their way of life was under fire, these people fought back. This is how change-back attacks work. They don't come from people who feel powerful, but from those who see themselves as victims of judgment. To stay on the path of integrity and avoid getting stuck in repetitive cycles of violence, we must *refuse to join our change-back attackers in their sense of victimhood.*

BREAKING THE DRAMA TRIANGLE

As we change our behavior, we may get caught up in a psychological dynamic described by psychiatrist Stephen Karpman as a "drama triangle." This pattern appears whenever errors of righteousness are running our lives. Recognizing the Karpman drama triangle, noticing every place we're stuck in it, and leaving it (Dante calls this "dishabituating") are your tasks at this point in your quest for integrity. It isn't the easiest section of our hike, but the view from above it is *fantastic*.

A drama triangle develops when we feel small and weak (as we all are during childhood). Other people may seem large and menacing (again, plenty of people are) and still others may appear to be our protectors (right again). But even as adults, many humans have a tendency to lock in this triangle as a way of viewing everyone, in every situation. Life becomes a play with only three possible roles: *victim*, *persecutor*, and *rescuer*.

We all know how confusing and scary it is to be little—and we all know fully grown adults who consistently feel that way no matter how big they get. For example, when boxer Mike Tyson famously bit off Evander Holyfield's ear during a match, he protested, "What am I supposed to do? I've got children to raise. He kept butting me." In other words, "I'm a victim of the situation! He made me do it!"

People stuck in the *victim* role always have targets of blame, people they see as *persecutors*. They often turn to others for help and support. These are their *rescuers*, who play the final role in the drama triangle.

Some people get stuck in just one of these roles for life. Perpetual victims never stop complaining about the terrible things persecutors do to them—but they don't take any action that might improve their situation. They rely on others to play the rescuer role. Many kind, empathic folks play that role all their lives, galloping to the aid of one victim after another. No one self-identifies as a persecutor: a violent or raging person (even Hitler and Stalin) will always claim that they're being threatened,

victimized. But everyone else can see they're playing the persecutor role to the hilt.

Like diamonds, drama triangles are forever—that is, the pattern may persist for decades, even centuries. The actors may
switch roles, but the pattern endures. If you want vivid illus-
trations of this, read about long-standing historical conflicts.
Each side will claim to be victims of the other's persecution,
and appeal for rescue to other actors. This pattern may be huge,
creating world wars. Or it may be tiny, creating the same damn
argument you have with your spouse once a week.

This is not to say that there are no real victims who genuinely need rescue. I've had many clients whose health, race,
gender, or economic situations made it hard for them to leave
terrible relationships or jobs. European Jews needed help to
resist the Nazis. People of color in America need support from
white allies to break patterns of oppression. But as we'll see in
a moment, even people who get caught in such horrific situations can avoid getting stuck in endless, fruitless Karpman
conflicts.

As a coach, I've seen the Karpman triangle play out in many
situations. It's particularly strong—and weird—in cases of domestic violence. Take Verna, who seemed from the outside to
have a perfect life, but who was actually being beaten by her
husband Tom. They went through the same triangular "dance"
over and over. First, they'd start to argue. Tom would become
so angry that Verna would become frightened and try to leave
the house. Immediately, Tom would go into "victim" mode.

Feeling the massive anxiety and rage of a child about to be abandoned, he'd physically attack Verna—all the time thinking of himself as her victim. Once Verna was too frightened and hurt to leave, Tom would break down in sobbing apologies, saying how he hated himself for harming her and begging her to forgive him. He'd become her "rescuer" when she needed one most (because she'd just been beaten by a man she loved). She'd respond to Tom's emotional distress by moving into the "rescuer" role herself, soothing Tom emotionally until they both felt calm and bonded.

Verna was terribly ashamed by her own behavior, knowing she should just leave Tom, baffled by the way she kept going back to him. But this pattern is all too common. The strange logic of the drama triangle means that whoever acts most victimized triggers a "rescuer" response, even in someone who has just attacked a loved one, or, stranger still, in the person they've just attacked. The period of connection just after the explosion of abuse is called the "honeymoon phase" by domestic violence experts. This intense, dysfunctional connection is mind-blowingly nonsensical from the outside, but the Karpman triangle is very powerful—so powerful that battered people may stay in this horrific pattern for years.

If you're feeling wildly masochistic and want to create a drama triangle of your very own, it's as easy as pie. Just choose a target of blame and cast yourself as the victim. Then sit back and relax, confident that the anger, arguments, cowering, and threatening will go on forever unless you choose some other course of action. And what might that be? Getting out of a triangle drama is also simple, though not easy. It hinges on one act of integrity: acknowledging that we're capable of choosing our responses to other people and situations, no matter what. We can end the futile drama of human conflict only when we accept that at a deep, existential level, we are free.

Choosing to reinterpret a drama triangle from the perspective of a free actor allows us to exchange a vicious cycle for its inverse. Dante learns this in purgatory when one of the souls he meets delivers a lecture on free will (just what you want when you're climbing a mountain). This soul—like the great moral leaders of history—tells us that our ultimate freedom lies in our capacity to interpret the world in new ways.

An author named David Emerald did just that after he studied Karpman's work. He developed a kind of anti-triangle, which he called the "empowerment dynamic." In this pattern, people who were once seen as persecutors become "challengers." They force others to rise to new levels of strength and competency. Rescuers become "coaches." Instead of jumping in to soothe and fix ("Poor you! Let me do that for you!"), they say, "Wow, that's an awful situation. What are you going to do about it?" And in the most empowering shift of all, Emerald suggests that victims become "creators." Where victims believe "This situation is unbearable and I'm helpless," creators ask themselves, "This situation is messed up. What can I make from it?"

Remember, creativity is the opposite of violence, which is pure destruction. *If we can find any way to see ourselves as cre-*

ators, *no matter what our situation, we can turn drama triangles into empowerment dynamics.* Instead of getting trapped in violence and hatred, we can use relationship dynamics to reach higher and higher levels of integrity.

Viktor Frankl managed to do this when he used his incarceration in Auschwitz as a way to understand how humans make meaning. Malala Yousafzai, a Pakistani teenager, did it by protesting the Taliban despite all they could do to oppress her, including shooting her in the head. It's how Martin Luther King Jr. and his followers responded to the unjust arrest of Black Americans by allowing themselves to be arrested and reframing it as a mark of honor. "They took something they couldn't fight," says Henry Louis Gates Jr. of Harvard, "and used it as a way to communicate truth."

All these people really, *really* would have been justified in seeing themselves as victims. Instead, they not only found ways to survive but also made massive contributions to humankind. Horrific attempts to victimize them led to almost superhuman levels of benevolent creativity.

So, while we may be genuinely victimized, we never have to accept "victim" as an identity. We have the freedom to respond to every situation with creative thought or action. Sometimes this means clarifying our thoughts. Sometimes it means speaking out. Sometimes it compels action. Always, it begins by observing our own raging thoughts and asking ourselves, "Can I absolutely know that I'm purely a victim, with no creative options whatsoever?"

I had a chance to try this in my own small way not long after my departure from Mormonism. One night—not to be virtuous, just to save my sanity—I flipped a drama triangle into an empowerment dynamic, and it changed my whole inner world.

Remember the weird fax that printed out in my office? It's not fun to get a note like that in the wee hours, telling you that rumors about you are Out There, and that you owe some anonymous person an explanation. When I first read the fax, I felt like a mouse trapped in a dark room with an unknown number of snakes. I wasn't sure who was hunting me or what their intentions were, but the fax showed they were out there. After a surge of fear, I also began to feel indignant. Just because something bad happened to me when I was a child, this person felt free to invade my home late at night and make demands on me? I felt vulnerable, scared, and angry. This is the energy of victimization and judgment. It sucked.

Fortunately, I was still in the middle of my Year of Not Lying at All. I'd gotten used to examining my own thoughts. So I sat with that creepy, menacing fax and began asking myself questions. "I'm like a mouse in a room full of snakes." *Are you sure?* "This fax is a totally unprovoked violation of my privacy." *Are you sure?* "I'm not safe." *Are you sure?*

As I asked each question, my mind began to lose its death grip on the thought "I'm a victim!" For some reason, I started thinking about how a football player might feel when several massive men try to knock him down. He doesn't see himself as terrified prey. He knows that in the process of playing the game, he'll get rushed. He does his best to avoid being tackled, but if it happens, he gets back up and takes it in stride. This is the energy of power—not invulnerability, but power. It will put breath in your lungs and strength in your spine.

Slowly, as that night went on, I shifted from feeling like a mouse to feeling more like a football player, simply because it felt better. Truer.

My inner teacher felt completely aligned with the thought that as a child, I'd been a victim. No question. But now I was an adult who had consciously decided to step outside the rules of my culture. I'd known that people would push back. I realized that the person sending that fax probably saw me as "attacking our way of life." After all, I'd told news reporters that I saw injustice in Mormon culture. I'd coauthored a study calling out the church authority structure. Of course players from the other team were trying to tackle me. I'd helped create my situation. The question was, What could I create from it going forward?

After that, I began to approach each change-back attack as a challenge to find creativity and peace. Situations I'd found terrifying became tolerable, even interesting. New ideas arose as I tried to figure out how I could react to social pressure without leaving my integrity. One of the processes that helped me most is the following exercise. I like to use it whenever I have a knee-jerk reaction to feel like a victim or pass righteous judgment. See how it works for you.

EXERCISE:
Instructions for my persecutor

Step one

Think of a person whose words and actions feel like an attack on you and your integrity. This person is trying to scare you, shame you, or force you back into old patterns that don't work for you. Who is it?

_____

Step two

Now you're going to write a letter to this person, asking them to completely support your truth.

Dear _____

I've decided to base my life on integrity, but you're trying to stop me. You're keeping me from my integrity by saying things like (fill in the blanks):

_____

_____

I want you to stop saying those things, and say these things instead (really go to town here, and ask them to say the most absolutely supportive things you can imagine):

_____

_____

You're also undermining my integrity by <u>doing</u> the
following things (think of everything this person does
that makes it hard for you to honor your truth):

_____

_____

I want you to stop doing those things. Here are the
things I want you to do instead (go ahead, ask for the
moon!):

_____

_____

Yours truly,

(Your name goes here) _____

Step three

Now (I bet you saw this coming) go to the name on the letter, cross it out, and put your own name there instead. Reread the letter as if it was written by your true nature to your frightened, socialized self. See where you have been saying and doing to yourself the very things that your persecutor is saying and doing. If you feel ashamed when your attacker is shaming you, question your thoughts about yourself until all your self-shaming dissolves, and no part of you believes that your true self is defective. Are people trying to scare you into accepting a subordinate role? Find the places where you're scaring yourself about the consequences of "misbehavior." Examine the beliefs that make you afraid, then use your observation and questioning skills on those beliefs until they give way.

> **Step four**
>
> Once you've altered your internal experience, change your external actions. Take the advice of your true nature. Stop saying and doing the things your persecutors have been saying and doing. Instead, say and do for yourself what you wish a "rescuer" would say and do. Get creative about ways to be true to yourself, without waiting for someone else to show up and do it for you.

This exercise does more than shift perspective from victimization to empowerment. It gives you clear instructions about your next best steps up the mountain of purgatory. Use it every time you feel attacked, and you'll find that *the person whose attack upsets you most is always showing you your next step on the way of integrity.*

You see, attacks cause emotional suffering only if a part of us believes them. When a challenger really bothers us, it's because that person believes things about us that aren't true—but shards of those same beliefs are still inside our own self-concept, hanging out in our blind spots. Letting go of belief in the attacker's lies (like the thoughts "I'm bad" or "I'm inferior") gives you access to the truth beneath them. Learning to hold—and repeat to yourself—all the supportive things you wish to hear from others puts you back in alignment with your inner teacher, your sense of truth. This heals the split in your worldview and restores a fundamental part of your integrity. Thank you, challenger.

PURGING ERRORS OF RIGHTEOUSNESS

African American feminist Audre Lorde once wrote, "When I dare to be powerful, to use my strength in the service of my vision, then it becomes less and less important whether I am afraid." When we focus on creative response rather than on blame and defense, fear drops from our attention. It gets edged out by the flip side of pride, envy, and wrath: healthy self-esteem, a sense of abundance, and the intent to make positive change.

When you pass through the gate of no looking back and people attack you for it, staying in your integrity will turn every potential conflict into a new chance to increase your creative power. You may even come to be grateful for these perfect instructions—all framed as attacks—about how to stop standing in your own way. As you leave the encultured patterns that once kept you in "known misery," you'll begin to climb faster and faster, more and more easily. And the higher you climb, the clearer and more beautiful the view.

11.

Fill Your Time with Life

I know a psychologist who sums up the way of integrity with this succinct prescription: "Know what you really know, feel what you really feel, say what you really mean, and do what you really want."

When I say this, many people react with confusion and alarm. They're not exactly sure what I mean, but it sounds dangerous. Especially the "do what you really want" part. I mean, if we did what we want instead of obeying cultural rules, wouldn't we all run around stealing purses, slapping neighbors, driving drunk while smoking twenty cigarettes at once?

Not if you've been using the processes I've described so far in this book.

Let's recap: as we embarked on the way of integrity, our task was to see through the fog of culture that blinded us to our true nature. (My experience with clients is that before taking that step, they literally don't know what they really know or feel what they really feel: "Yes, I'm *absolutely* comfortable in my uncomfortable position.") At the next stage, the inferno, we started removing cultural blinders, burning up beliefs that were untrue for us at a deep level. Once we connected with our inner truth, we took the challenge to stop lying—to start saying what we really meant. This is the point where we looked at how to cope with pushback from our culture.

If you've done all that, your next step on the way of integrity is to start spending your time doing what you really want. Ultimately, *all* your time.

If you followed this advice this without practicing and internalizing all the previous steps in this book, you really might run amok. When we're split from our true selves, what we really want is wholeness—but we don't even know what that looks like. We *think* it will come from dark wood of error rewards, like the wealth and power of Mount Delectable, or an endless supply of sex, drugs, and rock 'n' roll. The pursuit of these things, given the intensity of the pain that drives them, is so absorbing that we really are often selfish, greedy, and brutal. But real relief—the sort that brings us back to the person we are meant to be—comes only when we embrace our true natures.

Once we commit to being our true selves in every word and action, we emanate the love that is our essence. Having left the anguish of being split and come into the blessed relief of being whole and undivided, we want—deeply want—to offer the same relief to others. Your way of integrity might be to raise one happy child—or for that matter, one happy kitten. Or you may surprise yourself by becoming a social activist, or a healer of bodies, hearts, systems, the planet. You'll want to make the world a kinder, healthier, fairer place. You'll want to do it all the time.

Try it. You'll see.

THE LAST FEW STEPS UP THE MOUNTAIN

This chapter is about clearing away any errors of innocence that may still be dividing you from yourself even after you've stopped lying or getting stuck in your violent righteous mind. It's about honing your skills as a force for peace and love. Eventually, it will put you in a steady, unusual combination of effort and ease: finding and following your integrity in every moment.

This isn't work. It's play, as in "playing" a musical instrument or a skilled sport. It has nothing to do with inert leisure; it's getting enthralled in a meaningful challenge. Psychologists who study happiness know that this kind of effort puts us into a state called "flow." As we master it, our brains secrete hormones like dopamine and serotonin, which put us in bliss. It's human life at its most delicious.

Dante experiences flow as he gets to the upper reaches of purgatory. While clearing away falsehood and errors of righteousness further down the mountain was a difficult slog, he feels lighter and stronger now. He's free from so much suffering, eager to release whatever might still be dividing him from himself, surrounded by other happy souls. This is how you too will feel when you reach this point on the way of integrity. In fact, you may be ready to give it a try right this instant.

Many of my clients regretfully tell me, "I wish I could live my truth, but [my goldfish requires attention/my friends won't approve/I'm just too busy]."

Marc, for example, had been in the military all his life, but never enjoyed it. He muffled his misery and anger at work, then took it out at home by constantly griping at his wife and dog. "I can't stand my job or myself," he told me. "But I have only three years to go until I get my pension, so I can't quit."

Carol went to design school, but got married and raised two sons before she could launch her dream of becoming an artist. By age forty-seven she had an empty nest and a lifetime supply of ideas. "But I can't get started," she told me. "Everything's always distracting me—my friends, my husband, the appliances breaking in our house. If I could get some freedom, I know I could create beautiful things. But no one will let me."

Compare this to my friend Rayya, who was diagnosed with terminal cancer at age fifty-six. Rayya spent twenty years as a hard-core drug addict on the streets of New York, then got clean and stayed that way for another twenty. All of it had left her honest, blunt, and freakishly good at finding something to appreciate in every situation. She almost immediately decided to think of her diagnosis as an opportunity for a final, magnificent celebration.

"First I'm going to do every damn thing on my bucket list," Rayya told me. "I'm going to eat all my favorite foods, make great music, go to all the places I've loved, hang with everyone who makes me happy. Then, when I get too sick, I'll just score a massive speedball [heroin mixed with cocaine] and get so high I never come down. Kind of an awesome way to go, right? I've had an epic life, and I'm going to have an epic death."

But a few days later, after more medical tests, Rayya found herself in an odd dilemma. Her cancer was less aggressive than the doctors had thought. "I might have three to five years left," Rayya said. "What am I supposed to do? Go back to work until I'm too sick to move?"

"Well," I said, "you have that plan to do everything on your bucket list, right?"

"Yeah."

"So do it anyway," I said.

And she did.

For the rest of her life, Rayya endured great physical and emotional pain. But that time was also full of passionate, wild, raucous, tender, and hilarious adventures. Epic.

Rayya was well along on the way of integrity. She'd begun her adult life in the dark wood of error, numbing her pain with drugs. To get clean, she'd freed herself from many false beliefs, then climbed the first two levels of purgatory by committing to rigorous honesty and refusing ever to see herself as a victim.

But she'd never decided to devote all her time—every minute of it—to following her true desires. Rayya's cultural training told her to work until she dropped in her tracks—anything else would turn her "lazy." But there was no laziness in Rayya's nature. There was music, cooking, laughter, and loving. The fun never stopped.

Now, I have something scary to tell you: you don't have much time left to live. Whether it's five years or fifty-five, it's not all that long. You have no time to waste on suffering, no time to keep torturing your nature to serve your culture. The time for integrity is now.

THE POWER OF ONE-DEGREE TURNS

Rayya's cancer and intense personality helped her make a massive, sudden shift to pure integrity. But for most of us, it isn't the optimal strategy. We can start moving in the direction of our perfect lives immediately, but we can also go easy—in fact, we should. Psychologists who study change tell us that, paradoxically, positive transformation happens more quickly when we do it in small steps rather than heroic leaps.

Every day you make thousands of tiny decisions about what to do with your time. *Every single choice is a chance to turn toward the life you really want.* Repeatedly putting a little less time into what you don't love, and a little more into what you do love, is your next step on the way of integrity.

Earlier, I compared your life to an airplane. Imagine you're flying that plane on a ten-thousand-mile journey. If you change course by one degree to the right every half hour or so, you'll never notice a drastic change, but you'll end up in a completely different place than if you maintained your initial trajectory. I advise people to steer their lives with a series of "one-degree turns."

Start by noticing the amount of time you're spending with specific people or activities, and *see if it matches the amount of time you really want to spend with them.* Shift your schedule by a few minutes each day, spending a little less time doing things that don't appeal to you, and a little more doing what you love.

When I started coaching Marc, he didn't immediately quit the military. As he began observing himself more closely, he noticed that that he spent a lot of his free time watching TV, nursing his resentment, and snapping at his wife. His first one-degree turn was to take ten minutes away from a show he didn't really like and spend it playing outside with his dog.

Carol, the wannabe artist whose schedule was packed with obligations, realized that she was actually put off by the hidden hell thought "It's too late to be an artist." Once she questioned and disproved that belief, she set aside fifteen minutes every day to create art. Within a month she had several gorgeous paintings and a new sense of fulfillment. She said she felt younger, freer, and much more excited to be alive.

The following exercise may help you begin filling more of your time with what you really want, one-degree turn by one-degree turn.

EXERCISE:
One-degree turns

1. Make a list of five things you plan to do today.

   _____

   _____

   _____

   _____

   _____

2. Now list five things you have to do next week.

   _____

   _____

   _____

   _____

   _____

3. Make a third list of five things you'll spend time doing this year.

   _____

   _____

   _____

   _____

   _____

4. Looking at each item, answer this question: In an absolutely ideal world, what is the amount of time I *really want* to spend on this activity today/next week/this year? Please note that "zero" is an acceptable answer.

5. Compare the amount of time you plan to spend on each item with the amount of time you *want* to spend on it.

6. If the two are different, begin making one-degree turns in your schedule, spending ten minutes per day less on things you don't want to do, and filling those ten minutes with things you want to do.

If you can follow this exercise, *making small changes, not large ones*, your entire life will be transformed. Your time—that most limited of all resources—will fill up with a sense of happiness and purpose.

PRACTICE MAKES PERMANENT

Of course, if you take enough one-degree turns, you'll eventually encounter big choices. Once Marc started making small changes, gradually experiencing more and more happiness, he realized that he simply couldn't spend three more years in a job he hated. "I could die in three years," he said. "What good would my pension do then?"

He started looking up old friends who'd left the military, asking them what they'd done afterward. They helped Marc see that his skills were valuable in a lot of industries. He put out his resumé and got recruited for a job at an engineering firm, which he loved. Though his wife had financial fears when he quit the military, she quickly became a fan. "The man I married is back," she told me. "You can't put a price on that."

As for Carol, she gradually increased her art time until it filled her schedule—mostly. "I've found a balance," she told me. "It turns out I really don't mind taking care of people a few hours a day." She created a line of greeting cards she sells online. She says this brings in "a little money, and a lot of joy."

Because these people practiced changing in small ways, they were ready when big decisions arrived. Remember, following the way of integrity is a complex skill that puts us in flow. And skills like that require a lot of practice. My karate sensei used to make his students perform every new move very slowly a thousand times. Then we'd speed up the action while maintaining perfect form—a thousand times. Then we'd add power to the move, increasing the intensity gradually, another thousand times. "Practice doesn't necessarily make perfect," he'd say. "Practice makes permanent."

When we start living in complete integrity, practice makes permanent, physical changes in our brains. Neurologists tell us that the more times we repeat any action, the more we wire it into our neural circuits. To change a familiar behavior pattern (like anything we've been socialized to do), we must deliberately choose new actions, then repeat them until old brain circuits fade and new ones form. It's like do-it-yourself brain surgery. By repeatedly choosing the way of integrity, we unwire ourselves for cultural compliance and rewire ourselves for honesty and happiness.

BUT WON'T THAT MAKE ME SELFISH?

When I tell people they should always do what they really want, they often look shocked. "People can't just do whatever they want!" they protest. "If I started that, I'd turn into the most selfish person on the planet!" You may be having the same kind of thoughts.

Are you sure?

Can you absolutely know those thoughts are true?

Our culture sees most of life's rewards as a zero-sum equation: everyone's gain is someone else's loss. If one person gets more, another person gets less. If you make the honor roll, I flunk out of school. If you're rich and famous, it's because you stomped over hundreds of "little people." This is conventional wisdom. But it's not completely true.

Dante learns this from Virgil as they climb purgatory. He asks how everyone on the mountain can get into paradise. Like us, Dante has no experience of a culture where *everyone* gets to the very top of the pyramid. He asks Virgil how it's possible for people to share goodness while simultaneously creating more goodness to share. Everyone in purgatory gets a piece of the pie—and there's more pie left after they've all had their share than there was when the process started.

Virgil replies that there are two ways to do the math on

happiness. Dante's mind is still "fixed on earthly things," he says. If we think in terms of Mount Delectable rewards like money and power, things have to be divided up, so one person's gain is often another's loss. *But remember, we want these things only because we think they'll give us the feelings we yearn for—* peace, purpose, belonging, fulfillment. And when one person gets more of those truly innately delicious things, their joy isn't divisive. It's multiplicative. The more of these beautiful feelings we receive, the more we create. Giving doesn't impoverish us; it makes us richer.

To use a modern-day example, when a family adopts a puppy, each person doesn't diminish their love for all the others so that everyone can give a portion of affection to the dog. As the puppy wags and cuddles, she both receives and gives an affection that grows by the minute, for everyone. Each member of the family, and the group as a whole, gains more love. *Everything that truly makes us happy is limitless and multiplicative, not scarce and divisive.*

As we realize this, our fear of scarcity—the basis of greed—lessens. Recognizing that living our truth makes things better *for everyone* can give us the courage to make big decisions that move us toward integrity.

MY ONE-DEGREE TURNS

Early in my Year of Not Lying at All, I spent quite a lot of time trying to figure out what I really wanted to do. If someone said, "What shall we do for dinner?" instead of offering the reflexive people-pleaser's answer ("Whatever sounds good to you"), I was compelled by my no-lie vow to stop, look inside, and answer the question for real.

Tiny choices like these improved my life rapidly—and brought me to some huge decisions. Leaving Mormonism was one. Not long after that, when I complained to a friend about writing my PhD dissertation, she asked, "When was the last time you read a book for fun?" Oh, yeah, I thought, that's a thing. I'd spent most of my childhood on reading recreationally, but virtually none of my adult life.

That day I bought a novel. I read it all night long. By morning, I'd realized I didn't want to spend my precious time on Earth writing academic journal articles. I wanted to write things that people read for fun. So, though I finished my PhD, my chosen profession and my Harvard-shaped value system followed my religion and community of origin right out of my life.

Oh, and one other little thing: I realized I was gay.

It's not that I was in a sham marriage—I loved John deeply and felt deeply loved in return. But if we hadn't grown up Mormon, both of us would probably have identified as bisexual or gay earlier on. John's story is his to tell, but as we began following our integrity, we mutually decided to change the terms of our relationship. We unofficially "unmarried" each other, and waited to see what would happen next.

What happened was that we both felt freer and more loving toward one another. It became abundantly obvious that love was multiplicative, not divisive—just as Dante learned while he climbed purgatory. So my relationship didn't change as much as you'd think, not immediately. Still, I was rocked to my core. I'd never had a relationship with a woman—had never "experimented" at all. My one fantasy—albeit an extremely strong one—was that someday I'd have a really, *really* close female friend who lived next door, and every day we'd spend time just being together.

But gay? Me?

For months I felt waves of intense shame, guilt, embarrassment, and terror. After all, a Mormon authority had recently proclaimed that the "three great enemies of the church in the latter days" were feminists, intellectuals, and gay people. By the standards of the community where I still lived, I was a three-strikes evildoer. *And I couldn't lie about it, because I had promised I wouldn't lie, not once, not at all, for a whole year!*

My therapist joked that my biggest psychological problem was keeping my New Year's resolutions. But the real problem, I discovered, was that once again I didn't know what was true. Being gay was such a violation of my culture's values that I couldn't tolerate it. I spent sleepless nights knowing what I now knew, feeling what I now felt, and asking myself what to do about it.

Eventually, after making about a million one-degree turns, I reached a way of thinking I would later encounter in (surprise, surprise!) *The Divine Comedy*. For a medieval European Catholic, Dante sneaked a lot of subversive thinking into his masterpiece.

As they travel the upper reaches of purgatory, where souls

are cleansed of sloth, greed, gluttony, and lust, Virgil explains something that stuns Dante. All these "sins" are actually based in love. Sloth, greed, gluttony, and lust are simply unbalanced relationships with rest, abundance, nourishment, and sex. We can err by either compulsively indulging or *rigidly repressing* our natural relationship with these things. This lack of balance doesn't come when we allow union with our true nature, but when we split ourselves away from it. It's misguided *thinking*, not natural behavior, that causes us to stray from our innocence.

BECOMING YOUR INNER TEACHER

Once he's got that straight, Dante faces a cleansing fire that will burn the last of his corruptibility. He's scared, but he goes through it. Watching him, Virgil says that it's time for Dante to stop following the dead poet's lead. "Don't wait for my word or my sign," Virgil says. "Your will is free, upright, and healthy. To act against it would be to err." In other words, Dante is so close to total integrity that doing whatever he really wants—following the path that brings him the most joy—will take him straight to paradise. His inner teacher is as available to him as his outer teacher.

This will happen to you, too. As you practice the skills needed to live with integrity—noticing unhappiness, checking for false beliefs, freeing yourself from illusions, and moving into a truer course—practice will make permanent, freeing you more and more to be nothing else but your inner teacher, your truest self.

Of course you'll still encounter cleansing fires, those situations that test your courage to remain honest. Here's an example from my own life. Years later, I appeared on a live national webcast with Oprah Winfrey. Producers had given me a script, which specifically avoided mentioning being gay because Oprah had just done a show about Ellen DeGeneres's very public coming-out. But at one point, a woman in the audience raised her hand and told us that though she was married with three children, she had recently realized she was a lesbian.

I had a split second to decide whether to pretend I had only theoretical opinions about this woman's situation, or acknowledge that her experience was exactly like mine. I was terrified to break the rules by going off script, terrified to reveal myself so publicly. But my inner teacher told me silence would be a lie. So off script I went, and started talking to the woman about my own past.

At which point Oprah dropped her jaw, stared at me, and said, "Wait—you're *gay?*"

Live. National. Broadcast.

You may think that as a published author and coach, I'd feel secure and confident chatting with Oprah about my homosexuality while millions of people watched. Not so much. I literally felt as if I'd walked into a bonfire. The remaining shreds of the introverted Mormon people-pleasing girl I'd been burst into flames of embarrassment and sizzled away like bacon frying as we talked. Frankly, it was awful.

But not as awful as leaving the way of integrity.

I would never have been able to tell the truth at that

moment—would never have been on Oprah's show in the first place—if I hadn't practiced making one-degree turns toward doing what I really wanted. For years, every time I'd made a to-do list, I'd checked with my inner teacher to see if my plans reflected my true desires. Then I'd turned, small choice by small choice, toward my true nature. When I found myself facing a cleansing fire, I walked into it by sheer force of habit.

Here's an exercise designed to help you get so connected to your own inner teacher that you never have to leave the way of integrity.

EXERCISE:
Becoming your inner teacher

Short version

1. Tune in to your inner teacher (see Chapter 2).

2. Ask yourself: If I were absolutely free, what would I do right now?

3. Do it.

Longer version

1. Tune in to your inner teacher.

2. Ask yourself: If I were absolutely free, what would I do right now?

3. Now ask yourself: Why am I not doing that thing?

4. List all the obstacles to doing that thing:

_____

_____

_____

5. Trace each obstacle to the limiting beliefs that underlie it. Question the beliefs until you can see their falsehood. For example:

   • If you notice that you aren't following your true nature because of social conditioning, question whether that conditioning agrees with your truth.

   • If you doubt your own worthiness or capacity to follow your nature without causing harm, question your doubts.

   • If the obstacle is logistical, question the belief that you can't figure out how to solve the problem. Then solve it.

   • If the obstacle is lack of information, get the information you need.

6. Ask yourself again: If I were *absolutely free*, what would I do?

7. Recognize that you *are* free.

8. Do exactly what you want.

Many clients tell me their lives will go straight to hell if they actually follow this exercise. But their doomsday predictions invariably prove false. People who say "What I really want is to drink beer on a beach forever" get bored after three days and start developing career ideas. Parents who fear they'll abandon their children end up getting an occasional babysitter, which brings much more joy to their parenting. Folks who expect to start punching coworkers find that once they're doing what they want with their lives, free-floating hostility gives way to friendliness.

I hope that when you begin doing what you really want, you have sweet, anticlimactic adventures like these (not dramatic, disruptive ones like mine). I hope that once you find your true path, you never stray from it. But if you stumble, as we all do, that's okay. Just go back to the basic process of integrity. Slow it down, but keep it up. Repeat it a thousand times, by the numbers: notice the dark wood of error symptom, track the false belief that drives it, question the belief, tune into your true nature, and respond creatively according to your real values. Each time, you'll get better at it. A stumble isn't the end of the world.

Rayya had a significant stumble just months before she died. Fear and physical suffering—plus the whopping doses of opioids the doctors gave her to manage her pain—led her to a brief reprisal of the addiction she'd given up years before. But when Rayya realized this was going to ruin the last wisps of time she had left, she course-corrected. Being Rayya, she took a massive leap, not a one-degree turn (don't try this at home). She recruited another former addict to help her, gave up drugs cold turkey, went through a nightmarish withdrawal, and came out with more integrity than ever.

Shortly before her death, Rayya called me to make amends in case she'd done anything in her drug-addled state that offended me (she hadn't). Her energy on that call was astonishing: so pure and loving that, ironically enough, it almost made me feel high. She said, "I spent a lot of my life lying to get what I thought I wanted. Here's what I found out: if I live in the truth, I'll always come out okay. Because only the truth has legs. At the end of the day, it's the only thing left standing."

The one tattoo I have, printed on my right ankle, is that sentence: *The truth has legs.* It reminds me every day to fill my time with my best life, to honor my own integrity and the memory of my friend. She lived her last months and, in the end, died doing exactly what her true nature had chosen, surrounded by love, laughter, belonging, purpose, and peace.

Epic.

12.

Reclaiming Eden

Sharee was one of the most radiant people I've ever met. You'd never have guessed what an awful history lay behind her. She was raised in Kentucky as part of a small Christian sect that made Mormonism look like a frat party. At age fifteen Sharee got pregnant, dropped out of high school, and married her boyfriend, Nathan. By the time she was twenty-four (decades before I met her), they had five more children. That was when Nathan, a construction worker, fell from a scaffold and sustained significant brain damage.

With no income, huge medical bills, and eight mouths to feed, Sharee set out to find a job. She was hoping her parents and in-laws would help with childcare—but in their sect, women were absolutely forbidden to work outside their homes. Her mother-in-law blamed Sharee's sinful job plans for preventing Nathan's miraculous recovery. Exhausted, grief-stricken, and utterly lost in the dark wood of error, Sharee decided to kill herself.

Her plan was to jump off a cliff not far from her home, so her loved ones would think she had fallen. "I didn't want to leave my kids," she told me all those years later, "but I was just in too much pain. I was out of my mind." She left home one night and hiked until sunrise, when she finally reached the edge of the cliff. "At that point, it was basically a done deal," she said. "I was about to die. No question. So I sat down to have one last look at everything."

Watching that sunrise, Sharee let go of all her psychological connections to her identity, her culture, her family, and even her body. Then something strange happened. "It was like someone switched on the world," she said. "Like everything went from black and white to color. I felt totally free. There was all this energy pumping through me. It was *life*, and I loved it. I realized I didn't want to end my life, just the way I'd been living. When I thought of myself as already dead, I didn't care what anyone thought about me. It sort of gave me permission to stop worrying so much about everything."

Obviously, Sharee didn't jump. She returned home and scraped by with the help of some friends as she earned her GED, then a scholarship to nursing school. And though her life wouldn't be easy for several years, her inner world never went back to the gray wasteland it had once been.

I've met a few people like Sharee, individuals who burned up huge chunks of their socialization in one dramatic moment and felt abruptly, permanently freer. I believe a small version of this happened to me on the day I read the *Tao te Ching*, dropped a number of tormenting beliefs all at once, and felt my body flood with so much electricity I ran into a waterfall. In Japanese this experience is called *satori*, or "sudden enlightenment." In many other traditions, it's call awakening. It can happen in small, incremental ways or in huge, irreversible ones.

People from all over the world, at every point in history, have recounted having satori experiences. Sharing no cultural references or communication, they describe the event in very similar ways. Scientists have found that this "awakening" is associated with specific brain states. In other words, it's not only real but empirically observable. For people who experience a major satori, the whole world seems to change, because it changes the way they see the world. I believe that if you follow the way of integrity long enough, something like this will happen to you, too. At that point, you may not have the definition of a perfect life as seen by your culture. But you'll connect with ideas and states of mind that go *beyond* culture, to a way of being that's more vivid, fearless, and in love with life.

DANTE'S AWAKENING: THE THREE TRANSFORMATIONS

When Dante finally reaches the very top of purgatory, three things happen that ultimately propel him into awakening. First, he finds himself in a forest so lovely and harmonious he immediately recognizes it as the Garden of Eden. Second, he encounters Beatrice, his first love, who died very young. She flat-out orders him to wake up, saying she wants him to stop thinking and speaking like "one who dreams." Third, Dante gets dunked in two sides of a perfectly clear river. The first side makes him forget everything he's ever done wrong, while the second makes him remember everything he's ever done right. The last step in purgatory, for all of us, is to return to Eden and regain our lost innocence.

Okeydokey. How?

Let's take it one weird metaphor at a time.

The first transformation: Reclaiming Eden

As we saw in the previous chapter, practicing and perfecting our integrity skills gradually puts all the structures of our inner and outer lives into alignment. When we see something in our life that doesn't match our true nature, we leave or end it, replacing it with things based on our truth. This makes our lives work better and better. We create so much harmony that we eventually find ourselves in our own personal Garden of Eden.

In Sharee's case, a sudden inner fracture began a slow re-creation of her outward behaviors; her satori was dramatic, but her life changed quite slowly. For other people, inner beliefs disappear more gradually, but circumstances change quickly. How quickly? That depends on two things: how deeply they've been socialized, and how destructive their culture is toward the expression of their true nature.

For example, Derek and Jim were middle-class white guys

who had started a company right after business school. Over the course of twenty years, Jim had become increasingly narcissistic and dishonest. His tantrums and financial fudging almost brought down the company. Derek stayed loyal because he believed things like "He's my friend" and "I need to find a way to work with Jim." Those beliefs fell apart pretty quickly upon examination. Derek dissolved the partnership and started a solo business, which flourished. It was a textbook case of following integrity from difficulty to harmony.

Lucia had a rougher road to travel. As she followed her way of integrity, she stopped trying to fit American cultural norms by joining corporate America and (as she put it) "trying to succeed like a white person in a white world," and instead embraced her identity as a queer Latina. As she made many one-degree turns in her own life, Lucia also found herself unintentionally creating a kind of micro-Eden in her house. The place buzzed with friends who rarely felt safe anywhere else: people of all colors, genders, histories, and interests. No two of these people were alike, but Lucia lived a brand of inclusion that made them all feel secure and loved.

If you come to the way of integrity in a context of social injustice—racism, a repressive political system, religious fundamentalism—I have good news and bad news for you. The good news is that the system will cause you so much suffering it will be easy for you to see places where your culture doesn't match your truth (uh . . . congratulations?). The bad news is that you'll be "creating Eden" in adversarial conditions. Many people who've advocated simple changes toward integrity have been attacked by such systems. So as you keep making one-degree turns toward integrity, go gently and check in often with your inner teacher. The most dangerous places for creating change are also the ones where it's most desperately needed.

EXERCISE:
Creating Eden

By using the one-degree-change process described in the last chapter, you'll automatically form your personal Eden over time. But if you're up for something a tad more ambitious, try this:

1. Find one thing about your community (neighborhood, church congregation, workplace, nation) that strikes you as unfair or disturbing. Write it here:

   _____

   _____

2. Now answer the question from Chapter 7: In regard to the issue I've just written down, acting in accordance with my core values, *what positive thing can I create*? Make a note:

   _____

   _____

3. Now make a very small change, a one-degree turn, toward the step you just wrote down. Make one every day. Remember, huge transformations can happen in tiny steps. What starts as your own Eden can ripple out further than you'd believe.

The second transformation:
Total transparency and the beams of love

As he explores Eden, Dante comes to a river so clear it "hides nothing," like the pure core of our inner lives that harbors no secrets or lies. Social scientists tell us that "transparency" is a crucial condition for healthy families, teams, or governments. But this level of integrity requires a particular kind of courage: the willingness to be seen as we are.

As Dante stands by the river, he hears a host of angels arriving. They bring with them a great lady. Sure enough, it's Beatrice, Dante's first love, who's been dead for years. You'd expect what follows to be a tender scene like the end of the movie *Ghost*, where Demi Moore becomes capable of seeing her deceased partner (Patrick Swayze) and they share a moment of sweet, healing intimacy. This doesn't happen in *The Divine Comedy*. When his late girlfriend shows up, Dante finds her presence excruciating.

For one thing, Beatrice is no simpering ingenue. She has the bearing of general, and shines like lightning. In that unsparing radiance, Dante is transparent: Beatrice can see right through him. She's not cruel, but she pulls no punches. Facing Dante, she recounts how, after her death, she watched from heaven as he wandered away from love and into the dark wood of error. Beatrice tried to save him: she sent bolts of inspiration, appeared in his dreams, did everything short of grabbing him by the ears, which she couldn't do because she wasn't able to descend that far from paradise. Finally, she recruited Virgil to find Dante and guide him through hell and purgatory to the mountaintop. Now he's in enough integrity to tolerate Beatrice's celestial presence—but just barely.

Some Dante scholars seem a bit puzzled that Beatrice isn't *nice*, the way human cultures expect women to be. Shocking! But actually, I don't see this Beatrice as a literal woman in the first place. She feels to me like a version of that indescribably brilliant light I saw in surgery thirty years ago. It told me the same things Beatrice tells Dante: *I've always loved you. I've always tried to help you. You are meant to be happy. Don't ever forget me again.*

I don't know if Dante ever had an experience like my encounter with that light (they're a lot more common than most people think). But if we're looking at *The Divine Comedy* as a metaphor for his inner life, Beatrice might be Dante's soul—the pure radiance, love, and power that is the essence of his being, and everyone else's.

As Marianne Williamson wrote, "Our deepest fear is not that we are inadequate. Our deepest fear is that we are powerful beyond measure. It is our light, not our darkness, that most frightens us." I've seen this in every client who follows the way of integrity clear through to happiness. Culture has taught them to belittle themselves, to think, as Williamson says, "Who am I to be brilliant, gorgeous, talented, and fabulous?" But as their lives align with truth, they begin to shine—the way Sharee did, the way Derek did, the way Lucia and her friends did. They become radiant, as attractive as super-magnets. People start to notice them, and then can't stop looking.

And their initial reaction to this, almost always, is fear and shame.

Remember, culture imbues almost all of us with the "primal shame" that tells us our true nature is somehow bad. So we hide parts of ourselves, even from ourselves. Then we feel desperately alone, yearning to be truly seen and loved as we are. Yet when we first begin to reveal our true nature (Sharee getting a job, Derek ousting Jim, Lucia embracing her identity), primal shame can make us feel almost unbearably vulnerable. Dante can't even look at Beatrice, who sees and loves him through and through. He stares down at the grass, weeping tears of shame.

As you reach pure integrity and begin to form your own Eden, you may become much more transparent than ever before. You may blurt out that you love someone without knowing how they'll react. You may set firm boundaries, honoring a new level of self-respect. You may express unpopular political views at the neighborhood block party. You may hug a grieving stranger. You may start standing up for your truth in ways so brash you hardly recognize yourself.

In this phase, you may feel frighteningly exposed. As someone who's done a bit of TV, I know that when someone gets a reality-show "makeover," they most often feign delight for the cameras, then run home, scrub off their makeup, and go back to wearing lumpy, moth-eaten hoodies as if their life depended on it. Being seen in ways we can't control terrifies us all. It's important to recognize this fear, find the beliefs that drive it (usually cultural shame messages), question those thoughts, and move on.

The poet William Blake said, "We are put on earth a little space / that we may learn to bear the beams of love." Love-beams, like sunbeams, light up our lives. They're what everyone wants and needs. But especially at first, the light is too bright. We want to turn away, as Dante turns away from Beatrice. But she won't stand for it. She knows Dante needs to look at the love that's looking at him. And so do you.

EXERCISE:
Bearing the beams of love

1. As you move closer to full integrity, your one-degree choices will eventually put you in the company of someone you trust. It may be a friend, a twelve-step group, your partner, a sibling. We'll call them "the trusted other." When you've got someone in mind, move on to step 2.

2. Think of something you haven't told your trusted other, something that feels a bit too sensitive to share. Maybe it's something in your past that you're ashamed of, like being in an abusive relationship or failing at something important. Or maybe it's just a feeling of love, yearning, or hope that might make you feel vulnerable. Write it down:

_____

_____

3. Give this time, but notice that as you grow closer to your trusted other, *you both fear revealing and want to reveal the thing you're hiding.* As the desire to be fully known grows stronger, commit to telling your trusted other your secret when the situation feels right.

4. When the situation arrives (it will), tell your trusted other about your sensitive topic.

5. Now, here's the most important part: If their response feels uncaring or indifferent, shut down the conversation and start over with someone else. But if they respond with love and acceptance, *look into their eyes.*

I often use this exercise in groups. A brave participant will dare to talk about their anger or loneliness. Then, invariably, they drop their gaze. I ask everyone who feels compassion for the speaker to raise their hands and keep them up. Then I ask the speaker to look, one by one, into the eyes of all these sympathetic strangers. Eye-gaze is a powerful way to fire up the mirror neurons in our brains and shift the way we feel toward others. Over and over, I've seen this exercise powerfully "resocialize" people, reducing primal shame and creating the sense of being safe among humans. Take it at your own pace, but try it.

The third transformation: Oblivion and beauty

Beatrice certainly gazes into Dante's eyes, but he won't look up. So she goes to more dramatic measures. She tells Dante he's simply got to awaken, to "disentangle" himself from the fear and shame that make him "speak like one who dreams." So one of Beatrice's angelic companions drags Dante into the river. The angel dunks him twice, once by each bank. The first side is called the Lethe, Greek for "oblivion." This dunk wipes out every memory Dante has of ever doing anything wrong. The river's opposite side is the Eunoe (*eunoia* is a Greek word that means "beautiful thinking"). Once he's been immersed here, Dante can't help but remember everything he's ever done *right*.

This is a strange scene, certainly not part of the religious dogma Dante might have picked up from going to Sunday mass. I believe the poet created his double-dip in the Lethe and the Eunoe as a metaphor for something he literally experienced on a psychological level.

As I watch clients walk the way of integrity, I notice their thought patterns changing just as Dante's did in the river. Their inner torment (always based on falsehood) begins to dwindle. An image of themselves as worthy and loveable (based on truth) begins to grow. This can reflect a literal, physical shift in brain structure. Neuroscientists have shown that meditators who've spent many hours observing their thoughts and focusing on compassion have less neural activity in parts of the brain associated with negative emotions, and unusually dense neural tissue in areas linked to empathy, love, and joy. The longer these people practice, the greater the change. They are literally rewiring themselves for happiness.

Eastern religions, as well as many shamanic traditions, have pragmatic, methodical ways of creating this inner shift. Most of these methods involve long periods of quiet introspection—not learning new thoughts, but loosening our grip on all thought. Western religious practices like "centering prayer" have similar effects. But modern secular society doesn't have many practices for deliberately disentangling ourselves from fear and shame. Therapy can work, but it's very slow, and research suggests that just talking truthfully to a therapist is more important than any specific brand of intervention.

The most powerful practice I've found in American culture comes from the author and spiritual teacher Byron Katie, whom I introduced in Chapter 6. Katie endured horrible depression, anxiety, and agoraphobia for decades. At one point she became so unbearably unhappy that she checked into a halfway house for women with eating disorders—the only place near her home that offered inpatient care. She was so violently angry and unhappy that the other patients made her sleep in an attic room—they were afraid she would kill them in their sleep.

Then Katie had a total, abrupt satori. She woke up one morning unable to believe her own thoughts. Suddenly, everything in the world—including Katie herself—appeared to her as astonishing, fresh, gorgeous. She later wrote:

> I discovered that when I believed my thoughts, I suffered, but that when I didn't believe them, I didn't suffer, and that this is true for every human being. Freedom is as simple as that. I found that suffering is optional. I found a joy within me that has never disappeared, not for a single moment. That joy is in everyone, always.

Along with this perspective came a method for disengaging from thoughts that cause suffering. Katie calls this "the Work." As I said, it's the most powerful tool I know for giving people a double-dunk into the Lethe and the Eunoe. But before I show you this exercise, I want to tell you how it affected me.

SUMMITING PURGATORY, AGAIN AND AGAIN

I'm recounting a lot of my own story in this book because I want you to see that the way of integrity is reiterative: Dante goes through it only once in *The Divine Comedy*, but we may travel from the dark wood to the inferno and up purgatory many times as we clear out suffering in different areas of our lives.

So in my case, after Adam was diagnosed, I dropped my beliefs around intellectualism. After moving back to Utah, I repaired the damage caused by childhood trauma. Then I reconsidered my religion, then my career choices, then my sexual orientation, then my marriage. As I brought these issues into alignment with my integrity, I broke almost every rule of the various cultures that socialized me—and found myself happier than ever before.

Soon my Eden formed around me. John and I left—well, fled—Utah and moved to Phoenix, where we continued to co-parent our children, and got jobs teaching at the American Graduate School of International Management (Thunderbird).

Each of us ended up in committed gay relationships, so my kids now had four parents instead of two. My life looked totally bizarre from the perspective of any human culture. But my dark wood of error symptoms disappeared. I felt consistently calm and happy for the first time in my life. My "progressive and incurable" autoimmune diseases went into remission. That enabled me to write and sell my first book.

That first book did not do well, sales-wise. (If you are one of the approximately seven people who actually bought it, I salute you.) Aha, I thought. I can write books, but no one will read them. This freed me up to tell more truth. I began writing more transparently, churning out a memoir about my son that ended up more honest and intimate than I'd intended. I was stunned when that book became a best seller. The book tour never ended: I spoke in all fifty states and a few other countries. It sounds great, I know, and I was deeply grateful. I started writing for magazines, landing as a monthly columnist in *O, The Oprah Magazine*. But I struggled to take in so many beams of love from so many people.

This is when my way of integrity got scary again. I'd always felt that if I were lucky enough to gain any credibility in the world, I should use it to write about my experiences with Mormonism. I believed that many people—people with very little power—were living with the same kind of pain, abuse, and bizarre social pressure I'd experienced as a child. On the many occasions when someone told me, "Your father's work made me stay Mormon," I hadn't replied that my father may be a dubious spiritual anchor. To leave all these folks behind without speaking up for them didn't feel like integrity.

First I wrote a really bad novel about growing up Mormon. Using fiction, I thought, would allow me to tell my story without ruffling too many feathers. But my editor suggested that I scrap the fiction strategy and write the book as a memoir. I knew this would attract more than "beams of love." In fact, I honestly thought it might get me killed. But it felt like integrity. I doubled my life insurance, took a lot of deep breaths, and wrote a book called *Leaving the Saints*.

This time, I didn't have to grope my way to the inferno.

Oh, no.

It came right at me.

I could write yet another book about the hurricane of cultural change-back attacks that hit me when Mormons learned what I'd written. I truly didn't think I'd survive it. The threats rolled in, some including graphic descriptions of how my children and other loved ones would be murdered along with me. My siblings informed me they were planning to have me charged with federal crimes and put in prison.

During my book tour, Mormons showed up everywhere I went, trying to block my appearance on news and talk shows. My family and other church members waged their own publicity campaign, publicly denouncing me as a vengeful madwoman. Church members started an email campaign to get me fired from my magazine job; someone sent me a copy of the instructions, which spelled out how to write an email to Oprah attacking me, telling Oprah that the emailer was from a state other than Utah, and taking care not to mention that the writer was Mormon. Someone changed my Wikipedia page, erasing any reference to education and portraying me as mentally ill. I'd find out later that my teenage daughter had rewritten the post repeatedly, only to have the negative version restored within minutes.

This was my situation when I first encountered a copy of Byron Katie's book *Loving What Is*. I picked it up for two reasons. First, I'd taken to lurking in airport bookstores to avoid being recognized, and *Loving What Is* happened to be stacked near an excellent hiding spot. Second, I noticed that Katie's co-author (and, I soon discovered, her husband) was Stephen Mitchell. Remember the book of Chinese philosophy that made me run into the waterfall? The translator of that book was this self-same Stephen Mitchell. I bought *Loving What Is*, boarded my flight, found my seat, and scanned the cabin for angry Mormons (note: they smile a lot).

Once the coast was clear, I opened Katie's book. I learned that her Work is a concise, elegant exercise for releasing thoughts that cause suffering and finding a new perspective on life. It consists of four questions and something she calls a "turnaround." Here are Katie's brief instructions for doing the Work. I *highly* recommend that you study the way Katie uses the Work in her books, online videos, and live events. By the way, this is your exercise for this chapter, so grab a pen and dive in whenever you feel like it.

EXERCISE:
The Work of Byron Katie

Step one

Think a thought that makes you feel bad. Write it down.

_____

_____

Step two

Considering this painful thought, ask the following four questions. Don't give answers that are quick or glib: if you want freedom from suffering, let the questions sink into your consciousness and notice what arises from deep within you.

1. Is it true? (Yes or no. If no, move to question 3.)

2. Can I absolutely know that it's true? (Yes or no.)

3. How do I react, what happens, when I believe that thought?

4. Who or what would I be without the thought?

Step three

Consider the "turnaround," the direct opposite of your original painful thought. Reverse your painful thought in as many ways as you can. Try turning it around to the opposite, the self, and the other.

For example, if your painful thought is "Paul doesn't like me," an opposite might be "Paul *does* like me." Turning the thought around to yourself, you might say "I don't like me." Turning it around to the other (in this case, Paul), you may come up with the thought "Paul doesn't like Paul." Contemplate how any of these turnarounds may be as true as, or truer than, the original thought.

The first time I did this exercise, I had plenty of distressing thoughts to work with. I selected one that never seemed to stop repeating: "Something terrible is going to happen to me because I wrote that book."

The first of Katie's four questions, "Is it true?" felt comfortable to me; I'd been asking myself whether my own perceptions were true since I was eighteen. However, this particular hell thought, "Something terrible is going to happen to me because I wrote that book," seemed pretty solid. Angry people certainly kept telling me it was true. But in response to Katie's second question, "Can I absolutely know that it's true?" I had to admit that the answer was no. Not *absolutely*. (Kant again.)

Then I went to Katie's third question: "How do I react, what happens, when I believe that thought?" I noted my emotional and physical response. The thought "Something terrible is going to happen to me because I wrote that book" made me feel sick, frightened, and trapped. I'd long since learned that true thoughts didn't feel so much like poison. Noted.

Then I reached the fourth question, and this one swept me into the river Lethe. It's similar to the exercise in Chapter 11 where I asked you to imagine what you'd do if you were absolutely free. But this freedom is not in every deed, it's just in relation to one belief. It asks, "Who or what would I be without the thought?"

It took a long time for me to even imagine not having the thought "Something terrible is going to happen to me because I wrote that book." But eventually, I got there. The terrifying statement dropped away into the Lethe, into oblivion. I felt so calm and relaxed; just a person on a plane. It was wonderful to be in a situation where no scary people were likely to approach me and there wasn't much to do. I could just sit there, panting with relief. Nothing special was happening, and that "nothing special" was heaven. I basked in it for a while, then moved on to the last step of the Work, the turnaround.

This also took me a while, because I couldn't think of many convincing opposites for the thought "Something terrible is going to happen to me because I wrote that book." When I tried the turnaround "Nothing terrible is going to happen to me," it felt like a lie. Someone had already killed all the plants in my yard, terrorized my family. So I tried different turnarounds, until I made one that seemed nonsensical. That turnaround was "I'm going to happen to something terrible because I wrote that book." I thought about this for a while. As it sank into my understanding, I sank into the waters of the Eunoe.

"I'm going to happen to something terrible."

I remembered all those young Mormon women sobbing in my office at BYU. I thought about the friend I'd confided in who later took her own life. I thought about my father's lifetime of "lying for the Lord."

I'm going to happen to something terrible.

It wasn't a soothing statement. It was strange and fierce, the sort of thing Dante's Beatrice might say. It made me remember who I was: free, aware, lucky enough to have a little piece of the world's attention. It reminded me that I'd waited to write *Leaving the Saints* until I was sure it was coming from compassion rather than anger.

I was miles away from enlightened. But the statement "I'm going to happen to something terrible because I wrote that book" shattered much of my fear, permanently. I still thought I might be bankrupted, imprisoned, or killed, but I was genuinely fine with that. It felt much more peaceful than failing to challenge a system I believed was harming people. In this one area of my life, I had disentangled myself from fear and shame. I no longer spoke like one who dreams.

BEGINNING TO WAKE UP

Your dream—anyone's dream—is the version of reality our culture and our traumas have programmed us to see. If you keep following the way of integrity, the dream must end. Your Eden will form around you. You'll begin to open up, allowing your true nature to be seen, learning to tolerate the radiance of your own soul and the beams of love it inevitably attracts. Once you reach your whole truth in any area, you're likely to begin having moments of satori, where you feel a sudden burst of strange, irrepressible energy, where the whole world suddenly becomes more vividly colorful. You'll find yourself immersed in pure clarity, where your suffering disappears into oblivion and is replaced by beautiful thoughts.

The genius of Byron Katie's Work is that it shows you how to proceed beyond all your cultural training, all your painful beliefs. It will show you exactly how the direct opposite of your most agonizing belief is always your next step toward awakening.

For Sharee, the lie "I want to die" switched to the truth: "I want to live." For Derek, "I've got to find a way to work with Jim" became "I've got to find a way to work without Jim." Lucia exchanged the thought "I should be more normal" to "I should be *less* normal." These may not resonate for you, but for each of these people, the turnaround chimed the ring of truth.

This method reveals our most painful encultured lies as portals to enlightenment. Use it on whatever beliefs torture you most, and you'll realize that all that dreadful suffering was just reality trying its hardest to wake you up. When we let painful lies dissolve in oblivion and look at them from the opposite side, our own switched perspective tells us how to go beyond culture. This sets us free to be our whole selves. But it's not the end of the journey. As Dante says, when we reach this point, we are prepared to climb "unto the stars."

Stage Four

PARADISE

13.

Into the Mystery

Dante emerges from the Eunoe wide awake. Without self-deceit, fear, or shame, he's in a state of full integrity: body, mind, heart, and soul aligned with truth. And like that structurally integrated airplane I mentioned way back in the Introduction, he can fly.

Dante finds himself rising upward effortlessly, Beatrice by his side, until he enters paradise. At this point Dante does something unusual for any writer. He tells us to stop reading. Not mildly, as in "You can quit now if you like," but emphatically, as in "STOP READING NOW!" He compares himself to a ship that's about to cross very deep water, and worries that we're trying to follow him in "pretty little boats." He has zero confidence that we're up for it. "Turn back," he writes. "The sea I sail has never yet been passed."

Some commentaries on *The Divine Comedy* interpret this as Dante letting his arrogance out for romp, boasting that he's so stupendously talented no reader could possibly follow his brilliant logic and exquisite artistry. I disagree. I think Dante had a literal experience that blew his mind so completely he knew nothing he ever wrote could fully convey it: a massive satori.

Dante writes that once he no longer thinks "like one who dreams," he finds himself in a place so luminous he can barely describe it. His description echoes terms used by those who acknowledge the phenomenon of absolute integrity: "awakening" and "enlightenment." The imagery and concepts Dante uses to tell us about paradise are similar to descriptions of the enlightened state recorded by Zen masters, Hindu yogis, Gnostic and Sufi mystics, and shamans from many tribal cultures. This is why I believe Dante's *Paradiso* is an account of his own awakening. What reads like a fantasy could be closer to a literal description than most of us imagine.

Current research shows that the experience of enlightenment is a consistent neurological reality that can occur at different levels. If you follow the way of integrity far enough, you, too, may find yourself "rising" into it—maybe in small ways, maybe in big ones. In this chapter, we'll look at the pragmatic aspects of this esoteric concept, considering how it works and what to do about it.

HOW AWAKENING WORKS

Some people experience enlightenment as one huge, irreversible event. Others sense it in moments of insight and heightened perception that gradually increase and lengthen. Two modern authors who experienced a huge satori are Byron Katie and Eckhart Tolle. Both people emerged suddenly from deep misery into absolute bliss. Both were so disoriented by the experience that it took them years to readapt to functioning "normally" in society. Most people who follow the way of integrity experience a series of smaller moments of enlightenment, which begin to add up to a whole new worldview.

Either way, satori experiences are hard to describe, partly because our culture has no language for them and partly because, as Dante says, it's impossible to describe in words what it's like to transcend the state of being human. Centuries earlier, the Chinese philosopher Lao Tzu wrote, "Those who know don't talk; those who talk don't know." This seems to be a common frustration for people who experience enlightenment: language cannot communicate it. They could tell us about the taste of honey for years, they say, and we'd have less idea what they were talking about than if we tasted one spoonful.

Still, some enlightened people attempt to describe what they know, and Dante is one of them. Throughout his adventures in paradise, he tries to explain two basic perceptions that are alien to his prior human experience. First, he no longer feels any separation from anyone or anything. It's absolutely obvious to him that the entire universe is just one entity. Second, his personal will (Buddhists might call it his "ego") begins to dissolve, and diminishes steadily the further he goes into paradise. He finds himself directed by absolute love, which also motivates the actions of everyone else in paradise. The people he meets have their own identities and objectives, but at the same time they are all one, moved by love.

Enlightened people throughout history have described these same realizations. The sense of oneness and the dissolution into love show up consistently in people who have "awakened." In his classic work *The Varieties of Religious Experience*, psychologist William James summed up common elements that run through enlightenment accounts from every time and place. They include:

- A subjective experience of "inner light"
- A deepening of moral or spiritual values
- An increased sense of intellectual illumination
- A loss of the fear of death
- A loss of a sense of sin or guilt
- A lasting transformation of personality

Educated people in our culture either ignore such states of illumination, dismiss them as overheated religiosity, or see them as mental illness—despite the fact that people who've had them often abandon religion while becoming much more mentally stable, happy, and loving. "Who cares?" says our rationalist, materialist culture. "It's all nonsense! It's delusional to perceive an inner light, to have no fear of death, to lose all sense of guilt. *It's attacking our way of life!*"

Yes, it is.

And that doesn't make it any less real.

Neurologist Andrew Newberg, after a lifetime of studying the brain, writes, "Based on our scientific evidence, I now believe that the stories found in ancient texts are real in that they are related to specific neurological events that can permanently change the structure and functioning of the brain. The path toward Enlightenment is not only real, but we are biologically predisposed to seek it." Brain scientists are hard at work figuring out how and why.

THE NEUROLOGY OF AWAKENING

If you've ever learned the solution to a riddle and had that little burst of satisfaction Oprah famously called an aha moment, you've had a tiny taste of enlightenment. Imagine how it would feel to have that sudden breakthrough, that burst of illumination, solve every problem in your life all at once. Boom! Satori.

According to brain scientists, the feeling of an aha moment is associated with a sudden decrease of electrical activity in two areas of the brain. These are the same areas that seem permanently "switched off" in monks who've spent tens of thousands of hours seeking enlightenment through meditation. Activity in these brain regions correlates with two subjective feelings that underlie our everyday experience: the sense of being a separate thing, distinct from the rest of reality, and the sense that we're in control of ourselves and our situations.

Remember Dante's feeling that all reality is one united

thing, and all action is driven by love? That's what people feel when these "separateness" and "control" areas of the brain go quiet.

This experience is no less real than our usual perceptions, but it makes us much, much happier—and even a short experience of it can transform us permanently. A small mountain of research is showing that some substances, like psilocybin mushrooms, can turn off our usual brain patterns and allow more interaction between the other parts of the brain. The result? For many subjects under close medical supervision, one dose of these substances, one experience of the brain state associated with "awakening," can permanently end compulsive behaviors or leave terminally ill patients free from their fear of death.

You don't need a substance to have this experience. In culture after culture, people have found that processes similar to the methods in this book—watching one's thoughts and questioning them until they dissolve—has the same beneficent effect on the brain. Daniel Goleman of Harvard and Richard Davidson from the University of Wisconsin have done years of research on the neurology of meditation. They found that persistent self-contemplation and inquiry turns a temporary brain *state* of unity and love into a permanent, structural brain *trait*.

This doesn't require years of meditation in caves and ashrams either. As Newberg writes, our brains are biologically programmed to move toward awakening. This process kicks in every time we drop attachment to belief, shut down the

"separation" and "control" areas of our brains, and allow ourselves to align with our true nature. Want a taste? Try this:

EXERCISE:
Dropping into enlightenment

1. **Start by sitting with both hands outstretched, palms up.**
   Get comfortable. By actually lifting your hands, you're
   activating both hemispheres of your brain, so don't skip
   this step or the exercise won't work.

2. **Think of something you do regularly, even though you
   think you shouldn't:** obsessing about your ex, playing
   computer games at work, googling yourself. Call this the
   Forbidden Thing.

3. **Imagine that sitting in the palm of your left hand is a
   tiny version of a wild animal.** This is the part of you that
   wants to do the Forbidden Thing. If you're sleepy and
   irritable, it might be a napping tiger. If you're nervous
   and pent-up, it might be a trembling bunny. See it looking at you from the palm of your hand, wary and wild.
   Call it the Creature.

4. **In your right hand, picture a three-inch-tall version of
   your most socially appropriate self**—the one who believes
   the Forbidden Thing is wrong. This part of you is very
   well socialized. It would never stand by a buffet table
   eating all the shrimp or speak roughly to your mother or
   pick its nose. Call this version of yourself the Controller.

5. Notice that the Controller is always trying to dictate what the Creature does. **See how the Creature aches for freedom to just be itself. See how much effort the Controller is using to suppress the Creature.** Remember the times your Controller seemed to be running things, only to have your Creature break loose and do all sorts of Forbidden Things.

6. **As you observe these two versions of yourself, consider this:** Both of them are good. **The Creature is trying to be free. The Controller is trying to be socially acceptable.** Can you see how tired your Creature is of being yelled at by the Controller? Can you see that the Controller is just as exhausted?

7. When you can see this, **begin offering loving wishes to both the Creature and the Controller** at the same time. Silently say—to *both* of them—"May you be well." "May you be happy." "May you feel free." "May you feel safe." "May all your longing be fulfilled."

8. Once you can genuinely feel compassion for both your Creature and your Controller, ask yourself: At this moment, what am *I*?

You're not the Creature, nor the Controller. You're watching both of them. Caring. Meaning them well. At this point, you have moved into the part of your brain that calms inner conflict and emanates peace. Call this the Compassionate Witness. Feel that this is your core identity.

Welcome home.

"DON'T KNOW MIND"

As long as we dress enlightenment in mechanistic terms ("It's all just brain activity!") we can squeeze it into our cultural paradigm and feel marginally comfortable with it. But in fact, people who experience the internal sensation of enlightenment often have seemingly "miraculous" experiences that are impossible to chalk up to the voltage in their gray matter. I've had many such experiences, and seen them happen to my clients, as well.

For example, I once coached a woman I'll call Violet who said she sometimes had prescient dreams. At the same time, I was working (confidentially) with a movie star who lived in Hollywood. One day Violet mentioned she'd had a dream about me. Then she described, with incredible accuracy, a session I'd had a few days earlier with my Hollywood client. I'd met with this actress in her home, which was filled with exotic aquariums. As she recounted her dream, Violet named the client, described the house and the aquariums, even told me what we'd both been wearing.

What, exactly, was going on here?

I don't know.

Another client, Russ, was visiting New York when he got hopelessly lost. He parked his rental car to study a paper map (this was before GPS), and only then realized that the place he'd stopped was next to the cemetery where his father was buried. Russ's parents had divorced when he was five, and his father had basically disappeared, leaving Russ with an inferno full of hell thoughts like "I wasn't a good son" and "I'm not lovable."

When Russ was fifteen, his father died. The day of the funeral was the one and only time Russ had been to this cemetery ("I couldn't have found it on purpose to save my life," he told me). On the day he accidentally ended up at this very place, he got out of his rental car, walked to his father's grave, and stood there for a long time, letting go of all his hell thoughts. Eventually he reached a level of pure peace he'd never felt before.

At that moment, Russ said, he felt a tug on his pants leg and looked down to see that a small poodle had taken hold of his cuff. Russ crouched to pet the dog, and it bounced around him in "puppy play posture." A few seconds later the owner appeared, red-faced and apologetic.

"Axel!" she called. "Axel, get back here!" She turned to Russ and said, "I'm so sorry. He never does this! AXEL, COME HERE!" But the dog wouldn't come. Eventually the owner had to pick him up and carry him away.

"Here's the thing," Russ told me later. "My father's name was Axel."

What was happening here?

I don't know.

In fact, the further I go on the way of integrity, the more I know that I don't know much about how reality works. For an American, admitting to such total ignorance is anathema. We aim to know *everything*. We're socialized to think that not knowing is stupid and shameful. But in traditions like Zen, "don't know mind" refers to a way of thinking that's free from rigid concepts, as clear and fluid as air. "In the beginner's mind there are many possibilities," said Suzuki Roshi. "In the expert's there are few." From a place of enlightenment, the mind's job isn't to shore up beliefs, but to let them go.

Once you've dissolved many hell thoughts, you may accidentally begin applying your integrity skills to seemingly incontrovertible facts, like "It's raining." Can you absolutely know that's true? No. After all, you could be dreaming the day. You could be dreaming that you're reading this. You could be, as the ancient Taoist teacher Chuang Tzu wrote, "a butterfly dreaming that it is a person." The Indian sage Nisargadatta Maharaj once commented, "The only true statement the mind can make is 'I do not know.'"

"MAGIC" AND "MIRACLES"

As mentioned, I'm nowhere near enlightened. Nevertheless, I've had many mysterious experiences. I don't believe in "magic" in the sense that these events defy science; I just think there's a lot science hasn't yet figured out. And it seems that the more I dissolve my internal suffering, the more these mysterious things happen.

For me, these mysterious experiences rose sharply around the time my scandalous memoir was published. I had to burn through a lot of hell thoughts just to cope with my anxiety about what would happen when the book came out. A couple of weeks before the publication date, the *New York Times* ran an article about my book. I was amazed that they thought this newsworthy; I'd expected to ruffle feathers in Utah, but I never thought the rest of the world would care. Yet there I was, being interviewed by a *Times* reporter so expressionless he could have played world-class poker. I had no clue what he was thinking. I braced myself for anything that might happen on the day the *NYT* ran that article. Or so I thought. Nothing could have prepared me for what actually occurred on that day.

In the early hours of the morning in question, I snapped from deep sleep to intense alertness as if I'd been launched from a catapult. Something strange was happening. The best way I can describe it is to say my bedroom was filled with beauty. Nothing visible or audible, but some kind of exquisite presence that bypassed my senses and went straight to my emotions. Though I'd never felt anything exactly like it, I knew what it was. It was my father. Not the troubled personality I'd known since birth, but his essence, his true nature.

Imagine spending your entire life trying to listen to a symphony through a broken radio, hearing traces of gorgeous music distorted by static so bad it sets your teeth on edge. Then imagine waking up in the middle of the orchestra. No static. No separation. Just beauty.

I sat there for a long time, suffused with love. I wondered why this was happening. Was it because the *New York Times* article had hit the streets on the East Coast? I knew that my story was out now, just like the stories told by my father and his religion. We were even, and I was free to love him unreservedly. I sat wondering about this until the sun rose. Then I got up and prepared for yet another interview. During that conversation, someone called to tell me that in the early hours of the morning, my father had died.

Right in front of the reporter, I began to sob. The death of a parent is always intense, even if you've been estranged. But mostly I was crying because I felt another wave of that same beauty, that silent symphony of absolutely connected, pure love.

My father's passing ended most of the legal attacks targeted at me, but it gave extra vigor to the *illegal* ones. People who were already angry at me got even angrier. As I moved forward into my book tour, Mormons showed up at bookstores, TV studios, and radio stations, trying to block my appearance. Every time I dressed for a speech or book signing I couldn't help thinking about the death threats, wondering if someone in the crowd would have a gun, if these would be the last clothes I'd ever wear. But whenever I felt too scared to go on, I'd feel a calming surge of the sweet energy that woke me on the morning of my father's death.

Now, I'm not saying my actual father showed up in some metaphysical form to give me comfort and support . . . but I'm not saying he *didn't* either. To come down dogmatically on either side would be to claim I'm sure of something I don't understand, and that's not integrity.

I just don't know.

GOING BACK FOR THE LOST PIECES OF OURSELVES

"Don't know mind" is, above all, freedom from limiting beliefs. Knowing that you don't know everything doesn't turn you into a drooling ignoramus. On the contrary, it liberates your vastly intelligent true nature to see reality as it is, not as your culture taught you to see it.

As a character in his own poem, Dante the character just floats up into eternal glory. But Dante the actual person—after what I think was a real-life enlightenment experience—didn't disappear into the light. He stuck around to have a huge impact on society. Because he broke with tradition by refusing to write in Latin, using his own Tuscan vernacular instead, he unified different dialects and became "the father of the Italian language." He created images that still remain in our popular imagination. He made strong political statements about abuse of power among politicians and the Catholic Church. And, of course, he created a roadmap to enlightenment in *The Divine Comedy*. Dante became a real-life version of his own character Virgil, returning to the dark wood of error, helping lost people find the way to peace. Once he'd experienced freedom, he set others free.

This makes Dante a lot like all other enlightened masters. Since people who are "awake" experience everyone and everything as part of themselves, and since they are driven by compassion, their primary goal is to set themselves completely free by freeing other people. As Nobel laureate Toni Morrison said, "The function of freedom is to free someone else."

This is why great spiritual teachers like the Buddha and Jesus spent all their time trying to show others the way out of suffering. I've met at least three people who strike me as completely enlightened. All three have told me how they "awoke" from intense suffering, and all three now lead lives of continuous service.

The first is Byron Katie, whom I met after I'd been reading her books and doing her Work for a long time. After her abrupt, total enlightenment experience, people in Katie's hometown of Barstow, California, began talking about the "lit lady" who could heal people's hearts. Without ever intending to, she gradually went from local celebrity to world-famous spiritual teacher. This was not her goal. Her only goal, she says, is to "travel to the ends of the earth for any person that is suffering."

Case number two is Anita Moorjani. Anita was born into a South Asian culture in which, she told me, she was expected to enter an arranged marriage and spend her life doing housework. In her forties, Anita developed lymphoma, which progressed until she descended into her final coma. As family members gathered to say goodbye, Anita says she found herself in a luminous reality full of love and beauty. There she met her deceased father, who told her she needed to go back—she had a lot of life left to live.

This seemed dubious to Anita, given that her body was basically a skeleton weighing less than ninety pounds and riddled with lemon-sized tumors. Her father told her not to worry—now that she understood more about reality, her disease would be no problem. A stack of medical records attests to what happened next. Not only did Anita regain consciousness, but her tumors began to melt away. Within nine days, she was cancer free.

As news of Anita's recovery spread, an American publisher contacted her, asking her to write a memoir. Her book *Dying to Be Me* launched her as a spiritual teacher who, like Byron Katie, travels the world trying to help people escape suffering and live in joy.

Another person whose entire life healed, and who then began healing others, is a man I'll call Larry J., since that's how he's known as a twelve-step sponsor. He grew up on the streets of Brooklyn, experiencing many forms of neglect and abuse. He wanted to become a police officer—until, like every other Black person he knew, he experienced so much harassment and brutality that he later told me, "I wished death on every policeman." Larry started drinking early—early in life, early every day. As an adult his alcoholism finally became so disabling that he joined Alcoholics Anonymous and made the recommended commitment to "ninety meetings in ninety days."

"On the seventieth day," Larry told me, "I realized, 'Oh my God, I'm an alcoholic!'" He laughed uproariously at the memory. "Damn, I just had a spiritual awakening!"

But the story wasn't over. Larry thought, "Now I'm not drinking, my head's so much clearer I'll be a much better gambler!" Years later, flat broke and suicidal, he decided to try Gamblers Anonymous. This time, Larry followed the full way of integrity. He burned all kinds of inferno errors, what AA calls "defects of character." His first steps up purgatory were well-nigh impossible.

"My sponsor said, 'You got to tell your wife the truth.' I said, 'Man, I live on the fifth floor. She is going to throw me out of *a fifth-floor window.*'"

Larry's wife didn't leave—after four decades, they're still together. Larry gradually came to devote more and more of his life to helping others. "I work for the big boss now," he says. "I wake up every morning and say 'Who am I? Where am I? What am I?' Then I help people. It's something you don't even think about." He spends all day, every day, taking calls from people in various twelve-step programs, as well as local young people and other friends. People come to Larry aching, confused, and broken, and go away lifted by his wisdom.

These three people, from very different backgrounds, are like the same song being sung in slightly different registers. I believe they've followed the way of integrity all the way back to their own innocence, their own paradise. Now, like Dante's Virgil—like Dante himself—they spend their time finding people who are lost in the dark and guiding them toward freedom.

HELPING OTHERS ALONG THE WAY OF INTEGRITY

We don't have to be totally enlightened to feel ourselves drawn to help others. Whatever measure of integrity we find seems to turn us toward service. This started happening to me around the same time I wrote *Leaving the Saints*. While teaching at Thunderbird Business School, I often found myself advising students to abandon their cultural training when it ran contrary to their true nature. They began asking if they could pay me to advise them outside of class. Before I knew it, I was running seminars and seeing clients full-time.

This was confusing. I'd never set out to be any kind of counselor, and I'm very introverted. I decided to write down everything I thought might help people, so they could read a book instead of consulting me in the flesh. This strategy backfired: the book just attracted more clients. This was when I read in a newspaper that I was a "life coach." Once, when I spoke at a coaching convention, someone asked me for my marketing strategy. I truthfully answered, "Concealment and evasion." But people kept finding me, and when they did I always found that I wanted to help them. Every client felt like a lost piece of myself.

Over the years, as more and more of my clients and readers emerged from suffering, they began asking me to teach them my coaching methods. They felt connected to everyone who was suffering, driven by love rather than fear. They wanted— desperately wanted—to spend their lives trawling the dark wood of error for lost people, then Virgiling them back to happiness. So I trained a dozen coaches. Then another dozen. Today, there are thousands.

I ask all these folks to follow their own way of integrity, not mine. Each person's path is unique. I've watched many of these brilliant people gravitate to forms of service I couldn't have imagined: helping others while experiencing their own versions of paradise. They've told me about countless "miracles," some large, some small, that helped them along the way. Their own versions of paradise appear around them spontaneously.

After I'd spent years coaching and training coaches, someone asked me what I do for a living. When I told her, she said, "Oh, my God, how did you get that job?" Here's how: I started in the dark wood of error, went through hell several times, and clambered up purgatory until I reached a basic level of functioning integrity. Then I took countless one-degree turns in the direction of my true nature.

You can follow this same process to your own paradise, but your adventures on the way of integrity won't look exactly like mine. They'll be a three-dimensional self-portrait of your individual best life, your own specific enlightenment. But once you leave suffering behind, I suspect you'll spend at least part of your time going back to the dark wood of error, looking for suffering people—the lost pieces of yourself.

At that point you may fit in easily with the culture that surrounds you, or you may be a bit different. You could be so different you significantly challenge your culture. Like Dante, you may even transform it. Or, if you happen to be situated in a culture that's truly destructive to truth, you may shatter its false foundational beliefs, illuminate it by speaking a deeper truth, and help bring it all into integrity. This isn't an act of violence, but a natural creative consequence of living your personal truth.

At this particular moment in history, shattering culture may not only be the key to your own happiness, but essential for the future of humanity. As change accelerates, everything out of integrity in our culture is starting to fall apart. Overcrowding natural habitats transfers unknown viruses from animals to humans. Economic models originally built on slave labor are beginning to shatter at their foundations. Even the weather is turning into "global weirdness" because of human behavior. These are difficult, frightening times. It's hard to see how one small person can help. But you can. Your next steps on the way of integrity—*our* next steps—could change everything.

14.

Humanity at the Gates

If you've ever looked down from an airplane at a forest, you may have noticed that from high above, the trees look a lot like a bunch of broccoli—and also like some of the cumulus clouds around you. Or you may have seen a system of rivers snaking toward the sea, and realized that it looks very similar to the shape of a plant's roots—and also a lot like the nerves and veins that interlace in your own body.

This isn't a coincidence. Bunching and branching tend to occur when similar natural patterns repeat over and over again at different sizes. These patterns are called "fractals," and nature is full of them.

Fractals form because of the interplay between the basic shapes and forces that make up the material world. For example, a molecule of water—two atoms of hydrogen and one of oxygen—is literally shaped like a little triangle. When water molecules interact with each other at low temperatures, the hydrogen atoms stick together in characteristic rings of six. That's why, though snowflakes are infinitely varied, they're always variations on the basic shape of a hexagon.

When basic fractal shapes add up, they form similar versions of themselves at different sizes. This principle is an underlying feature of physical reality. It happens when shapes *reiterate*, when one pattern shows up over and over again because the forms and forces creating them happen over and over. The basic shape of a tree trunk is reflected at a smaller scale in each branch, a pattern that shows up again in each twig. Again, no two of these shapes are identical, but they're all very similar.

You can see beautiful versions of fractals by looking online at what happens when mathematicians simply reiterate certain equations (google "fractals" or "Mandelbrot sets").

Something similar to "fractaling" happens when people change their behavior, as you will on your way of integrity. The "shape" of your life—your words and actions—will shift in ways that affect the people around you. As those people change, the shift in their lives will affect the people around *them*. The pattern of integrity recurs in the same shape but at a larger scale. As a twig is to a branch is to a tree trunk, so one human's integrity is to a couple's, a family's, a nation's. This is how individuals and small groups may end up influencing huge numbers of people.

For instance, as you work through this book, you might get more honest with yourself about what you really need to be happy. This might make you more straightforward about stating your needs to your best friend or your partner. If that works out well, it might create a base of experience and emotional support that could help you start acting more assertively at your job. This, in turn, could influence everyone on your work team, creating more openness and clarity in the whole group just as it did in your intimate relationship and your inner life. The "fractal" of your integrity would replicate itself at different sizes.

As you reach higher levels of integrity, the sense of connectedness and love we saw in the last chapter will turn you toward helping others in some way. Remember, this is an inevitable result of the unity and compassion that emerge as we come closer to pure truth. At this point, your effect on the people around you gains velocity and power. "Fractals" of your integrity will show up in larger and larger ways, each slightly different but similarly beautiful.

Of course, darkness has its own fractals. A value system built on avarice, ambition, and oppression shows up in unprincipled leaders, corrupt groups, and then entire national cultures. This often makes the news and appears overwhelming. But positive qualities spread and replicate as fast as—maybe faster than—negative ones. Byron Katie, Anita Moorjani, and Larry J. made no effort to gain "followers," but people were drawn to them by the dozens, then hundreds, then thousands. People like Lao Tzu, the Buddha, and Jesus have influenced lives by the billion.

My point is that as you follow the way of integrity, solely to end your own suffering, you will end up helping the whole world.

And oh, my, does this world ever need it.

THE WORLD IN THE DARK WOOD OF ERROR

Right now, humanity as a whole has an enormous case of dark wood of error syndrome. The most dominant societies on Earth are riddled with false, divisive beliefs. We have deep cultural tendencies to separate and "other" people from different categories of class and race. We falsely divide human beings from nature. We've been doing this for several centuries, and the fractures of integrity affect us collectively in the same way they affect us individually. I have no idea what will be going on in the world as you read this book. But as I'm writing it, in mid-2020, things are not looking good.

Despite achieving so many Mount Delectable goals (fancier technologies, more billionaires), humanity as a whole is not feeling better. Let's consider those dark wood of error symptoms. How is humanity's mood lately? Studies consistently show that, as one Gallup poll put it, "Collectively, the world is more stressed, worried, and in pain today than we've ever seen it." What about physical illness? Two words: global pandemic. Relationship problems? According to one expert, ideological conflict "is tearing at the seams of democracies around the world."

What about careers? Economically, we're looking at a situation similar to the Great Depression, only worse. Addiction to all sorts of activities and substances is at an all-time high. And let's not forget what scientists keep telling us: the harm we're doing to the biological systems that keep us alive may already be irreversible.

In short, humanity is not in structural integrity; if it were an airplane, it would be nosediving. The human population is bigger than ever, growing faster than ever, and self-destructing all around us. Rivets are popping. Engines are catching fire. We're losing altitude and the ability to steer. Since history began there have always been doomsayers predicting that humanity is headed to hell in a handbasket. Now, by any logical measure, we're watching it happen.

Despite all this, the typical "fractal" of humans, from individuals to governments to whole populations, is still focused on climbing Mount Delectable, looking for more money, power, and status. These goals are not the solution; they're the root of the problem. The only thing that will keep us from destroying ourselves at a collective level is exactly what keeps us from destroying ourselves at an individual level.

You know how this process works, because it's the same at all levels of human groups. First, we have to collectively identify places we've deviated from the truth as a culture—for example, by believing that we aren't connected to one another or the natural world. Then we burn up our false assumptions, recognize our next steps toward truth, and change our actions.

The whole human species desperately needs to find the way of integrity.

BECOMING THE CHANGE YOU WISH TO SEE IN THE WORLD

Looking at the scale and intensity of humanity's problems, it's easy to panic or despair. What can you, personally, do to help—one tiny person among more than seven billion? It may seem that following your own way of integrity will just give you a slightly more comfortable seat on the *Titanic*. But remember, nature works in fractals, and total integrity often causes whole systems to adjust course. As you follow your own way of integrity, the effect on everyone and everything around you may be greater than you can imagine.

The bad news is that if you don't find integrity yourself, even your best intentions will only replicate the dysfunctions of your culture. You can't build a high-performance airplane out of broken parts. The good news is that once you've aligned your whole life with truth, you'll automatically begin working to repair damage wherever you find it. You won't be able to witness suffering without responding in some way (your unique, particular way). As you make your one-degree turns toward your own happiness, you'll stop being part of humanity's problems and become part of the solution.

One thing that can happen at this point is a sense of increased social pressure. I've seen this in many of my clients and coaches as they "become the change they wish to see in the world." High levels of integrity draw attention, and more attention can be scary. It's like driving a compact car around a parking lot at five miles an hour, then suddenly finding yourself in an eighteen-wheeler barreling down the freeway at seventy-five. As the speed and momentum increase, your driving skills need to be more and more impeccable.

If you begin to feel overwhelmed by other people's attention, or swept up in the social energy of larger and larger groups, it's helpful to review your basic integrity skills to help you stay the course. Here's a reminder list:

- Notice your own dark wood of error symptoms even when they're very slight—a touch of irritation here, a wave of fatigue there. Immediately address *any* level of suffering in yourself. Even a slight drift off course can have serious consequences as your fractal gets bigger.
- Connect frequently with soul teachers who can ground you in your own integrity. Read their books, watch them online, connect with them in real life.
- Practice connecting with your own sense of truth, your inner teacher, every day. Notice the difference between thoughts that give you that ring of alignment and those that make you feel fragmented or off-center.
- As loud cultural "voices" push you in various directions— often contradictory ones—remember to leave them all behind and check in with your sense of truth whenever you feel confused.

- Acknowledge your own mistakes as soon as you notice them. Abandon all cowardice: when you break through denial, acknowledge your errors and move bravely to a more honest position.

- If you learn something that contradicts what you've always believed, don't reflexively double down on your opinions. Remain open to the idea that even your most basic beliefs may be wrong. Have the humility to let them go when your inner teacher realizes you've been mistaken.

- Catch yourself whenever you begin "othering" people. With divisiveness so prevalent and all forms of attack escalated by the echo chambers of the internet, it's tempting to generalize and join the fray of destructive attack. Make sure your anger against injustice finds modes of expression that purposefully create things (including boundaries!), rather than randomly destroying them.

- Refuse to betray yourself by believing anything that clearly causes suffering. For example, if someone says you're inferior to others, don't buy it. If someone says you're superior, don't buy that either. As Byron Katie says, "Don't believe things onto yourself."

- Once you've found clarity within, refuse to lie—and remember that there are times when silence is a lie. Say what you really mean when it feels right, even though others might not approve.

- Make sure you spend your time doing what you really want or moving toward what you really want in a series of one-degree turns.
- Be transparent: hide less and less of yourself. As Mark Twain said about doing right, this "will gratify some people and astonish the rest." The astonished will separate from you. The gratified will bond with you more closely. You will gather a community of like minds.
- As you meet and interact with these people, really listen to them. Look them in the eyes, hear the kindness in their voices, feel their acceptance. Allow the "beams of love" to light up your inner life.
- Forgive yourself for violating your integrity when you didn't know better. Let go of your mistakes. Remember and value everything you've done that accords with your sense of truth.

Does this all feel like a grimly virtuous way to live? In fact, it's the opposite. Your way of integrity will lead you to serve the world in ways that increase your own happiness. As Larry says, on the path to happiness, our final destination is service.

HOW INTEGRITY SPREADS

I've watched many people follow the way of integrity, and virtually all of them began contributing to the common good in ways that were very specific to their own true natures. The most common thing I hear from clients and coaches at that point is "I can't believe I get to do this!" Whether they're engaged in service as their full-time occupation, or doing it on the side while raising families and holding down other jobs, they feel lifted, illuminated, and miraculously supported, like Dante in paradise. Remember what the poet learned in purgatory: love doesn't divide the pool of goodness available to all humanity, but multiplies it for everyone.

Whatever you do to heal the world, it will replace dark wood of error symptoms with purpose, happiness, vitality, love, abundance, and fascination that specifically match your true nature. Maybe you'll simply spend all your time "Virgiling": connecting with people who feel lost and miserable, helping them burn up their own internal suffering and then change their behavior to claim integrity. Or maybe you'll help the cause of truth through some form of science, service, political action, or artistic expression. Remember how much Dante managed to change his culture. (True, he was a genius, but he was also one solitary man trying to light up the entire Dark Ages.)

In my own life, following the way of integrity has led to situations that fulfill long-term heart's desires, even though they may not be everyone's cup of tea. I'm not really sure how they happened, but I know that if I hadn't been so focused on staying in integrity, I wouldn't have stumbled into so many wonderful opportunities.

For example, I was born obsessed with animals. I mean *obsessed*. By age two I could name every animal in my family's book of seven hundred mammal species. Since we didn't have a television, we'd go to my grandmother's house every Sunday to watch *Mutual of Omaha's Wild Kingdom*, a program about wild creatures and ecosystems. I had endless fantasies about going into the wilderness and connecting with animals myself. I planned to be a zoologist or ecologist.

Somewhere on the path to adult life I dropped this idea and began climbing Mount Delectable toward full professorship in a prestigious, accredited blah blah blah. But then I hit the various "life accidents" described in this book: my son's diagnosis, reemerging childhood trauma, my tell-all book and the reaction to it, coming out as gay. These events stripped away almost every part of my psyche that wasn't devoted to finding peace.

Then, on a book tour in South Africa, I met a family who devote all their time to something they call "restoring Eden." Starting with an immense barren cattle farm near Kruger National Park, the Varty family corrected watercourses, cleared invasive plants, and let indigenous fauna and animals return. Now they run a game preserve called Londolozi (taken from a Zulu term that means "protector of all living things") and also help thousands of rural South Africans reach higher levels of income and education.

Talking to these folks woke up a part of me that I'd split from my consciousness somewhere on Mount Delectable. I wondered where my own particular skill set could contribute to restoring Eden. Over the following years, the Vartys and I developed change-your-life safari seminars together. We now run them annually at Londolozi. Our first-world guests come

to South Africa, connect with nature (in the world and in themselves), and return home feeling restored. I donate all my own
earnings from the seminars and about a month of my time to
the cause of restoring Eden. What do I get out of the deal?
Oh, well, only the chance to realize my wildest, most precious
childhood dreams.

Here's how it feels to me as I look into my own memory:
I'm a little kid, staring at my grandmother's TV, longing intensely to be in nature with wild animals. Then, suddenly, I'm
a middle-aged woman sitting in a grassy South African meadow
while monkeys and nyalas forage around me. I'm laughing in
an open Land Rover as a baby hyena tastes my shoe. I'm reaching out my hand to let a friendly wild ostrich touch it with her
beak. I'm standing in the dark, alone except for an elephant
who's grazing an arm's length from me, his huge head blotting
out a patch of stars. And amid all these incredible gifts, I'm
doing "work" that helps heal the land, plants, animals, and some
of the world's most vulnerable people.

How did I get this job? By going through my own hellgates,
burning my own falsehoods, and bringing my own life into
alignment, one-degree turn by one-degree turn.

Of course, this isn't where I intend my service to end—I
have no idea where life will take me as I uncover more blind
spots and integrate more truth. But this is where the way of
integrity has led so far. Yours will take you home to your own
true nature, where you'll find your own longed-for rewards,
your own greatest joy. I've seen this happen hundreds of times.

Here's what some of my clients and friends are doing as the fractals of their integrity spread out around them:

- Seth helps wealthy landowners create farms that provide organic food for the local poor, reduce animal suffering, and grow plants that are particularly good at pulling carbon dioxide out of the air and replacing it with oxygen.
- Amira learned techniques for releasing her own trauma, then began teaching them to individuals and groups in her native Syria.
- Liam spends part of every day learning and posting online about various forms of social injustice. His funny, insightful, sometimes painful rhetoric has raised donations for more than a dozen helping agencies.
- Jasmine is having a baby and planning to raise her child with love, tolerance, and the intention to do good in the world.
- Zoe travels widely to study the ocean and its creatures, writing books and articles about how to stop the destruction of marine ecosystems.
- Grace helps shelter animals find happy homes.
- Khalan makes podcasts in remote wilderness locations, speaking about the intersection of personal growth, spiritual awakening, and connection to nature.
- Alex is a nonbinary person who writes popular online fantasy novels about gender-fluid worlds, creating new ways for people in this world to imagine gender roles.

None of these people, so far as I know, started out with a plan to do what they're now doing. Each of them grew up in cultures that pulled them away from their true natures. Each suffered dark wood of error symptoms, and each went through a personal inferno to dissolve their belief in cultural assumptions that didn't work for them. Each turned slowly but consistently away from their Mount Delectable pursuits to do things that made them happy. They all faced opposition and "change-back attacks" from others but refused to abandon themselves again. Now they serve the world not to be virtuous but because doing what they're doing fulfills their deepest yearning.

FRACTALS OF ENLIGHTENMENT

In the end, I believe, people who follow the way of integrity can illuminate even the darkest times. This is why, through thousands of years of history, human civilization has slowly, erratically, haltingly inched closer to ideals like equality and freedom. It's why unusual individuals who have left culture to find their own truth (the Buddha walking away from his palace into the jungle, Jesus retreating into the desert) have changed billions of lives. It's why Dante's *Divine Comedy*, that succession of strange stories and images, is widely considered one of the greatest works of human literature.

These people get our attention because part of us is inexorably drawn to integrity. At some level we know that lies hurt us, lame us, ground us—even if we don't know we're lying. We can feel in our marrow that the truth sets us free. At some point, everyone who wants to escape suffering begins fumbling in the dark toward awakening. As a species, not just as individuals, we are biologically wired to seek enlightenment.

Here's an exercise that will not only help you steer toward your own pure integrity but also act to help everyone and everything else. So far we've talked about your individual integrity fractaling out to the world. Now we're going to invert the process (since fractal patterns can move in either direction, small to large or large to small). This exercise will help you see connections between things you do to improve your own life, and things that you can do to affect the rest of the world.

EXERCISE:
You are the world

1. Sit with your eyes closed and picture Earth from space, a perfect sphere of blue, green, brown, and white, hanging in a pitch-dark vacuum.

2. As you look at your home planet, think about the problems and sources of suffering that seem to threaten it most.

3. Let yourself focus on something you find especially troubling. It might be racism, political corruption, poverty, climate change, cruelty to animals, war, or crime. Whatever sparks the strongest reaction in you, allow it. Don't try

to get the "right" answer, to choose what's most virtuous or politically correct. Feel what you really feel.

4. "Zoom in" on the issue you've identified. Though it will be painful, really focus on what's going wrong. Remember everything you've ever learned about it. Know what you really know.

5. As you let yourself feel outrage or despair about this issue, write down everything that's wrong about it. Say what you really mean. Make a list. If necessary, continue the list on a separate sheet of paper.

The global issue that bothers me most is creating all these problems:

_____

_____

_____

_____

_____

_____

_____

_____

6. Now write down what must happen to fix this problem. You don't need to have sophisticated answers, or even logical ones, at this point. Just say (or write) what you really mean: "People have got to stop seeing each other as inferior!" "We must not put any more garbage into the ocean!" "We've got to start treating animals as fellow beings, not objects!" Make another list:

Here's what someone (or everyone) should do to fix these problems:

_____

_____

_____

_____

_____

_____

_____

_____

7. Go back to your image of Earth. Now replace that image with your own body. If you have a negative reaction to that, know that your contribution to the planet is touched by that negativity.

8. Look at the problem you've chosen as your area of focus. Ask yourself: Is there any way in which your treatment of yourself mirrors this problem? Here are some examples:

- You may worry about polluting the land and sea but still put a lot of toxic substances into your own body.

- You may be angry about some human beings seeing others as inferior while seeing yourself as inferior in some way.

- You may hate cruelty to animals but drive your body—an animal—to keep overworking, staying cooped up when it longs to go outside, or forcing it to do work that it hates.

- You may be distressed about poverty while "impoverishing" yourself by denying yourself things like relaxation, kindness, play, or free time.

When you think of a way you are inflicting on yourself the problem you see in the world, write it here:

Here's how my "global issue" shows up in my own life:

_____

_____

_____

_____

_____

_____

9. Now look at your list of things "someone or everyone" should do to fix the problem. Can you apply any of these "fixes" to restoring your own happiness in the area you've just identified?

Ways I could help myself feel better in relation to this problem:

_____

_____

_____

_____

_____

_____

10. Today, spend at least twenty minutes applying what you've just written down. Take at least ten minutes to move toward healing this wound in yourself, and at least ten more working to heal it in the world. Do what you really want. Remember, huge changes happen in tiny steps.

THE TIPPING POINT OF AWAKENING

When we first begin following the way of integrity, it's like cleaning a dirty windowpane, where false beliefs have muddied the clarity of our minds. At first we can only scrub away in the dark, not even able to see what we're doing. After a while, glimmers of light start to sparkle through here and there. At some point the process accelerates rapidly. As bigger areas come clean, we get more motivated, more able to see how the process works. At some point, the whole windowpane effectively vanishes and lets light pour through unobstructed.

I believe this process may apply not just to individuals but to groups of people and humanity as a whole. Throughout history, individuals who are "awake" have been points of clarity where light shines through to others. And as Margaret Mead famously said, "Never doubt that a small group of thoughtful, committed citizens can change the world. Indeed, it is the only thing that ever has." Groups committed to truth and compassion become patches of translucency, even transparency. As this process continues, it's conceivable that humanity as a whole might someday reach the tipping point of enlightenment.

If that ever happened, unexpected things could follow fast. In 2020, after decades of unheeded warnings that we must reduce our fossil fuel consumption, a microscopic virus managed to dramatically alter the behavior of the entire human race in just a few weeks. Almost immediately, the air and water became clearer than they'd been for a century. Deer appeared in the streets of Japanese cities. Bears and wild boars showed up in parts of Europe where they hadn't been seen in living memory. Kangaroos bounded down the streets of Adelaide. When things return to their true nature, they can heal more dramatically and quickly than you might expect.

So follow the way of integrity for your own sake, to leave suffering behind you and experience as much happiness as possible. But don't be surprised that as you do this, your own life will become a clear space through which more and more light shines for others. Our whole species seems to be headed for apocalyptic destruction—but are we sure that will happen? Can we absolutely know it will? Who would we be, what would we do, without that story?

Maybe we can realize the opposite of our worst fear. Maybe we can reach the point where everything reverses, where going down becomes going up. Every individual who develops a clear mind becomes part of a fractal that brings us into alignment with one another and with nature itself. As that pattern spreads, humans may begin to live in a whole new way. Our scrappy, inventive, unthinkably destructive species could end up heading beyond the inferno, all the way to paradise. By following the way of integrity, we just might save ourselves.

15.

The Great Unbuilding

Many people find Dante's *Paradiso* strange and hard to follow. The plotline of the epic all but disappears. Dante starts using language strangely—for example, making pronouns into verbs. He says he isn't sure whether he's a physical body or just pure consciousness. He seems to be moving at light speed through more and more dramatic levels of brilliance and beauty, but Beatrice tells him he's not really moving at all: in paradise, since everything is united, everyone is everywhere.

These ideas, strange though they sound, aren't like the incoherent fantasies of a lunatic, or even a pulp-fiction writer. They match the reported perceptions of reality from people who've been through enlightenment experiences. They also correlate with the way science now describes reality, even though these truths haven't made it into conventional wisdom. For example, we know that at the speed of light, time stops. Traveling at the speed of light, then, one really can be everywhere at the same time. We also know that what we call "matter" may exist only as energy until we measure it. In fact, the most austere version of quantum physics tells us almost exactly what Beatrice tells Dante: that everything in the universe is one single thing (energy field), and that we see it only as bits of matter because our way of perceiving (epistemology) can't take in reality as it actually is (ontology).

It's vanishingly unlikely that Dante just happened to make up incredibly counterintuitive ideas that parallel other enlightenment accounts, as well as quantum physics. I think it's more probable that when people search long and hard for truth, as Dante did, they begin to see things in ways that go beyond their culture's typical worldview into something more accurate.

Western materialism assumes the same reality as Newton's physics: everything is made of chunks of matter bumping into each other. But for at least a century we've known that this isn't accurate. Particles really do exist primarily—maybe only—as clouds of energy. What Einstein called "spooky action at a distance" really does affect them. The universe is more like Dante's paradise than his easier-to-understand descriptions of the inferno or purgatory.

If you follow the way of integrity far enough, your life may go beyond *our* culture's definition of "normal"—not because you're departing from reality, but because you're connecting with it. As the windowpane of your mind becomes clearer, more free from error, you may feel yourself not as separate from the world, but as existing in a continuum with everything around you. This continuity may show up in coincidences so improbable they almost couldn't be accidental, or circumstances that align themselves as if to reflect what you imagine. You may begin experiencing a world similar to Dante's paradise. At that point, there's no predicting what you'll do.

REALITY AND MAGIC

The further I've traveled along my own way of integrity, the stranger the experiences I've had myself. When I write about these experiences, readers with New Age inclinations often seem to believe that I've developed miraculous superpowers, or learned to control reality with my thoughts. Personally, I don't believe in miracles—only in things science doesn't yet understand—and I've never been able to control anything with my thoughts, including my thoughts. The New Age fads bother me so much that these days I actively avoid talking or even thinking about "magical" things, the way I once actively avoided people who wanted me to coach them.

But running doesn't work. Experience has convinced me that the closer we come to our integrity, the more "magical" our lives become.

For example, about a decade before writing this book, I began to wake up many mornings knowing—not just thinking, but *knowing*—that I lived at the edge of a national park in California. This made no sense. I'd never lived in California, much less next to a national forest. But lying on my bed in Phoenix, I *knew* what I'd see when I opened my eyes: an oak forest, a black horse standing in a green field, ridges of mountains fading to the horizon. Over and over, I was genuinely shocked to find myself still in Arizona.

Eventually these morning visions got so clear and compelling I started looking for "my" California property online. It wasn't hard, because I could lie in bed (eyes still closed) and walk through the whole place mentally, noticing exactly what was there. For a few weeks after I started searching the internet, I saw nothing like the property I'd been viewing in my fantasy excursions. And then, by George, I found it.

And so, on my fiftieth birthday, I moved with my family into a small house nestled up against the Los Padres National Forest, in central California. There was no good reason for this, only an irresistible longing to be at this specific place. From the beginning, I felt intensely connected to the land, plants, and animals. Then I developed a new incongruous obsession: meditation. I'd been "sitting" on and off for years, for the same reason I took vitamins and exercised: because I'd read that it was good for me. This was different. The need to meditate felt overwhelming, irresistible.

This seemed even more odd because at first, meditating was the opposite of fun. For about a year, I spent most of my daily meditation time feeling absolutely terrified. My mind flooded with urgent messages like "This can't be right! I should be doing something productive! I need to get a job!" But I'd been using the processes I've described in this book for a long time. Clearly, my thoughts caused suffering. So I didn't obey them. Instead, I watched and questioned them until they dissolved.

By two years in, the windowpane of my mind was much cleaner. My panic disappeared. My body often hummed with the electrical sensation that had chased me into that waterfall twenty years earlier. I learned to tolerate it, then experience it as pure physical bliss.

One day it occurred to me that I could sprinkle myself with birdseed before settling into my usual outdoor meditation. The first time a songbird bird landed on my knee and looked searchingly into my eyes, I thought the love would obliterate me, the way Beatrice's love in paradise almost obliterates Dante. I soon got used to watching little birds stop in the air above me and fall toward me, braking with their wings and extending their feet just prior to contact. One day two chipmunks had a territorial dispute in my open hands, pushing and shoving one another like tiny little sumo wrestlers. That will always remain one of the high points of my life.

Sometimes I heard a pure, ringing tone that seemed to come from the land itself. Often my vision changed, and the whole forest would pixelate into showers of light. Time would seem to stop, or reverse, or collapse. One day I had the thought "How strange that this body had three children" and then immediately realized it wasn't true. Every atom in our bodies is replaced every seven years, so not a single atom of the body I have now was present when my children were born. In reality, my body is not a solid thing, but a constantly shifting assortment of molecules swirling around a wisp of consciousness.

After a few years living away from almost any human cultural influence, I began to see all matter this way. It felt to me—feels to me—as if the entire universe is being projected onto an infinite screen called "now," and that this "now" is in fact the only material thing that even appears to exist. The future isn't here, and the world that's slipping into the past (at this moment, and this one, and this one) is irretrievably gone. Nothing real could ever vanish that completely.

In short, after I moved to the forest I got really weird. Most of my encultured beliefs simply went away. In their place was a perception of an interconnected, benevolent reality in which human consciousness and the other aspects of the universe are continuously interacting.

AT HOME IN THE SEA OF PEACE

A Jamaican friend once confided in me that she'd had a number of "paranormal" experiences. When I told her that similar things had happened to me, she let out a long sigh and said, "Oh, good! Is not I crazy me-one!" This beautiful little bit of language meant "I'm not just going nuts over here all by myself." And though our culture is insistently mechanistic and materialistic, there's good evidence that my strange experiences are far from unique. Is not I crazy me-one! Millions of ordinary people, not just me, experience reality as a web of connection.

In 2018 a group of psychologists led by J. D. W. Clifton published the results of a five-year study, for which they analyzed enormous amounts of internet data looking for major trends in human attitudes. They found that our culture is divided between people who see the universe as dangerous, frightening, and meaningless, and those who see it as "safe, enticing, and alive." The researchers called these two perspectives "primal world beliefs." They described how, because perception is selectively screened and interpreted according to belief systems, people in either camp can find abundant evidence to support their worldviews.

When I moved to California, I had our culture's "normal" primal world belief. I felt like a physical self, frightened and doomed along with every other human. But those first years in the forest, following the way of integrity, took me to the other side of the primal world belief divide. When I look around me now, everything appears "safe, enticing, and alive." The acronym for this is "sea." From this perspective, we're all intermingled drops in what Dante calls *"lo gran mar de l'essere,"* the "great sea of being." Absolutely united, perfectly unique, and constantly communicating.

As this internal shift occurred, life seemed to deliver more and more of the things I'd longed for during my life. I began to imagine that the universe works like this: whenever we humans long for something, the Powers That Be immediately send it. But everything we've ordered is always delivered to our real home address: peace. Go back to the resonance of the statement "I am meant to live in peace." Can you feel yourself relaxing as your whole self aligns with that idea? This is why, when we struggle for things in a state of desperation, they don't come to us—nothing works when it's misaligned. But when we return to a state of peace, the things we've "ordered" can finally reach us.

It boils down to this: peace is your home. Integrity is the way to it. And everything you long for will meet you there.

While I was living in the forest, making virtually no attempt to contact anyone, several of the soul teachers I'd met in books connected with me in real life. I met with Byron Katie and Stephen Mitchell at a video shoot, and afterward, Katie said she "knew to" cancel their schedule and spend an entire day driving me back to the woods. We've been friends ever since—something that still amazes me, after the many years I spent as an obscure person learning from their books. Not long after that, I was invited back to Arizona to interview yet another of my soul teachers, Anita Moorjani.

As miraculous as all this felt to me, I realize that social connections between humans who share common interests is nothing magical. But other beings I loved and imagined—specifically, wild animals—kept reacting to me in more and more surprising ways. They often came when I "called," not with my voice or a dog whistle, but with my imagination.

This happens all the time at Londolozi, but of course wildlife there is thick on the ground. The same can't be said of the Sedona resort where I met Anita Moorjani. As I arrived there, on the night before our interview, I remembered that I'd once discovered javelina tracks in the surrounding desert. Javelinas (members of the peccary family) look like furry, dainty little pigs. Peering into the darkness, I found myself wishing I could see one while I was in Arizona. But my interview started early, and I'd be going straight from there back to the airport. Oh, well.

Early the next morning, after I met Anita—a radiant, irresistibly huggable human—there was a knock at the door of the hotel suite where we were filming. An assistant went to answer. She found no one at the door—no one human, anyway. Standing there was a fine male javelina, peering up as if to say, *You rang?*

The assistant yelped, "It's a pig!" We all rushed to the window, hoping to get a glimpse of this shy wild animal as it galloped into the underbrush. Instead, the javelina just stood there. We opened the door. He didn't move. We cautiously went outside. Not only did the big male remain within a few feet of us, but about twenty more javelinas followed him. As they milled around us, munching cactus and nursing their adorable striped piglets, a hotel employee stood nearby wringing her hands and saying, "They're aggressive! They're very aggressive!" Maybe in her reality. In my reality, they were furry enlightened beings, companions in paradise.

Perhaps that resort had become a hotbed of tame-ish javelina activity since I'd last visited—but those animals could have gone anywhere on the huge resort. Instead it was like *Casablanca*: of all the hotel rooms in all the buildings on that property, those javelinas came to ours. We never did figure out exactly how that big male knocked on the damn door.

On another occasion I set out to drive across a long stretch of wilderness in Wyoming. As I began my drive, I thought, "I've never seen a pronghorn antelope. I'd like to see one today." I felt a strange, distant twinge, as if I'd moved my hand, except that my hand happened to be many miles away.

Hours later, as I drove through a seemingly endless "big sky" prairie, a white smudge appeared on the horizon. I pulled over and parked to stare at it. The smudge grew rapidly until I could see what it was: a herd of pronghorn antelope, running flat-out, raising a cloud of dust. They came straight to my car—the only human thing in all that broad plain—and stopped. I wept helplessly while they stood around me, their nostrils flaring as they caught their breath, their angel eyes watching me calmly.

You rang?

Once when my family went out for a drive at Londolozi, we stopped near a pride of lions. Adam was riding shotgun in the open vehicle. As we sat in silence, a huge male lion got up and padded over until he was almost nose to nose with Adam. As he stared into my son's face with his golden, serial-killer eyes, I confess I felt a bit jittery. But later, when I asked Adam if the lion made him nervous, he said, "No, because I was feeling him. And he was feeling me back."

"Oh?" I said. "And what was he feeling?"

"What lions always feel," said Adam.

"So . . . what do lions always feel?"

"Peaceful."

I think Adam is right. He and the lion could "feel" each other because both of them were in pure integrity, a state of complete peace. In this sea of being, they were both connected and individual. Dante says that in paradise, people literally intermingle with one another, not needing language to communicate because they share a state of peace. There, they mutually understand one another because they *are* one another. As you move closer and closer to pure integrity, as the windowpane of your mind grows more and more transparent, you will begin to love everything, and it will be obvious to you that everything loves you back.

THE STILL POINT OF THE TURNING WORLD

One day as I sat down in the forest, a thought appeared in my head, almost like an inaudible voice. It said, very clearly, "Your name is stillness." Suddenly I felt as if an invisible hand grasped my mind and pulled it deep, deep, deep down, into an infinitely small point at the center of my heart. There I found myself in absolute stillness, unlike anything I'd ever felt. The best adjective I can think of to describe that stillness is "quenching." It satisfied me like a drink of sweet, pure water after a long drought.

After that, the phrase "Your name is stillness" worked for me like some kind of enchanted password. All I had to do was repeat it in my mind, and down I'd go, like a pearl diver, to the same never-changing, always-renewing freshness. I'm telling you, if there were a drug that could make us feel that bliss, I'd be on it right now. I'd want you to be on it, too.

One day an Australian writer named Rowan Mangan came to visit us in our forest home. I was delighted: I'd met Ro at Londolozi, and we'd hit it off immediately. We shared our literary interests, as well as degrees in social science and an obsession with "restoring Eden" before humans destroy the world. A few days into her California visit, Ro showed me a poem she'd written. It was called "The Turning." In this poem, a divine force from the distant future reminisces about the time humans "almost broke the world."

"You tore at this world, and I watched," says this omniscient narrator, referring to the time we are living now. "I felt the air's grim thickening, saw the waters rise." But then, just when the damage seemed irreversible, humans changed course.

What crucial inspiration turned you at the last?
I'll never know what broke over you,
and with what calamity, clamor
or grace—

but when you knelt, as one, it was a mighty sight.
You placed your hunger on the ground
and left it to lie among the gadgetry of old logics,
beside the corpses of cruelty and greed.

. . . So then came the time of the great unbuilding,
where everyone's name is stillness.

The poem goes on, but when Ro read that line I interrupted, feeling the now-familiar electrical buzz in my body. I'd never told anyone about the strange magic password I'd been repeating every day for months: "Your name is stillness."

"Where did you get that phrase?" I asked. "The line about everyone's name being stillness?"

"I don't know," Ro said. "Just my imagination."

The field of imagination, of physical being without physical limits, may be what connected me with wild animals like the javelinas and the pronghorn antelope—and also with other humans. Certainly, my imagination and Ro's somehow landed on the same phrase when we were literally occupying different sides of the planet. Perhaps it's in our imaginations that fractals of awakening first begin to spread, clearing one mind, then transferring light to another.

Imagining may be the key to finding paradise, in our individual lives and then in all life, all consciousness. Dante seems to think so. At one point in the *Paradiso*, he tells us very pointedly to use our imaginations to picture beauty that "exceeds our sense." Three times in quick succession, he says *"imagini"* and then describes dazzling arrays of shining stars and particles. He asks us to "retain that image like a steadfast rock." By doing this, the poet tells us, we perceive something like a shadow of what he saw in paradise.

Again, Dante's images mirror descriptions of the universe from people who've had enlightenment experiences. The ancient Buddhist masters described the structure of reality with a metaphor called "Indra's net." Picture a multidimensional spider's web stretching out infinitely in all directions. At each intersection of the web hangs a multifaceted diamond. Every diamond glows from within, and also reflects all the other diamonds. And in each reflected diamond is the reflection of all the other diamonds. The pattern continues ad infinitum, repeating at different scales from the inconceivably tiny to the unthinkably immense.

IMAGINATION AS SALVATION

These images may be pretty, but what do they have to do with your real life? Dante and the awakened ones might say that imagination *is* our real life. The way we see determines what we see, whether our primal world belief shows us a universe that's dangerous, frightening, and meaningless, or safe, enticing, and alive.

This is why humans have been able to create a reality that "exceeds the senses" of previous generations. Imagining something unheard-of, then holding that image with rocklike solidity, is a "magic" that humans have been using since history began. It's how someone in ancient Mesopotamia invented the first cuneiform alphabet. It's what allowed someone else, this time in China, to come up with the idea of typesetting. It's what made Steve Jobs drive his coworkers half crazy, yelling at them and berating them until they actually crafted the "insanely great" devices only he could see in his mind's eye.

Right now, I'm using all these once-imaginary things—alphabet, printing, and an app on my iPhone—to transfer my thoughts to yours. It's not magic, but it's pretty damn close.

If anything can save us at this point, it will be the kind of magic we work by clearing our minds so completely that we can see beyond anything our combined cultures have ever created, and then hold that image constant and still until the world turns around it. The process that takes each of us out of individual suffering and self-destruction is the same one that might spread through larger and larger populations, until our whole species shifts to more enlightened ways of being.

Here is an exercise that takes your imagination out to play. Maybe (I don't believe this, but I don't *not* believe it) this will also connect you, through the medium of imagination, with everything that is.

EXERCISE:
Imagini, imagini, imagini

In the last chapter I asked you to picture your mind as a window, and the quest for integrity as a way of cleaning that window. In this exercise, you'll visualize something similar, but more complex and detailed. Take some time by yourself in a quiet place, then follow the steps below.

Step one

Imagine that you can see Indra's net. Picture the multidimensional web, extending infinitely in all directions. At each intersection of the web is a clear, glittering diamond. Each gem contains infinite information and glows with its own light. Each also reflects the light of all the others.

Step two

Imagine that you are one of the jewels on the net, a diamond with thousands of facets. Your essential nature is absolutely pure and clear, but some facets are coated with mud (error or illusion). The mud keeps some of your brilliance from shining outward, and also prevents you from reflecting some of the images shining toward you from surrounding diamonds.

Step three

Imagine that each time you release an error and begin living according to your integrity, you clear the mud off another facet of yourself. More light shines from you into the entirety of Indra's net, the universe as a whole. You also receive more light from every other jewel. The closer you get to complete integrity, the more brilliantly you shine outward, and the more beauty you absorb inward.

Step four

Imagine that your diamond-self has reached a state of total clarity. At this point, every thought you think immediately beams out into Indra's net, enriching and illuminating the entire universe.

Step five

Imagine that everything you hold solidly in your mind creates new things, ideas that have never yet existed. Once you've reached total clarity, your life cannot help but reflect every new image that occurs to you. Indra's web immediately picks up and begins giving form to every image you think.

Step six

Imagine the best possible thing that could happen to you, your loved ones, the whole world.

Step seven

Imagine something even better.

Step eight

Imagine something even better.

Step nine

Hold that image steadfast, like a rock. Write it down. Draw a picture of it.

Step ten

See what happens.

BEYOND IMAGINATION

Over the past few decades, more and more thinkers and teachers have begun to suggest that humanity is on the verge of a "transformation of consciousness." Eckhart Tolle describes this happening the way a virus spreads: first a few cases here and there, then clusters appearing in proximity to each other, then what looks like explosive growth that could eventually affect almost everyone on the planet. We've all seen what this "exponential growth" looks like as we watched the global pandemic that began in early 2020. We've watched internet images and ideas "go viral" in much the same way. If enough people reach a critical threshold of integrity, we might see a virtual explosion of awakening.

I like to imagine this, as opposed to the more likely scenario that our species will soon expire in an inferno of its own making. If the transformation of consciousness is real, what lies before us is not a time of building but of unbuilding, not thinking harder but thinking less. (As Lao Tzu puts it in the *Tao te Ching*, "In the pursuit of knowledge, every day something is added. In the practice of the Way, every day something is dropped.") As integrity scours the mind clean, we transcend the clumsiness of language and culture and join the limitless intelligence of our true nature—of all nature. This could allow us to create solutions that, as you are reading this, have never existed even as thoughts.

There comes a time when, like Dante, we will follow the way of integrity to places even our imaginations can't reach. Remember how the poet warns readers to turn back before reading the *Paradiso*? He says flat-out that he's headed for waters no one has ever sailed before, and we simply can't go there. By the end of *The Divine Comedy*, he has traveled beyond our usual conception of reality into a place beyond space and time.

In the last few lines of his epic, Dante uses a literary device that also shows up in Rowan Mangan's poem: switching from the past tense to the present ("So then *came* the time of the great unbuilding, when everyone's name *is* stillness."). It happens at the apex of paradise, as Dante draws close to the ultimate source of the universe. He describes this source as an eternally opening rose—an image that isn't Christian but very like the Asian concept of the universe emerging from a many-petaled lotus blossom.

As Dante's perceptions begin connecting with this unspeakably brilliant unfolding light, his language goes from past to present tense. He's no longer telling his story as something that happened to him, but as something that *is happening* to him. Now.

I don't believe Dante means the "now" of 1320—the date when he physically finished writing *The Divine Comedy*. I imagine that as he writes the poem's final lines, Dante turns from the page and looks straight out at his audience—at you, reading this, in this moment. He has moved into the eternal present. "Eternal" doesn't mean something that lasts for a long time, but something *outside of time*. Remember, Dante is becoming identified with light, and at the speed of light, time no longer exists. A photon can be anywhere, everywhere, at every moment in history.

The moment we call "now" is like the line where the plane of eternity intersects with the plane of time. From this precise moment we can see time stretching out infinitely in one plane, and eternity in the other. Dante is present here, in the eternal "now," because we are all present here. We have lost our distinctions and blended into something infinitely varied yet absolutely united, an ultimate integrity with everything that exists, will ever exist, or has ever existed.

So, although each of us is still active in the line of time, clearing facets of our minds and lives, emerging from confusion and distress into clarity and joy, part of us is already in the plane of eternity where Dante is, right now, writing *The Divine*

Comedy directly to us. We can meet the compassionate eyes looking across the centuries, seeing us *now*, understanding us *now*, encouraging us *now*. We can see one another past the ups and downs of a million lifetimes, past crusades and plagues and world wars and moon landings. Because we are all one thing, one being, each experience is all experience.

This is the place where Dante says even "high imagination fails." There is nothing left to do at this point but release one final error: the belief that there has ever been any distinction between the separate scraps of matter we imagine we are, and the all-inclusive truth that extends beyond anything we can conceive. When we fully dissolve the lie of being isolated within ourselves, we join Dante and everyone else, everything else. We forget ourselves as small, doomed beings on a threatened planet and remember ourselves as *l'amor che move il sole e l'altre stelle*, "the love that moves the sun and the other stars."

ACKNOWLEDGMENTS

I don't think I've ever been so grateful to so many people for helping me write a book. First, my heartfelt thanks to the many clients who have shared their experiences with me, and to all the fellow coaches who have studied my methods. It's such a joy to seek the way of integrity surrounded by like hearts and minds. Many of you may see flashes of yourself in these stories.

My brilliant work team carved out time and gave me endless support as I wrote this book—just when the 2020 pandemic brought upheaval to all our lives. Such deep thanks to Jennifer Voss, Carmen Shreffler, Christina Brandt, Lara Endorf, and our very own "manifester of miracles," Jennifer Falci. We have been through twelve kinds of adventure together, and I couldn't ask for more stalwart companions.

I've been blessed to have learned from many world-class teachers in my life. In particular, Byron Katie, Anita Moorjani, Larry J., and Alexandra Barbo have given me key insights that made it into the center of my life and the pages of this book.

I'm lucky enough to have friends who are also part of my heart's family. Particular thanks to Paula Keogh, Rennio Maifredi, Susan Casey, Jennifer Johnsen, Katja Elk, the Varty family, and Maria Shriver—bright spirits, brilliant minds, generous souls.

I'm also grateful to have a terrific literary team. My agent, the wonderful Linda Loewenthal, not only took on this book in proposal form but combed through many initial drafts, improving the writing and contributing inspired ideas. Pamela Dorman and Jeramie Orton believed in the project and worked on the editing process throughout the COVID-19 lockdown of 2020, proving their tenacity and commitment even in the worst of times. Karen Wise caught and corrected many of my mistakes with the very quality her name describes. So much gratitude to all of you.

I live in a web of kindness woven largely by my beloved next-generation family: Adam Beck, Elizabeth Beck, Sam Beck, Kat Forster, and Scott Forster. Sam, a gifted writer, generously read and commented on an early draft. Kat's keen editorial mind corrected not only my writing but also my thinking over several drafts. What a gorgeous bunch you are. I adore the whole damn lot of you.

Stephen Mitchell has been an extraordinary guide for me since I first read his work decades ago. Without our friendship and his encouragement, this book wouldn't exist. Over many conversations, Stephen gently urged me to develop my original ideas, clarify my thinking, and bring more discernment to everything I thought and wrote. I never imagined receiving so much time and attention from one of the world's foremost spiritual writers. I'd call it a miracle, but that would never pass Stephen's standards of proof. I'll have to settle for expressing my heartfelt love and thanks.

My dear friend Elizabeth Gilbert has been a huge part of this book's creation. She listened to me read the entire manuscript over the phone during lockdown and turned some of the words into gorgeous art in her journal. Liz is more committed to the way of integrity than almost anyone else I know, and her spirit lights the world. Thank you for everything, Lizzy. You will always be most in show!

Finally, and most of all, I am grateful to my beloved partners, Karen Gerdes and Rowan Mangan. Karen has been my lifeline for so many years, as vital to me as my bloodstream. Rowan's incredible mind, heart, talent, and devotion have made this book—and my life—better than I could have imagined. Karen and Rowan, in being with you I am truly awash in the great sea of being, where the whole universe feels safe, enticing, and alive.

If I had known that I would meet all these people at some point in my life, the way of integrity wouldn't have felt nearly so difficult. May everyone who reads this book be as lucky as I am.